A Feast *of* Losses

Thursday July 12th

Back to the lands of Yesterdays.
is a solace Just divine
Back to friends of yore
Back trough the dark and veary ways.
Where hearts of friends are awaiting me
warmd by the sun above
Back to life light and health Once once more
and to the land of beginning again
where brocken dreams come True
where skies are always blue . Y.H. Dine, July 12, 51

A flicker of hope is again awackened in me

I buried my pride and wrote to Roz lynn that

I want to come back to her, there is where my
only hope of survivel is, I hope one will be
kind enough to give me one
more chance I'm tired of this Idle lazy life
I must do something to Keep me
ocupied I realy feel Phisicaly well to be able
to work. I have two good Jobs
promised right here in Mt Vernon work
that I know well if I could only get started
I know I can do twell, both all beginnings is

A page from Yetta Dine's diary.
Collection of Gretchen Kunitz, M.D.

A Feast *of* Losses

YETTA DINE AND HER SON, THE POET STANLEY KUNITZ

Judith Ferrara

TIDEPOOL PRESS
Cambridge, Massachusetts

TidePool Press, LLC
6 Maple Avenue, Cambridge, Massachusetts 02139
www.tidepoolpress.com

Printed in the United States

Library of Congress Cataloging-in-Publication Data

Judith Ferrara, 1942–
    A Feast of Losses: Yetta Dine and Her Son, the Poet Stanley Kunitz
    p.cm.
    978-1-7367720-6-5
    1. Ferrara, Judith 2. Stanley Kunitz—biography
    3. Yetta Kunitz Dine—biography/memoir 4. Poetry
    5. American-Jewish Literature 6. Immigration—Worcester, MA
    7. Lithuanian-Jewish History 8. Death with Dignity
    9. Mother-Son Relationships
    I. Title.

    2023934252

Book and jacket design by Ingrid J. Mach

Note: The graphics on the front cover, title page, and that serve as
paragraph spacers are derived from traditional Lithuanian embroidery
patterns.

To

GRETCHEN KUNITZ, M.D.
CAROL STOCKMAL
JOHN GAUMOND

Contents

List of Illustrations

Foreword

SHORTLY AFTER MY father's death in 2006, I opened the door to the study of his West 12th Street apartment. The walls were lined from floor to ceiling with a lifetime collection of books. This was his sanctuary. He had painted the wooden floor bright green, and it always struck me as his way of bringing nature into his hallowed place of work and contemplation. How would I decide where to allocate his books and papers? Several years previously, he had sent the bulk of his papers to the Princeton University Library, but being a man who rarely discarded anything, he stuffed the one musty closet in the room with old shoe boxes of miscellaneous papers, letters, and black and white photographs. My daunting task was to comb through these materials, determining the fate of each item.

Poets House of New York, an organization which my father co-founded and dearly loved, agreed to take the entire collection of books. It took more than a few days for their staff and interns to pull the thousands of books off the shelves and haul them away. The papers and photographs were another matter.

I sat on the floor surrounded by shoe boxes and began the process of sifting through the remnants of my father's life. I unearthed a wealth of materials that for whatever reasons, my father had not included in the Princeton papers. Among these discoveries were the original handwritten pages of my grandmother Yetta's memoir. Her penciled words were faded, yellowed and frayed by time. Also in the collection were a diary and letters written to and from family members in the last years of her life.

I first learned of the existence of the memoir in the late 1970s but did not read her words until 1985, when my father transcribed and published an excerpt in a collection of poems and essays: *Next to Last Things*. My grandmother was a somewhat mythical figure in my mind because she died in 1952, when I was two years old. I knew very little about her life because my parents' marriage ended when I was young. My father spoke little of his family. I learned more when he published *The Testing-Tree* in 1971 and *Passing Through: The Later Poems, New and Selected* in 1995. As a body of work, "Journal for My Daughter," "The Portrait," "An Old Cracked Tune," "My Mother's Pears," and "Halley's Comet" opened the door to my family's history, or at least, my father's rendering of it.

What would I do with my grandmother's papers ? I knew without hesitation that I would take the collection back with me to California. My intention was to learn more about the grandmother I never knew beyond one photograph of her and a hand-crocheted cotton bedspread from the 1930s given to me by my father. I knew that at a young age Yetta emigrated from Lithuania, that she became an accomplished seamstress, that she taught herself English, that she revered Nietzsche and Spinoza, and that Emma Goldman dined at her table. I also knew she had a life replete with losses, most notably the premature deaths of her husbands and her daughters, leaving her only son and her daughters' heirs as her immediate family.

Years passed and the memoir sat untouched.

In 2010, I visited Worcester, Massachusetts, for the first time. The occasion was the dedication of my father's childhood home, as a Literary Landmark™. In 1979, Carol and Gregory Stockmal purchased the home and began to lovingly restore it. In 1985, the Stockmals fortuitously met and befriended my father. The story of that encounter and subsequent relationship is recounted in the Afterword to this book. In 2008, after Gregory's untimely death, Carol dedicated herself to allowing visitors into her home, creating a public window into my father's history in early 20th century Worcester. Judith Ferrara, a Worcester writer and visual artist, volunteered to work with Carol on a docent program that offered tours focused on the Stockmals' friendship with my father, and the rich poetic links to her home and neighborhood. On several occasions, I had met the Stockmals when they came to visit my father in Provincetown, Massachusetts, but it was on this visit to Worcester for the dedication that I met Judith and learned of her interest in my father's life and work.

As Judith's research uncovered more history about my father's family, we began an email correspondence. When she inquired as to the existence of my grandmother's memoir, I was delighted to inform her that the original memoir, along with her diary and letters were stored in my attic. I sent these materials to Judith. Through extensive research of family and library documents, historical records, and personal conversations, she became intrigued with Yetta's story and began the formidable task of unraveling the complicated threads of her long life.

Yetta's is a heartbreaking story that is revealed because of Judith's unwavering dedication to this project. For this, I am humbled and grateful. Judith's work has brought to light pieces of family history previously unknown to me. She has drawn a vivid portrait of a remarkable woman. The story of my grandmother's inauspicious beginnings and of the hardships she endured throughout her life illustrate a universal immigrant story. Yetta was an intelligent, fierce, and loving wife, mother, and businesswoman who deeply loved her family. Even as death neared and sadness and frailty engulfed her, she planned to ask my father for assistance in moving back to New York City to find a job and enroll in college. Until her last days, she strove to rise above what she saw as her own ignorance, something about which she was deeply apologetic and ashamed. She never let go of the dream to better herself—the same dream she had in 1890, when she arrived on America's shores.

I like to believe that some small remnant of Yetta, like a piece of dressmaker's cloth, resides in me. I know we would have enjoyed each other's company.

Gretchen Kunitz, M.D.
September, 2021

THE PORTRAIT

My mother never forgave my father
for killing himself,
especially at such an awkward time
and in a public park,
that spring
when I was waiting to be born.
She locked his name
in her deepest cabinet
and would not let him out,
though I could hear him thumping.
When I came down from the attic
with the pastel portrait in my hand
of a long-lipped stranger
with a brave moustache
and deep brown level eyes,
she ripped it into shreds
without a single word
and slapped me hard.
In my sixty-fourth year
I can feel my cheek
still burning.

—Stanley Kunitz, *Passing Through:*
The Later Poems, New and Selected

PORTRAYED IN STANLEY KUNITZ'S POEMS AND INTERVIEWS
AS AN UNFORGIVING AND UNAFFECTIONATE MOTHER, YETTA
DINE REVEALS A MORE COMPLEX NARRATIVE THROUGH HER
RECENTLY RECOVERED LETTERS, MEMOIR AND DIARY. THEY
PROVIDE VITAL INSIGHTS INTO THE LIFE AND WORK OF A
MAJOR AMERICAN POET.

Prologue

I cried to the mourner on the stair,
"Mother, I hate you for those tears."

—From "The Signal from the House,"
Stanley Kunitz, *The Collected Poems*

In 1945, Yetta Dine's son, poet and editor Stanley Kunitz, "suggested that she occupy herself with putting down on paper ... the untold story of her life."[1] She gladly took up the task with the expectation that he would edit and publish it.

Publication did come about, but not until three decades after her death and in highly edited excerpts which pale in comparison to her own words. Untouched since 1985 and recently recovered and transcribed, Yetta Dine's complete, unabridged, and minimally edited letters, memoir and diary provided the foundation for this biography. As the project grew, another distinct voice emerged: her son's.

If Yetta were not the formidable and dramatic presence in her son's poems and interviews, then perhaps she would be a minor figure in the drama of Stanley Kunitz's life and poetry. Immigrant by choice, seamstress by trade, and a natural storyteller, she was no stranger to metaphor and might have argued: "To appreciate the garment, examine the fabric."

Because of Stanley Kunitz's long life and influence in the poetry community, he was interviewed frequently and spoke of his relationship with his mother: Yetta Dine was a strong but unaffectionate mother, whose "fierce love I never doubted."[2] His poetic mother

7

figure is cold and unforgiving, as seen in "An Old Cracked Tune": "my mother's breast was thorny." In "The Portrait," the memory of her slap burned on his cheek decades later. He justified his decision to customize his portrayal of her in this way: "All creative writing is fiction, a distillation and transformation of reality. That's what makes it a work of art."[3] Excerpts from poems rooted in Kunitz's family relationships are an invitation to locate and read them in their entirety, then ponder that transformation.

With the publication of this book, Yetta Dine's voice can now be heard in discussions about her son's life and work. Her writing reveals an outspoken, shrewd, compassionate, independent, resilient, and loving individual with strong family ties. To his credit, Kunitz's writing assignment helped his mother to discover the special satisfaction of producing a compelling first-hand account of a life threaded with success but penetrated by profound losses.

Despite its mid-twentieth-century origin, Yetta's observations provoke readers to think about economic and religious oppression and the challenges of immigrant life, subjects that reach across the decades to touch us today.

Her 1951 diary was written in a rest home after she suffered a stroke. Even then, her longing to be published was undiminished. She fought to resurrect memories of "a few sweet drops" in her "bitter cup" while delivering a blunt and cautionary tale about end-of-life hardships.

Taken as a whole, this book challenges the reader because it presents three situations: first, a precise and relevant rendering of one woman's struggles; second, a mother-son relationship complicated by his representation of her in poems and interviews; third, one person's prescient arguments for death with dignity.

This hybrid biography-memoir-diary fulfills her wish and presents Yetta Helen Jasspon Kunitz Dine: daughter, sister, Lithuanian-Jewish immigrant, wife, widow, mother, grandmother, great-grandmother, mother-in-law, great-aunt, seamstress, businesswoman—and writer.

CHAPTER ONE

The Letters:
Tarrytown, New York, 1945

> She was wearing a mourning bonnet
> and a wrap of shining taffeta.
> "Why don't you write?" she cried
> from the folds of her veil.

—From "Quinnapoxet," Stanley Kunitz, *Passing Through:
The Later Poems, New and Selected*

STANLEY KUNITZ'S REPUTATION as a twentieth-century American
literary figure was nascent in 1945 when he suggested that his
mother write her memoir. Although proud of the forty-year-old's
scholastic and literary accomplishments, Yetta Dine could not know
that he would become the 1959 Pulitzer Prize recipient in Poetry,
or be honored as Consultant in Poetry to the Library of Congress
in 1974 and 2000 Poet Laureate of the United States, or win the
National Book Award in 1995.[4] She did know that World War II
was raging and her son—in fact, her only surviving child and three
of four grandsons—were in the military, and she was overcome with
worry. By 1945, tragedy and reduced circumstances resulted in her
living with great-niece, Rosilyn Levitan.

YOU ASKED ME TO WRITE SOME OF MY MEMORIES

Inside apartment 110 at 74 South Broadway, Tarrytown, New York,
seventy-eight-year-old Yetta sat alone and balanced a tray on her

lap, the portrait of a lady at her improvised writing desk. February's stillness was interrupted by the shuttling of pen across paper. Yetta was writing to her daughter-in-law Eleanor and "Only Son" Stanley, who was stationed in Washington, D.C.

Yetta had done her best to keep Kunitz from being drafted. She signed the deferment application stating that he was her sole support, but it had been denied. Another plan, to have him classified as a conscientious objector, had failed. The official verdict was rendered: Even if "he were deferred as conscientious objector, he still will

Private Stanley J. Kunitz, United States Army, Alexandria, Virginia, 1945.
Department of Special Collections, Princeton University Library

be subject to limited service, so he couldn't support his mother."[5] Kunitz reluctantly took leave from his poetry writing and his editing job at H.W. Wilson. On January 11, 1943, he was inducted into the army in Allentown, Pennsylvania.[6]

After Basic Training, he requested and received an assignment to the Public Relations Department of Air Transport Command Headquarters at Gravelly Point, Virginia, across the Potomac from Washington, D.C. He became a publicist for the army and would be "editing an orientation bulletin that goes out weekly to our stations throughout the world."[7,8]

IT KNOCKED ME OUT

O ruined father dead, long sweetly rotten
Under the dial, the time-dissolving urn,
Beware a second perishing, forgotten,
Heap fallen leaves of memory to burn
On the slippery rock, the black eroding heart,
Before the wedged frost splits it clean apart.

—From "For the Word Is Flesh," Stanley Kunitz, *Intellectual Things*

Yetta Dine's mood was darkened by her latest loss.

Her younger brother Abraham Jasspon was born in Lithuania, as were all six children raised by Harry Jasspon and Ida Wolpe. Abe was the brother left behind with her ailing mother in Lithuania. In 1891, she had saved money from her first job in New York City to pay his passage to America.

Abe lived and died in Worcester, Massachusetts. He married Dora Levine in 1897, and their first son, Harold, was born in 1899. Their second son Leon died of pneumonia at five weeks old. Abe held jobs as a dry goods merchant, wrapper cutter, grocer and tobacconist and lived at multiple addresses in Worcester, never far from his sister, Yetta. When her second husband Mark Dine died in 1920, Abe lived with her at 4 Woodford Street. After she lost joint ownership of Woodford Street, she lived with him in his 933 Pleasant Street apartment. The 1940 census and Yetta's letter combine to describe his ending: Abe Jasspon was divorced and living alone in a rooming house.[9]

Her son would need to know about his uncle and of the new baby in the family, her great-nephew's grandson. Kunitz was involved with his own life and out of touch with Rosilyn, her sister Florence, and brothers Harold and Benjamin Levitan. She and her niece's family were always close, but now Kunitz, Eleanor, and four grandsons embodied her shrinking immediate family.

Monday, the 27th

Dear Stanley and Eleanor,

I got home Tuesday in time to listen to Eleanor's radio talk, and I enjoyed it very much.

I had to see the dentist Tuesday morning. The same day, or rather in the evening, I got a telegram that my brother Abe passed away. The news was not unexpected. I knew that he was very ill. Yet it knocked me out, and I was terribly upset that I could not go to the funeral. It was too late. He was 76 years old and had a very lonely life. So, his troubles are ended.

At the very same hour, I received a telegram from Michigan City, Indiana that a baby boy was born, a grandchild to my [great-]nephew. One life gone, another arrived.

Stanley, when you asked me to write some of my memories, I did not know if you really meant it.

I thought about it and wondered who would be interested enough to waste the time and read it, unless you could take out some of it like a chemist does, with all the tons of material used to extract an ounce of something worthwhile.

So, I decided to try. I'm all alone, because Rosilyn went to Boston.

I scribbled a few pages as a very poorly made sample, but I want to know if you think you could do something with it.

I know you can add the collar and trimming. I could elaborate on each subject for pages and pages. It is not fiction. It is all facts. If you think it is worthwhile, let me know, and if you want me to really do it, I'll try to improve my writing and spelling. I hope you will be able to read it and understand the subjects. You could add on a lot by using imagination and history, especially about the Polish Revolution. I really enjoy writing it and living over my childhood, although it was not a very pleasant one.

Hoping you are both well and not working too hard.

With love,
Mother

P.S. I received a letter from Slater. He is to report to Norfolk, Virginia on March 12th. Buddy is to report to San Francisco on March 13th. They are both coming to Tarrytown next week, so there it goes.

While Kunitz encouraged his mother's writing venture, problems with finding a publisher for his second book of poems, *Passport to the War*, were fresh in his mind. He had sent his manuscript to Harpers, but it was rejected. Viking would publish it if he would write a novel. Saxe Commins at Random House turned it down "because people are not reading poetry." Harcourt Brace wrote that "because of the war, poetry like [his] will have to wait." Knopf asked to see the manuscript but passed on it. He mended his damaged self-confidence and shipped it to Macmillan, who rejected it. Finally, Henry Holt & Company accepted it.[10]

It is fair to wonder how Yetta felt when she read her son's two published collections. She would have read poems from *Intellectual Things* (1930): "For the Word Is Flesh," "Poem," "Vita Nuova," and from *Passport to the War* (1944): "Reflection by a Mailbox," "The Tutored Child," "The Signal from the House," "Father and Son," "Night Letter," "The Hemorrhage," "The Illusionist," "The Guilty Man," "The Fitting of the Mask."

Haunting lines signaled an unraveling of family secrets:
from "Father and Son,"

> ... "Father!" I cried, "Return! You know
> The way. I'll wipe the mudstains from your clothes;
> No trace, I promise, will remain...

from "The Guilty Man,"

> Father, the darkness of the self goes out
> And spreads contagion on the flowing air.

and from "The Fitting of the Mask,"

> ...the youth, the undefeated,
> Whose falcon-heart, winged with the golden shout
> Of morning, sweeps windward from his native city,
> Crying his father's grief, his mother's doubt.

The poems from both collections held father references but were written without naming Solomon Kunitz. The husband and father whose memory she had attempted to erase was being memorialized by her son in poetry.

As miserable as her son was in the army, he seemed happy in his second marriage. Colorado-born Californian Eleanor Evans was a woman with talents and skills that included little theater actress, writer and librarian.[11] Her first marriage to artist, educator and arts administrator Joseph A. Danysh ended in divorce.[12] Kunitz wrote to a former colleague at Worcester's *Telegram & Gazette* that he was married to Eleanor Evans of San Francisco, "a swell gal with a stage and library background".[13]

Evans and Kunitz met in New York City at the home of mutual friends, poet and playwright Ettore Rella and his wife Jessie.[14] Their 1939 Richmond, Virginia, marriage license listed both addresses as New Hope, Pennsylvania, a fourteen-acre farm Kunitz had purchased in 1935 with his first wife poet Helen Pearce whom he had divorced in 1937.[15]

Stanley and Eleanor Kunitz, c. 1940.
Department of Special Collections, Princeton University Library

In January 1943, while he was in Basic Training at Fort Benjamin Harrison, Indiana, Kunitz wrote to poet Genevieve Taggard, describing his ordeals: "bronchitis and exhaustion" and "lying sick on a hospital cot ..."

> We have closed our house in New Hope, and when I left, Eleanor was trying to rent it, preparatory to leaving for Washington, where she is now (presumably) looking for a job ... I miss my girl, and when I think of the good life I had and of the sweetness of the warmth which I was privileged to share, my heart turns on its hinge.[16]

Eleanor arrived in Washington, D.C., and found a job, thereby ending their separation and confirming Kunitz's confidence in her: "Eleanor is capable & high-spirited—she'll pull through."[17]

> Eleanor is here ... she's the gal who names all the Liberty and Victory ships ... we have a small basement apartment at the edge of the city.[18]

15

Eleanor and Stanley Kunitz, 1945, Alexandria, Virginia.
Department of Special Collections, Princeton University Library

When the United States entered World War II, the military enlisted merchant ships to carry supplies overseas. German U-Boats systematically torpedoed the newly designated Liberty ships. In 1943, the government began a new ship-building program and launched the faster, larger Victory ships.[19]

Eleanor's experience as an actress meant that she could be placed front and center in media efforts to support the costly project. Radio interviews would have been a natural part of her job, as was her being photographed for a *Woman's Home Companion* article.[20] Yetta must have felt proud to alert family and friends about her daughter-in-law's public role in the war effort.

When Kunitz was on leave, he and Eleanor visited Tarrytown. There he asked his mother to write down her memories, his solution to help allay her sadness and offset her mounting worries.

Yetta was still mourning the loss in 1940 of her daughter Sarah, whose husband Percy Baker had recently remarried.[21] This resulted in two significant changes: Her teen-aged grandsons Stanton and Lawrence (Buddy) had a new stepmother, and she needed to find another place to live.

She landed in Tarrytown, at the apartment of her great-niece, Rosilyn Levitan, who was soon to be married to divorced stock-broker Nathan Moses. Here was another possible destabilization—might this mean another move for her? Where and with whom might she live next?

As if that were not enough, World War II continued, and three of her four grandsons were on active duty. Yetta joined the ranks of worried relatives who remembered World War I and its death toll. The navy welcomed twenty-year-old Ensign Slater Isenberg and his nineteen-year-old cousin Lawrence (Buddy) Baker, who was in the Seabees, a nickname given to construction battalions. Her eldest grandson Stanton Baker was an anti-aircraft gunner in the army.[22]

Letters were Yetta's lifeline; news, or lack of it, created more knots of anxiety. Her son's suggestion that she record her memories made sense: Keep busy to hold her sadness and apprehension at bay.

RAW MATERIAL THAT NEEDS TO BE SHAPED

Yetta Dine was both alight with the early success of her writing and aware of her limitations.

Dear Stanley and Eleanor,

I have already arrived in New York and scribbled a few more pages. Maybe you will have time to look at them over the weekend.

I would like your opinion: Did I travel too fast through time? I'm writing the way I would be telling my experience. It is raw

17

Yetta Dine, Stanley and Eleanor Kunitz, Tarrytown, New York, c. 1945.
Department of Special Collections, Princeton University Library

material that needs to be shaped or molded. I'm no artist and my English vocabulary is very limited, as you know.

What do you think? Will you be able to extract something from the crude material? If you will be able to read it, please let me know.

I'm waiting for Buddy to come tomorrow for the weekend. It will be his last visit to me for a long time. Even if I live until his return from a journey like his, which is so uncertain, I will miss him. He is such lovable boy. Slater is also coming someday next week to say good-by.

I was so busy with my trip that I had no time to brood over the journeys my two grandsons are to take in a few days.

I'm waiting to hear from you. I hope my letter will find you both in good health.

With love, Mother

Lawrence "Buddy" Baker, United States Navy, verso "LH Baker."
Department of Special Collections, Princeton University Library

The envelope included one afterthought—an unattached paper scrap measuring 8½ by 3¼ inches, pierced with a dressmaker pin:

If we only could have all this valuable blood for our soldiers on the battlefield, how many lives could be saved.

In the space of a few weeks, her memoir pages mounted up and so did her satisfaction with her son's assignment.

I'M TRYING MY BEST TO CALM DOWN

Thursday, March 22nd

Dear Stanley and Eleanor,

Thanks for your encouraging letter and forgive me for not answering sooner.

I've been upset by having Buddy and Slater go. Who knows if I will live to see them again? Buddy spent three days with me, and he stopped by again on his way from Albany. Now he is on his way to the Philippines. Slater also came and spent three days with me and left for Norfolk, Virginia. He is still there.

I have not heard from Stanton since March 2nd, a letter that was mailed February 18th. But Percy received a card March 9th that said he was on a navy transport. Why and where he was going, no one knows.[23] You know how much these boys mean to me, and how I feel about seeing them all gone.

I'm trying my best to calm down, but it does not come very easy.

In order to distract myself, I worked more than a week with a decorator to help make up some drapes and curtains. I made twenty dollars which I can make use of, as I need to have new glasses and pay my dentist bill.

However, I did some scribbling. If you will find time to read it, write me what you think of it.

I know my writing is very bad as I had no desk and had to write on a tray in my lap. I'm having my vanity from the

Stanton K. Baker, United States Army, c. 1945.
Department of Special Collections, Princeton University Library

bedroom suite made into a desk. It will be very convenient for me, and it will look much nicer.

I thought of re-writing before I send it to you, but it would take too much time. My English would not improve. You are used to my misspelling.

If you could patch together what I'm sending you and put each pattern where it would fit best.

I will write more about the family as I go along. I started to write and found myself on Henry Street. I have so much to tell about all the people who came into my life on that street.

I shall try again and do the best I can.

Eleanor's picture in the magazine is splendid. It is the real Eleanor. I would like to have the picture if you could spare one.

If I believed, and if I knew that you also believed in God, I would have asked you to pray for my three lovely grandsons who are floating on the blue oceans, heaven knows where.

I can't understand about Stanton. Rosilyn called up Percy, and he told her that I should not expect mail for some time, but not to worry. I fear I'm not being told the truth.

Be well, my dear ones, and forgive me for writing about my troubles.

With love, Mother

She turned over the letter to add a request.

Eleanor Kunitz, c. 1945, *Woman's Home Companion.*
Department of Special Collections, Princeton University Library

Eleanor, dear,

If by chance you happen to be in Norfolk, you might call up Slater. I just received a letter from him. He does not know how long he will be there. I hope you keep well. I know you are taking good care of my Only Son, and Your Only husband.

Mother

Ens. Slater K Isenberg
BOA Lewis Park
Norfolk. Va.[24]

Please write soon so I get some mail to cheer me up. I will not hear from Buddy perhaps for two months, and from Stanton, I don't know when. I need some encouragement in my present mood. I'll have to go into New York shortly about my glasses which have not changed in fourteen years. My health is pretty good, better than it has been for a long time, despite all the worries.

Ensign Slater Isenberg, United States Navy, verso "1944."
Collection of Slater Isenberg

Yetta's daily routines in Tarrytown included attending Hadassah and Red Cross meetings, working on committees, going to the library, and keeping an eye out for sewing jobs.[25] She could still be useful, somewhat independent and connected to her family, spread out over the world as they were. Her newest vocation energized her, and she savored the satisfaction a completed memoir might bring.

CHAPTER TWO

Lithuania: A Life With No Future
1866–1890

Your story flickers on your bedroom wall.
Deaths, marriages, betrayals, lies,
   close-ups of tears, forbidden games,
   spill in a montage on a screen,
with chases, pratfalls, custard pies, and sores.

—From "The Magic Curtain," Stanley Kunitz, *Passing Through:*
The Later Poems, New and Selected

WRITERS AT WORK

IN 1945, TWO WRITERS held the prism of Lithuanian history up to the light. Yetta Helen Jasspon Kunitz Dine (1866–1952) was a native who lived there until her early twenties. Her life story had been deemed worthy for examination by her brilliant son, but she soon realized that she lacked scholarly resources and told him so. From her point of view, the Polish-Lithuanian Insurrection of 1863–64, which took place shortly before she was born, was a harrowing family story.

The other writer, Constantine Jurgėla (1904–1988) was born in New Jersey and spent a decade in Lithuania when his parents returned there. He joined the Lithuanian army in 1919 and fought to expel the Russians. When he came back to the United States in 1924, Jurgėla earned law and history degrees and became a noted Lithuanian historian, as well as the chief of the Lithuanian service of Voice of America.[26]

Map of Lithuania, 1867–1914.
From Wikimedia Commons

While Yetta sat at her improvised writing desk, Jurgėla was deep into an ambitious book, which was still two years away from publication. Either from experience or research, both writers knew that Lithuanians lived for centuries in a web of oppression, alliances, invasions, and reprisals. Yetta Jasspon was born in a *shtetl* or market town near the provincial capital of Kovno during Russian occupation. Her town, Yashwen, or Josvianiai, was home to a diverse population of Lithuanian Catholics, Jews, Poles, Germans, and Russian Orthodox settlers.

A third writer, Masha Ralsky Greenbaum, was born in 1927 in Lithuania to a well-to-do Jewish couple. Her father Sholem Ralsky was a chemist transferred by his employer to Kovno, where he headed a tobacco-processing factory. When World War II ended in

1945, Masha, her mother Judith and sister Susannah were liberated by the British from the Bergen-Belsen concentration camp; her father had perished.[27] She eventually moved to Israel, where she matured into a historian with a storyteller's gifts and poured decades of research into a book which was published in 1995: *The Jews of Lithuania: A History of a Remarkable Community, 1316–1945.*

Constantine Jurgèla's *History of the Lithuanian Nation* provided background support for some of Yetta's memories. Historians have biases, and Jurgèla was not without his. Despite their centuries-long presence in, and contributions to, Lithuanian society, Jews were mentioned infrequently, and then without admiration. Jurgèla took on the history of Lithuania from 1200 through 1920 and admitted the task of doing justice to his subject "was hardly possible in a single volume: each writer, of necessity, 'selects' the events for his comments."[28]

Jurgèla and Greenbaum's complex and thorough histories more than fulfilled Yetta's need for background information about one specific insurrection: 1863–1864. Both also supported her observations of family life in the village of Yashwen. In the service of giving context to Yetta Dine's memoir, what follows are highly compressed syntheses gleaned from both historians.

RESISTANCE

The armed uprising of Polish and Lithuanian insurgents against Russia in 1863 had one purpose: to secure independence and be freed from Czar Alexander II's restrictive policies against Polish and Lithuanian Catholics, several of which he inherited from his father Nicholas I's regime.[29]

Census-taking, payments and bribes made up the system of regulations for conscription into the Russian army. In the early 1860s, sixteen to eighteen-year-old Lithuanian sons were drafted. Soldiers who were both Lithuanian and Jewish were treated with special vengeance.[30] While some served, others fled either abroad or into the forests, where they joined groups of insurgents. Yetta's brother, Max

Jasspon, would attempt the former solution to avoid conscription.

Two factions arose within the ranks of Lithuanian rebels. The Whites formed a partnership between Lithuania and Poland and worked to create a government free from Russia. The separatist Reds wanted land reform and freedom from all foreigners, including the Polish Lublin government. Lithuanian and Polish insurgents carried out punishments for treason or desertion. Double-barreled shotguns, scythes, hatchets, and ropes for lynching were used against anyone suspected of siding with the Russians. "Death verdicts were punctiliously carried out by the insurgents."[31] One such incident nearly claimed the life of Yetta's father Harry Jasspon and resulted in permanent damage to his health.

As with previous rebellions against Russian rulers, the rebels' defeat in 1864 brought fierce retaliation.[32] Russia granted Lithuania's Polish cohorts some concessions, but the plan for Lithuania was more severe. Jurgėla documented policies known as compulsory Russification, which were designed as a shroud of extinction for Lithuanian nationality, culture and history.[33] In the second section of Jurgėla's book, "The Period of Resurgence (1795–1918)," he deconstructed Russia's pattern for their burial garment.

THE SHROUD

Cut away. Fit. Trim. Discard. Rework. Insert. Stitch. Land is the fabric of a nation. Lithuanian nobles who did not swear loyalty to the Czar were relocated to Russia. Confiscated estates were colonized by Russians, who were largely unhappy being transferred to the Northwest Territory, as Lithuania was renamed. "Russian authorities abetted the Orthodox settlers to assault and rob the Catholic native gentry."[34]

When Alexander II freed the Lithuanian serfs in 1861, gentry could remain if they agreed to sell off land parcels to peasants. This was an unsavory carrot, because the gentry were permitted to select the plots and sold those with poorer soil. Peasants were permitted to purchase up to 161 acres of land, except that all peasants were

Catholic, and Catholics were restricted from purchasing land. The restriction was lifted when they converted to Russian Orthodoxy and swore loyalty to the Russian government.[35]

Those who refused to convert saw many of their churches closed and transformed into Orthodox temples, which were added to the list of new ones. Fewer Catholic churches meant that people needed to travel for Sunday Mass and religious holidays, which was a boon to merchants in towns such as Yashwen. Priests were restricted to their residences and laws forbade them from leaving their parishes without specific permission from the government. Parochial schools were stitched closed.

A country's future is its children. Laws made it illegal to teach them to read or write Lithuanian. If parents were caught hiring tutors, heavy fines were imposed. All non-Russian teachers were dismissed from state schools and replaced with "Russian teachers, who were former non-commissioned soldiers and misfits, armed with loud, vociferous patriotism, vodka and the knout."[36] Teachers distributed only Russian books to students. Yetta's brother Max attended one of these schools.

Censorship and control of information are the undergarments of oppression. All official correspondence and documents were to be written in Russian. The vibrant Lithuanian printing press, responsible for sustaining its highly literate population, came to a halt, and its books were banned. A network of book smugglers arose. Searches were followed by arrests, banishments, and executions.[37]

Alcohol consumption spawned a temperance movement in Lithuania that had grown powerful by 1858, and taxes from liquor sales were lost. Growers, brewers and Jewish saloon keepers (who had no voice in the government) objected. In 1859, the gentry succeeded in pressuring the government to ban temperance societies and overtly encourage liquor consumption.[38]

◆◆◆◆◆◆◆◆

INTERSECTIONS

While reading Masha Greenbaum's history of Jews in Lithuania, two expressions came to mind. Both employed the word "running," an ironic echo of the Jewish diaspora.

The first was "running the gamut": Jews were protected or persecuted at either extreme of tolerance and intolerance, frequently at the same time. A deadly pogrom could be in progress just as the Czar realized that losing a segment of the Jewish population would jeopardize a source of expertise or income. He and/or the nobles would then attempt to suppress the violence.

The second expression was "running the gauntlet": Life as a Jew in Lithuania could be described as a long, mad dash between rows of economic and religious persecutors. Constant exposure to danger and uncertainty tore at their lives.

Together, Masha Greenbaum and Yetta Dine provided the warp and weft of Lithuanian Jewish history. Examples of bribery reported by Yetta are documented as a way of life by Greenbaum.[39] Yetta's description of the custom of families serving meals to yeshiva students is documented in Greenbaum's book as a tradition of community support practiced since the 1600s.[40] In Greenbaum, Jewish wives like Yetta's sister Sifre Gordon were expected to become breadwinners if their husbands chose to continue devotional studies.[41]

"Let them teach real religion: Love thy neighbor as thyself"— Yetta's use of aphoristic declarations reflects the influence of the nineteenth century's Musar movement, led by Rabbi Israel Lipkin of Salant.[42] Its appeal lay in the premise that ordinary people, not just rabbis, could do good deeds and have high moral values. Teaching ethical behavior to merchants in their business dealings would result in prosperity and acceptance into society. All occupations (at least, those which Jews were permitted to practice) should be useful: Merchants, doctors and lawyers should demonstrate their ethical commitment to the community in all interactions. Simplicity was the best Musar platform, and adages were used to communicate easily how to behave: "Treat others as you would expect to be treated."[43]

Yetta stitched adages into the tapestry of her memoir as a way of capping thoughts about religion and ethics. Her son recalled: "I was raised in a Jewish community ... In our household the emphasis was never on religious practice, but on the ethical tradition." Her ethical treatment of Dine Manufacturing Company workers, "precipitated by her reluctance to discharge any of her employees in a time of depression," ended in bankruptcy.[44]

JEWS IN LITHUANIA

Yetta's father Harry claimed to be descended from Sephardic Jews who fled from Spain in the sixteenth century—according to her, Jasspon translated meant "I am Spanish."[45] As early as 969, Jews fled wars or expulsion from other regions in Europe, the Near East and Asia into Lithuania. Anti-Semitism existed there to a somewhat lesser degree because Lithuanians were relative newcomers to Christianity, having been forcibly converted from paganism to Catholicism by the Poles; they had less history with the Crusades and Rome's representation of Jews as Christ-killers.[46] In Lithuania, Jews formed an international merchant class and were welcomed by aristocrats into the feudalistic society as a stabilizing influence.[47]

Through the granting of charters by the nobility, Jews' rights were spelled out and protected. However, depending upon the decade, the current regime, and the strength of anti-Semitic influences that seeped in from other countries, those rights and freedoms were modified or withheld. Periods when land ownership was possible but restricted were followed by confiscation; Jews were eventually herded into the Cherta, commonly known as the Pale of Settlement. Yetta Jasspon was born into one of the largest ghettos in history, which was established in 1835 and lasted until 1917: nine provinces in Russia, with six in Lithuania and Belarus, of which Kaunas (Kovno) was one.[48]

Inevitably, when Lithuanian monarchs married, went to war, were overthrown, united with Poland against the Russians, submitted to partitioning and colonization, or died, the Jews' fate was in jeopardy. Charters, mercurial as they were, controlled where they could live and how they could earn a living. During Yetta's time, Jews could become shopkeepers or innkeepers, run saloons and engage in a few trades.

Because Catholics were forbidden by Rome to lend money and charge interest, Jews became bankers; they collected taxes and managed absentee landed gentry's estates. Jews were middlemen for sales of goods. However, as important as these roles were to the economy, they were not warmly accepted by the populace. When a Lithuanian middle class developed, Jewish middlemen disappeared because they were redundant. It was a push-pull relationship between Jews' functioning role as contributors to the economy and their persecution, as they maneuvered for a place in a changing society.[49]

FLICKERS OF AUTONOMY

Czar Alexander II, who ruled from 1855–1881, enacted policies toward Jews which became the baseline for Yetta Jasspon's childhood and young adulthood. Greenbaum's subheading for his regime was "Fear Sets In." During the first half of his reign, he behaved as if he wanted to appear enlightened. He freed the serfs, granted local rule in rural communities—even minorities—and modernized the judicial system to include trial by jury.

The Czar opened Russian schools, again including Lithuanian minorities. Some Jewish students were enrolled by families who looked to assimilation as a path to emancipation, while other families struggled with exposing their sons to secular study and maintained their strict yeshiva attendance.[50,51]

Alexander II decreed that Jews, who were exempt from military service, could be conscripted into the Russian army for a sixteen-year term.[52] It was a fate that Yetta's brothers would resist when they came of age.

Surrendering none of his powers, Alexander II's rule was absolute.

After a failed assassination plot in 1866, he became a suspicious, angry despot who repudiated many reformist policies.[53]

Lithuania's seat of government was in Lublin, Poland, where the Russians appointed a Jewish council for self-governance; their rules governed daily life, including levying of taxes and settling disputes.

Among the council's functions was the supervision of schools, where, for a time, the Hebrew or Yiddish language was permitted by the government. Meanwhile, Jewish boys and girls could also attend government schools, where Talmud study was systematically undermined by secular subjects. Young Jews would grow to rebel against learning confined to the study of the Torah by reading forbidden books. The Jasspon household was an observant one, and a young Yetta recalled the shocking discovery of Russian and German book reading by her brother and cousin. Conflicts arose among Jewish groups—those who saw advantages to assimilation and opposing conservatives who clung to the traditional religious curriculum.

It was a time when the dye of change penetrated the fabric of society. Ideas inherited from the Scientific Revolution and the Enlightenment resulted in people questioning orthodox religious belief, as well as encouraging them to abandon old ways of understanding the world and the afterlife. As Yetta observed, by the mid-nineteenth century, "People were hungry for knowledge." Traditional Judaism was itself threatened by internecine struggles among newer factions, some stretching to embrace a combination of Torah and secular study.

Greenbaum documented how, despite having lived in Lithuania as a minority for generations, Jews' enforced outsider status contributed to constantly precarious conditions. Unlike the immigrant Germans (Prussians), Poles, and Russians, they had no homeland to either turn or return to. During the nineteenth century, a movement took hold among Jews: Instead of waiting for the Messiah to lead them to the Promised Land, the Zionist movement encouraged immigration to Palestine and/or strong community support for those who chose to settle there. Yetta was in the second group, having decided in 1890 to follow brothers Max and Charlie to the United States and lend her support from there.

It seems worth noting that, at the age of sixty-one, Yetta Dine finally traveled to Palestine for the vacation of a lifetime in 1927.[54] That same year, Masha Greenbaum was born in Kovno, Lithuania and would survive Bergen-Belsen concentration camp to become an Israeli citizen.

THE FATE OF LITHUANIAN JEWS

The assassination of Alexander II in 1881 fueled four years of pogroms that devastated Jewish communities. His successor Alexander III, who ruled from 1881–1894, used violence to punish the Jewish minority, who were deemed guilty of "exploitation of peasants and financial manipulations." The press was openly anti-Semitic; agitators read the charges aloud to illiterate peasants.[55] Alexander III reversed his father's reforms and blamed minorities, especially Jews, for all manner of misery. Widespread murder, looting and destruction of Jewish businesses attracted international outrage, but to no avail. Pogroms continued and more restrictions for the remaining Lithuanian Jews were enacted.

Yetta was typically reticent about acknowledging unspeakable events in her memoir and wrote only one sentence about the pogroms: "From the middle 1880s, there was large-scale emigration, especially of the Jewish people after the pogroms started in Russia." She was explaining her decision in 1890 to follow brothers Max and Charlie to America, conflicted as she was about leaving her sick mother and younger brother Abe.

Anti-Semitism had simmered or flamed in Lithuania for centuries. Belief in the horrific myth of blood libel, wherein Jews were accused of murdering Christian children and using their blood in rituals, ended in deadly retaliation. When pogroms raged and thousands were slaughtered, their homes and businesses were left in a wake of destruction. Further, Jews were blamed for epidemics, famines, alcoholism, and economic downturns. Who would embrace the lies and act on them? Many people did.

Lithuania's ebb and flow of tolerance and persecution of Jews saw the beginning of the end in 1941, with the invasion of the Nazis. According to Greenbaum, by the conclusion of World War II and the Third Reich's Final Solution, the 200,000 Lithuanian Jewish citizenry was reduced to 1,700, less than one percent.[56] While she credited some Lithuanians with the perilous work of helping save Jewish lives, she did not look away from those who were complicit in the Holocaust.

Greenbaum noted that it was not until 1990 that the independent Lithuanian Supreme Council acknowledged and condemned the extermination of the Jews. They stated "with sorrow that Lithuanian citizens were among the executioners who served the occupiers."[57]

In 1945, the same year that eighteen-year-old Masha Ralsky was liberated from a Nazi death camp, Yetta Helen Jasspon Kunitz Dine sat in her great-niece's Tarrytown, New York, apartment. Pencil sharpened and memory intact, she began her account of life in Lithuania from 1866 to 1890.

◆◆◆◆◆◆◆◆

THE MEMOIR BEGINS: YASHWEN, PROVINCE OF KOVNO

> I have walked through many lives,
> some of them my own,
> and I am not who I was,
> though some principle of being
> abides, from which I struggle
> not to stray.

—From "The Layers," Stanley Kunitz, *Passing Through: The Later Poems, New and Selected*

Without my consent, I was brought into the world much too early in the year 1866—and if I had my choice, it was also in the wrong place, Yashwen, a God-forsaken town in the Province of Kovno, Lithuania.[58] The population of about 300 families consisted of Poles, Jews, Germans and Lithuanians. The latter were the majority, about 150 families: Jewish about 100, Poles, 40 or so, and a few Germans.

The Lithuanians and Poles had small farms, and their entire families worked in the fields in the summer. In winter, women would spin yarn of wool and flax and weave cloth to make into garments for the family. The men worked in the forest cutting timber. Their pay was about one-and-a-half rubles per six-day week. The hours depended on the daylight.

Jewish men were traders, merchants and saloonkeepers, with a few artisans, such as tailors and shoemakers. There was one coppersmith.

The Germans made earthenware pottery, such as you see now in 57th Street antique shops. German cabinetmakers and woodworkers made everything: spinning wheels, barrels, tubs, pails, boards,

Without my consent one I was brought in the World in the year 1866. (much to early If I had my choice) and in the wrong place,

A Gods forsaken town in Lithuania in the Province of Kovno.

The population about 300 families consisted of Poles, Jewish Germans and Lithuanians, the later ware the majority, about 150 families, Jewish about 100, Poles 40 or 20, and a few Germans.

The Lithuanias and Poles had small ferms, their whole families worked in the fields in the summer, In the winter the women would spin yarn of Wool and Flax and weeve cloth to make into Garments or Clothing for the Family, and the man used to work in the Forest getting timber their pay was about One and a half Rubbels per week of 6 days, the hours dependent on the lenght of the day from day break until dark

The Jewish ware traders Store keepers a few Artisans such as taylors Shoe makers, One Copersmith

The Germans made Potery or earthen wear, such as you see on 5th St in the antic shops. Cabinet makers that made every thing, Gunning, Wheels Barrel tubs pails boards Rolling pins spoons, and numerous other articles There was also a Black smith and a locksmith,

every thing that was made, or say manufactured was sold by the local cummunity and the surounding vilages that came to church

The church brought most of the busines in town perhaps 50 surounding vilages had to come to this Catholic church, the only one in the district

Memoir, page one: "Without my consent …"
Collection of Gretchen Kunitz, M.D.

rolling pins, spoons, and numerous other articles. There was also a blacksmith and a locksmith.

Everything made was sold to the local community and the surrounding village people who came to the Catholic church, which brought most of the business into town. Perhaps fifty surrounding villages had to come to this Catholic church, the only one in the district.

All the Gentiles were Catholics, and the population was very poor, with the exception of a few Jewish store or saloon keepers.

The farmers had homes built adjoining their farmland, and all the houses looked alike. They were built of logs with straw roofs. Living quarters and stables or barns were attached. The house had one large room, with a large wood-burning oven built of clay, which served all purposes: baking, cooking, heating; people slept on top, with chickens underneath. Ovens had no chimneys.

The furniture consisted of benches near the walls. There were sometimes ten or twelve people in the family. They needed the benches for sleeping if the top of the oven could not accommodate the whole family. Small windows did not take up any wall space, and the only door opened into the stable or barn. Every household had a couple of spinning wheels and a homemade weaving machine. Yet, they seemed to be happy and never complained. The priest had promised them a place in heaven, and they were content.

They produced all their food stuffs on the farm. Everyone had a couple cows, goats, sheep, pigs and poultry, like geese, ducks, chickens and turkeys. Surplus livestock was exchanged or sold for commodities they had to get in the stores. Most of the money they got from selling the farm stuffs and livestock went to the church and the saloons (which one of the two is the greater evil?). They had to get drunk at least once a week, and the five saloons in town did a good business.

The town never changed in population or otherwise. For instance, the pasture was two to three miles from town, and it belonged to everyone. A shepherd and a few small children were in charge of the herd. They were paid for the season by the town.

All livestock had to travel miles before they reached the pasture. About 5 a.m., hundreds of cows, goats, sheep, pigs and geese were led to the pasture through the whole length of the town, which had two streets like a T. I wondered why each farmer could not have his own pasture on his land, which was behind his home.

The church was in the center of the town, but it had a long drive, perhaps a quarter of a mile, with a large tract of land beautifully laid out with lawns, flowers, gardens and a large orchard. The church's well-built and well-kept buildings were surrounded by a high iron fence.

The church was very large, as it accommodated hundreds of people. The bells could be heard for miles. It had three priests and an organist who lived on the premises.

The priests' house had many rooms and was nicely furnished. They even had a piano. As children, we used to sneak behind the fence and listen to the music. This was the only piano in town or in the whole district.

We also used to watch the priests walking in the gardens with their "sisters," as they were supposed to be. My Mother and I noticed that every priest had good-looking sisters, who were dressed in style—taffeta dresses with hooped skirts and white ruffles. No one else in town wore dresses like that.

They were called *panenka,* which means mademoiselle or "doll." No one ever knew their names. At that age, I could not understand why people would say that they were someone else's sister, not the priests', then smile about it.

All business was done on Sunday when the villagers came in by the hundreds, either by horse carts or on foot. The few that had shoes or boots would carry them and put them on near the church. But very few had them because they were too great a luxury.

In summer, everyone was barefoot. In winter, they wrapped their feet in rags and woven sandals made of bark from young trees that were laced up with hemp rope. They must have been very comfortable and warm.

The villagers were self-sufficient. Very few commodities were brought in from the big cities. Of course, the landlords lived differently. They sold lumber and everything you could think of in large quantities. It amounted to thousands of rubles yearly.

The owners were seldom on their estates. They spent their fortunes in Monte Carlo or Paris, where they gambled away thousands. Then they had to mortgage their estates or get money in advance for their crops. They were always short of funds.

Their children were sent abroad to be educated. They and their kind ruled Poland after World War One, and they are the ones who were not satisfied with the [Polish] Lublin Government supported by Russia.

The Jewish population lived in the center of town around the market square. All the stores and saloons were located around the square. The majority owned their homes, which were connected with the businesses. The homes were also built of logs, but they looked much nicer. The logs were square and the walls inside were plastered. Some homes had wood floors. Ovens had chimneys, and sometimes were covered with tile.

My own home, where my Mother and I were born, had a tile oven that heated three rooms. It was very comfortable. There was a large brick Dutch oven in the kitchen for baking and cooking. The kitchen was a large room with a vegetable storage cellar for the winter.

Several outbuildings were used as barns and warehouses for grain. We had cows, horses, a couple goats and, of course, chickens. Why they bothered with chickens, I don't know. In those days, you could get eggs for ten kopecks a dozen.

The poorer homes only had one or two rooms with clay floors. They did not have plastered walls, but all had chimneys that carried the smoke out, instead of going into the room like the Gentile homes.

Everyone lived in peace, without police protection. If a dispute arose, it would be settled by arbitration with the rabbi as judge. The Christians would fight and settle it in the saloon, but there was never any serious trouble until the uprising of the Polish revolution.

My Mother, Ida Wolpe, was a native of the town perhaps for six or seven generations. We were told that her ancestors were all business people and men of learning. They were a large family and settled all over Poland and near the German border.

My Father, Harry Jasspon, said that he was a descendant of Spanish Jews from the sixteenth century. He and his ancestors were proud of their Spanish origin. So, they took the surname of Jasspon. In Russian it was Yaspan, which means "I'm Spanish."

He was a learned man who loved to give orders, and his orders were law. My Mother was a good-natured, hard-working woman, who was Father's slave (in those days, all women were slaves to their husbands).

AN INCIDENT

Since ever I could remember, Father was always in poor health because of an incident that happened before I was born.

One of his businesses was to supply food and grain for the Russian army horses. When the Polish-Lithuanian revolution started, the Russians persecuted those who supported Poland, and the Poles did the same to those who supported Russia.

The Poles had Father on the list of Russian supporters. He knew that could mean death. He decided to go to Warsaw, where he knew two leaders of the rebels, Graf Radziwill and Graf Aginsui.[59] He left Mother at home with two small children.

It took weeks before he could get in touch with them. Finally, they promised him freedom if he would stop supplying the Russian army. They told him he could return home, and in case someone molested him, they gave him a letter signed by both that he was not to be troubled anymore.

Father returned home late one evening, happy with what he had accomplished and told Mother not to worry.

The next morning a group of rebels came and took Father out of bed. They told him not to bother dressing because they were going to hang him. They had the rope.

They walked him through the street to the river, which was not far. There was a tree where many innocent people were hanged by both Russians and Poles. Father in his haste forgot about the letter, but Mother ran after them, crying and waving the letter. She reached them just in time to save Father's life.

How history repeats itself almost a century later. Europe suffers again, only in a crueler way and on a larger scale.

Father was free but ruined financially and broken in health. It took months before he could do anything. No one was sure what would happen from day to day.

> ... one day my teacher in the 6th grade—her name was Miss Ryan—asked me to tell a story before the class. I rose and told what had happened to my mother's father in Lithuania. When I finished, Miss Ryan said to me, "Stanley, thanks so much, but next time will you please tell us something more pleasant?" I never forgot that.
>
> —Stanley Kunitz, from "Stanley Kunitz on Paul Celan and the Poetry of the Holocaust."

After the revolution was suppressed, he tried again to earn a living for the family, which had increased in size by that time. We were six children; the oldest, Sifre, was married.

JEWISH LIFE IN YASHWEN

The life of Jewish people in a small town had no future. It went on from generation to generation, with children following in the footsteps of their fathers. The sons of tailors became tailors and shoemakers pursued that profession.

The synagogue in every Jewish community was not only the house of prayer but also the house of learning. Every male child had to study ten hours a day from the age of five until at least thirteen. Girls' education was voluntary, not compulsory. Very few of the older generation could read or write.

All of a sudden, a certain change took place. The younger people in the synagogue where they studied the Talmud became hungry for knowledge. They had Russian and German books, which was a crime then. Learned young men from the large cities came to the towns and opened schools for girls and boys alike. The old people protested, but it did no good.

The Russian government also opened an elementary school for boys only. My oldest brother, Max, was the only Jewish pupil. Up to that period, all the Christian people were illiterate.[60] Education was not compulsory, yet they took advantage and sent one boy from the family to school. It went to about the fifth or sixth grade.

When my brother entered that school, his knowledge was far above the Russian teacher's, who could not understand how one could obtain so much knowledge by himself without instruction. The instructor at the school knew only Russian. At that time, my brother must have been fifteen years old and had mastered German, as well as some French. He had learned the languages in secret with the aid of dictionaries. According to the Jewish tradition, it was a sin.

Max became the instructor's pet. The whole class were beginners—it took them a term to learn their ABCs, which they wrote in large letters.

RECORD KEEPING, CONSCRIPTION AND BRIBES

Another change took place, I think in 1872. Until then, there was no record of births and deaths. No one ever knew their exact age.

In fact, I did not know the date when I was born. I knew it was on a Jewish holiday in the year 1866. Every year on that holiday, I was a year older. When I was in my fifties, I wrote to a Jewish newspaper to find out on what date that holiday was in 1866. They answered that it was September 22nd, which also happened to be the date in 1890 I landed in America. It really was my rebirth, and I consider it my real birthday. I regret that twenty-four years of my life were wasted. It was supposed to be the best part of one's life.

Conscription for military service was established. Every man at the age of twenty-one would have to serve three years in the army. Russia always had an army, but the system was different. Only the very poor and the peasants would serve six years.[61] How did they get them? They were rounded up in the towns and villages and taken far from home against their will. They were sent away, the way the Germans did since Hitler.

Even after conscription was established, it was considered a disgrace for a Jewish family to have a son in the service. Every family tried to avoid it by different means.

A census was taken all over the country, and from that date all births and deaths had to be recorded. Father was chosen recorder for the Jewish population of the districts because he knew the Russian language fairly well. He liked the honor and authority and also received a small fee for his work.

I really think that time was the turning point from ignorance and slavery to freedom and knowledge. People became restless and dissatisfied with the heaven promised by their religious leaders. They also wanted a share of comfort and knowledge in their lifetime. The younger people left the small towns and went to the big cities searching for something they themselves did not know.

Books and poems in all languages suddenly appeared and called for youth to wake up. Religion declined, especially among the Jewish youth. The Catholic church was not affected by the change. I don't think it ever will.

Father resumed business after the revolution. Sailing was hard on account of his ill health and lack of capital, but he still maintained his position as ruler of the community. Certain business he undertook was more for the sake of authority than for the profit derived.

For instance, he was also the collector of taxes. The Jewish communities had to pay a certain lump sum, which was derived in the following way.

A tax was put on the slaughter of cattle and poultry according to the Jewish ritual, which all Jewish families observed in those days. Bids would be sent to the government for the privilege of collecting this tax. The government would set a minimum, and the bidding went up. The highest bidder got the contract for all Jewish people of that district. It had to be paid in advance for a year. As long as I can remember until his death, Father held the privilege to sell tickets for the slaughter. It was fifty kopeks for a steer or cow, thirty kopeks for lamb, sheep, goats and calves, seven kopeks for geese and turkeys, three kopeks for chickens and ducks. Sometimes, the income would not cover the price of the contract, but there was a prestige to own that privilege or contract, which came directly from St. Petersburg.

The auction, as you would call it here, was held in Kovno, the capital of the Province. Some bribing had to be done, and Father knew all the government officials and knew whom to bribe. Any business done with the government had to use bribes.

Father also had a business producing lime, which was done in a primitive way. He had several pits where lime was burned and sold to the government for use in building railroads or any government buildings.[62]

Officials had to be bribed in a big way. The price obtained was below cost of production, but it was made up by short measure with the consent of the officer in charge.

I remember an episode when I was about eight or nine years of age. When the Vilna to Libau railroad was built, Father obtained the lime contract. It was to be delivered to Kaidan, halfway between Libau and Vilna, six miles from our town of Yashwen.

The lime was carted by horse and wagon, with each cart carrying ten barrels the size of sugar or flour barrels in this country. The price for delivery was a ruble-and-a-half per load. It took a full day for a man and two horses.

One day I got on one of the carts and went along with a load of laundry. When we came into Kaidan, there was a vast square of land with a post in the center. Two officers were checking each load and giving receipts. The team would drive up to the post, and the officers would give the driver a receipt. I noticed that he did not empty the load. The officers motioned him to drive on. He did and came again to the same spot, and it was repeated. Some of them got three receipts for one load. So, they collected three times the amount for carting, and the officers also were paid for each extra receipt, which also was the invoice. No business could be conducted with the government in an honest way.

The officers' pay was small and not sufficient to pay for their vodka and caviar. So, they always managed to supplement their pay with bribes, and the merchant managed to get a living from this dangerous business.

The export business was not very profitable either, as Father had to be advanced capital from the German merchants. It took lots of money and storage space. We had the latter. We five children all lived at home, but no one ever earned any money.

My oldest brother, Max, continued to educate himself now more in the open than in secret. Our house was full of Russian and German books. Father also had a large amount of Hebrew literature, which was displayed on shelves where they could be seen. Some books were very old, and he claimed that were brought by his ancestors from Spain. He treasured them dearly.

His health kept on declining, and he had to stay home a great deal. Because his businesses required travel, the situation became worse from day to day. He tried to hold on and not lose his authority. People still came to him for advice or to fix up something with the government officials, all the way up to the governor himself.

Meanwhile, according to the census, Max was almost twenty-one. He would have to go into the army if there was not enough money to bribe him out.

My brother really was only eighteen, but at the time of the census, Father listed him as three years older, and my two younger brothers as three years younger. There was a law that the oldest son at twenty-one would be exempt if the quota was filled and if his younger brothers were under ten. Unless the country was at war.

So, my brother became twenty-one at the age of eighteen, and Russia was at war with Turkey. Max left home and went to Germany to hide out. He liked Germany and would have remained there if he was allowed, but Germany would not allow Russian citizens to reside in their country. He was expelled from Germany after a year of hiding and returned home in secret. He hid in the hay barn where we brought him his meals.

After a few weeks, he left for America, which was a disgrace for any respectable Jewish family. America was a place where only horse thieves would escape to. My Father passed away in the spring of 1878, a few months after Max left. I was twelve years old.

Despite all the businesses Father had—census-taker, tax collector, lime pits, export company—we were left penniless. Mother struggled to support the family. We still had two cows, one horse, a goat and chickens. Mother secretly sold whatever she could to marry off my older sister Rebecca.[63] Her jewelry included gold and some stones, a heavy gold chain and a string of mother-of-pearl. Other valuables were table silver, gold-plated wine cups of various sizes and shapes, with matching small trays or plates. They were seldom used, but the pleasure and prestige of having them is beyond imagination.

Mother must have suffered to part with all these valuables. No one knew about it because she went to Kovno and sold everything to a dealer. She could have almost doubled the price if she sold to private people, but she wanted no one to know about it and no one did, except the older children in the family.

Mother was reconciled because she had raised the money for the required dowry. My sister was married and left home with her husband, a nice respectable young man from the city of Shavel, about sixty miles from Yashwen in the same province of Kovno.[64] She lived there and bore fourteen children. My sister died on the road when they were evacuated in World War I.[65]

I think eleven children survived and were scattered over the world in South Africa, the United States and Mexico. We don't know the fate of those who remained in Lithuania, where they returned after Germany was defeated. Nothing has been heard from them since 1939—another repetition in another generation.

MY FAMILY'S SINS

Father was a native of Vilna, the largest city in Lithuania, a city of Jewish culture and Talmudic studies with its population of more than fifty percent Jewish. It remained a city of learning until Hitler overran it. He destroyed all the schools and libraries that had existed for centuries since the Jews were expelled from Spain and emigrated to Eastern Europe. The fate of the Jewish people in Vilna is well-known: more than ninety percent were annihilated.

Father came to Yashwen in 1846, when he married Mother's older sister, who died six years later, leaving one child. Mother took care of the child, and in a year or so was married to Father. She was sixteen, and the child who was my oldest sister was six. Her name was Sifre, and my Mother loved her just as she did her own children. We never knew the difference. We were six in all, including Sifre. I was the fourth, with two brothers younger than myself.

Father was Lord and Master, and we all feared him and would never dare to contradict or disobey him. We had to do what we were told.

On the Sabbath and all Jewish holidays, dietary laws were strictly observed in line with all other Jewish homes.

On Friday evening, Mother used to light several candles and a kerosene lamp. According to Jewish custom or law, it was forbidden to put out any light, even to touch it. The candles would burn until they were gone, and the lamp would either burn as long as it held kerosene, or a Gentile would be called in to put it out. We always had a Gentile to make the samovar and the fire on Saturdays.

I remember one Friday night when I was six or seven years old. Everyone had gone to sleep. Some of the candles still flickered, and the lamp was burning. The smell of kerosene was not very pleasant. I was watching the shadows on the wall, and in the dimly lit room, I saw Father come out of the bedroom. And there he was at the table, blowing out the lamp and the flickering candles.

I became scared, worried and afraid of his being damned. Although

I feared Father, I loved him just the same and did not want him to be punished. We were always told that God punishes us for every sin committed.

The next morning, I waited for a chance to tell Mother. I did not know if she heard Father when he came into the other room. When I finally told her, she said in her calm way, "You did not see Father do that. You just dreamt about it." But I knew better even then that it was not a dream. She told me not to repeat the dream. I did not repeat it, but I kept thinking about it.

A few months later, I came upon another sin in our house. Part of the house had two separate rooms, one with a window that faced the garden. My older brother Max always used to lock himself in that part of the house, and we never could see what he was doing. He kept some of his books there, and other things that he experimented with.

On a hot summer Saturday afternoon, I went into the garden and looked in the window. There was Max, smoking a cigarette and writing in his Russian book. He was with a cousin of ours, who was a year or so older than my brother. He was standing behind Max, also smoking a cigarette, dictating to him.

I became frightened and went to look for Mother. I would not dare to tell Father. I told her what I had just seen, and again in her calm way, she said, "You have not seen that. You just imagined it. Don't tell anyone and don't look in the window when your brother and cousin are studying."

My cousin, also named Max (his surname was Shabishewitz), had the most brilliant mind. He and my brother were inseparable. They studied the Talmud (and also forbidden literature) together. In the synagogue, they were under the supervision of my sister Sifre's husband, Aaron Gordon, who was an ordained rabbi but never used it as a profession. He always had great hope that the two Maxes would someday become great men in Jewish life. Of course, he never knew about the forbidden literature.

NAMING

There was a Max or Maxim, as they were called in Russia, in every branch of Mother's family. They were named after my great-great-grandfather, who was supposed to have been the most learned man in his time. Mother used to tell us of his greatness. He was very pious and could perform miracles. Everyone in the family would come to get his blessing, so it is no wonder that every clan of the family who had a son named him Max. His real name was Myer but was altered in later generations to Maxim in Russian or Mark in German or American. The only miracle that was proven is that he lived to the age of 101. Mothers hoped that his namesakes would also live to an old age and some of them did.

My four grandsons did not inherit the name of this famous ancestor. My daughters selected fancy-sounding names, such as Stanton K. and Lawrence Herbert Baker, Slater K. (K. stands for Kunitz) and Conrad Herbert Isenberg.

They happen to be good students and nice boys. I don't think their names have anything to do with it. My children never forgave me for the names, especially the names I gave them and changed them later.[66] I always believed that each person can make his name worthy or even famous, but the name itself can never do that to its owner.

Max Jasspon and Max Shabishewitz did not follow the footsteps of the man they were named after. Year after year, the two cousins studied together. Another cousin, a Max Wolpe (Mother was a Wolpe), became a professor at a college in England.

COUSIN MAX DISAPPEARS

When my older brother Max became twenty-one at the age of eighteen and left home to avoid military service, my cousin was despondent. He decided that he wanted to go to the university to study medicine or science, but his Father would not listen to him. He did not want his son to become an infidel.

Their house was next to ours, and we were always together. He had two sisters, one older than he and one younger. Their Mother died when they were very young children. She was my Mother's sister. My uncle was well to do, but very stingy. Max decided he was going to the university, whether his Father agreed or not.

In January, Max started to make a very dangerous plan. His Father went to Kovno, and Max and his sisters were home.

One evening, my father had a celebration at our house for members of the synagogue. The sisters and Max stayed until late. When they went home, they found the door open. All the silverware was piled on the table, ready to be taken away. Their Mother's jewelry, which was of considerable value, was gone. Max gave the alarm, but there was no trace of the burglars. The girls were frantic, especially with the loss of a string of real matched pearls. They also feared that their Father would blame them.

When my uncle returned and was told of the loss, he, too, became frantic. He told his children to get out of the house.

In secret, my uncle used to keep his cash under a beam of the ceiling. To his surprise, the 300 rubles he had put there were also gone. He could not understand how the burglars knew where he kept the money, when his own children never knew.

Time went by. Month after month, there no trace of the jewelry, the money, or the burglar.

The following July, Max also disappeared. Then everyone understood that he had planned and committed the burglary. There was no way to find out where he went. Almost a month went by.

One day, Max was brought back as a prisoner, with his hands in chains. That was the end of a perfect crime.

He had left home with the intention of getting to Warsaw and enrolling at the university with his 300 rubles in cash, hoping to realize another thousand rubles from the jewelry. With that, he could manage to accomplish what he wanted: to become a doctor. His plan was good but had an unhappy ending.

In Russia, you were not allowed to travel without a passport. Max knew that but was afraid to get one, because his Father would discover that he intended to leave home. So, he took a chance and left without a passport. Traveling without one was a crime in Russia in those days. He was halfway to Warsaw when he was stopped and immediately arrested. He was put in jail, where the jewelry and money were stolen.

When he was sent back home, it was not by train. They walked prisoners from town to town, where the jails were their lodging. When Max finally reached home, he was a wreck and had a nervous breakdown.

It took a long time before he became well, mentally as well as physically. He never became a doctor but made good anyway. He got married and lived in Kovno. One of his sons is a lawyer in New York. In 1928, my brother Max and his wife Annie visited Max, after fifty-two years of not having seen each other.

I often wonder if cousin Max's son in New York or his other children ever knew of their Father's experience. Brother and cousin passed away just a few months apart the following year.

THE STORY OF GETCHEL

It was the duty of every Jewish family to help support yeshiva students, even if it meant depriving their own families. Everyone always managed to have a good meal for these future teachers of the Jewish tradition. And that is why at no time, wherever Jews lived, no matter under what hardship, you could never find one male who could not read Hebrew and did not know the Old Testament. I think that is why the Jew has survived.

Father married his first wife, my mother's sister, in the same way, from the very same school or yeshiva where he selected Aaron Gordon as a husband for his oldest daughter, Sifre.

A colleague of the two Maxes, who studied under my brother-in-law, was a stranger. His only identification was that he was called Getchel. He came to our town to study, and the custom was that every town would have accommodations in the synagogue for such students from thirteen years of age up. The synagogue would have lodging, and the meals were donated by the Jewish people. Every young man was given certain days with each family. The poorest family gave at least one day of each week, while the more well-to-do would give three or four days a week.

Students had no social life and never went to visit except for their three meals each day in different homes. People seldom knew their names. They were identified as the tall fellow, the dark-haired or blonde one, or the short one. Once in a while, they were known by the town they came from. No one ever bothered to know anything about them; they came to study, and they would be the future rabbis to teach the law of Moses to the next generation. Such students would remain for a couple years and then go to the theological seminary either in Vilna or Volozhin where they completed their studies.

Not all became rabbis or teachers. Some of them would marry a rich man's daughter and become businessmen. Any well-to-do man who had a daughter would go to such a school and select a husband for his daughter according to his social standing. When my oldest sister, Sifre, was not quite seventeen years old, my Father went to Vilna to select a husband for her. For a couple years, he gave them free board and room and established a business for them. Such was the custom between families and students.

Radicals who were suspected of revolutionary activities would also come to the small towns like Yashwen. They found synagogues to be safe hiding places. They hid their identities and, being practically isolated, pretended to study the Talmud. They were all brilliant young men of higher education, which they had to hide from their fellow students and teacher. Generally, these boys would not stay more than a few months.

Father always had two students for the Sabbath, which was an honor. I still can remember when they came with Father from the synagogue. They would always avoid looking at my sister, who was almost of marriageable age, because this was forbidden fruit for them. They would talk very little during the meal, and if they did say anything, it was to the younger children. Occasionally, they would give a look at my sister from the corner of their eye, when no one was looking. My sister always would dress up for that occasion and try to attract their attention at the table.

One of these students was Getchel. He was a year or so older than my brother. They became friends, and the three of them, Max, Max and Getchel, studied together. My brother-in-law, Aaron, was surprised by his keen mind and his extraordinary knowledge, calling him a genius and arranging for Sabbath meals at his home.

Getchel lived at the synagogue with all the other boys and obtained his meals in the same way. He never looked at women when someone was present. Everyone in town admired him, and he was well-liked. He could have had fourteen days' board, instead of seven.

My brother and cousin became very much attached to him. I noticed that Max always came back from the synagogue with Russian or German books. He never would say to whom they belonged.

Getchel remained in town for almost two years. Then rumors started that Getchel was not as pious as he pretended to be, that he was more interested in Tolstoy, and even in the poet Heine, who was a convert.[67] People actually saw that Getchel had books of that kind, but my brother-in-law would not believe it and said, "It's impossible!"

When Getchel was approached on the subject, he said nothing. Instead, he packed up and left. Nothing was heard from him, and eventually he was forgotten.

In 1893, in New York, my brother-in law became very ill. He had a stomach ailment that he suffered from for some time. He tried many doctors, but no one could do anything for him. A friend who came to visit suggested that we call in a specialist who someone else had recommended, a certain Dr. Jacob Goldenberg. He arranged for the doctor's visit.

When Dr. Goldenberg came in and looked at the patient, his face turned white. He recognized his beloved teacher, and the teacher recognized his beloved pupil, Getchel, that genius. How happy Getchel would have been if he could have helped his beloved teacher, but it was too late. My brother-in-law passed away a few weeks later.

The story Getchel told us was as follows: When he left Yashwen, he made his way to Germany. He went to Berlin and obtained private pupils in order to support himself. He prepared himself for three years and finally succeeded in entering the university. He studied medicine and graduated with the highest honors.

Getchel remained in Germany for a number of years, then came to America where he became a well-known doctor. It had been nineteen years since he left our town and many friends behind.

If there is a will, people will find a way. Can anyone imagine how many hardships Dr. Goldenberg endured before he reached his goal? Why do parents and teachers object to new ideas? Why do they try, from generation to generation, to keep their children in ignorance? They tried to have us believe things they themselves did not believe. What reasons were behind all this nonsense, especially with my own people?

Governments, like Russia under the Romanovs or the present Japan, control the churches. They want to keep their people in ignorance in order to hold on to their power.

Why did the Jewish people feed their children with fear and superstition? We had great men through the ages. Yet they forbade us to ask questions. More than three centuries ago, when Benedict de Spinoza dared to speak his mind, he was excommunicated. The Jewish people had no state to protect, no power they could lose. Wherever the Jew lived, he was always in a minority without any voice in the government or any rights whatsoever. Why didn't they want their children to obtain knowledge and find themselves a better way of life?

Who was it that started the march against the will of their elders, and despite any hardship, tried to get in line? Who abandoned the hope that miracles would happen and the idea of a messiah? For almost two thousand years, the Jew lived in exile, a stranger in every land. They did not try to better themselves, always feeding each other with false hope. Why were our ancestors always afraid and against any progress?

What did the Jew have to lose? He never got credit if he accomplished something in science or inventions. The country he lived in would always claim the credit of any discovery the Jew made. And he would remain an alien, just the same.

My own parents were not fanatics. Yet, we would be punished if we did not accept and obey the customs that they themselves disobeyed in secret.

I suppose other religions do the same thing. Their clergies are all educated men in science and biology, yet they, too, teach things they know not to be true. Why do they all try to teach these things, especially in a free democratic country?

I admire clergy who are unafraid to speak their minds, like Dr. Fosdike, John Hines Holms of the Community Church and Dr. Stephen Wise.[68] When I resided in New York, I always went to hear their lectures. I once heard Dr. Wise in his Sunday morning sermon at Carnegie Hall. He expressed his belief that the Ten Commandments were not handed down by God himself to Moses on Mt. Sinai. But he did say that the Ten Commandments were the best document ever given to mankind, and if they were only obeyed, we would need nothing else. Of course, the next day, the Jewish press came out against him, calling him an unbeliever not worthy of his position as rabbi. The same thing happened to Dr. Fosdike and John Hines Holms. People simply don't want to hear the truth.

While working at the Red Cross, I happened to meet a certain Miss McAlister, who was interested in Girl Scouts. We occasionally discussed religious beliefs. Her mail used to come to the Red Cross address. Shortly before this country was at war with Italy, she received a letter from Rome. So, I made a remark, joking that she was corresponding with the pope. She joked back, saying, "Maybe he will be pope someday. Anyone who goes into the priesthood hopes that someday he would become bishop, cardinal and even pope."

She knew this young man from college days. They went out together a lot. He used to visit her when she became a social worker.

On one of his visits, he told her that he was going to become a priest. She did not know if he or his family had decided for him. They kept up their friendship after he entered the seminary. She told me that he was an exceptionally bright fellow.

Before leaving for Rome to be ordained, he came to see her. She asked him if he really believed what he was going into, to preach and teach everything that science and biology proves untrue. He said, "Of course not. But it is a lovely fairy tale to have people dream about."

Millions are spent in teaching these fairy tales, which to my opinion are misleading people. These "lovely fairy tales" breed a lot of hatred and even create wars. Why do they teach these fairy tales in a democratic country? What benefit do people derive from this? Why are money and time spent on this? Let them teach real religion: Love thy neighbor as thyself.

MY FIRST JOB

At the age of fourteen, I left home and went to Kovno to earn my living as a salesgirl. My pay was fifteen rubles per year with board and room. I felt very happy and considered myself lucky to live in the capital, where there were streetlights, sidewalks, paved streets and a nice park where a military band played every evening.

This is how I got my first job. Miss Amsterdam's father was the chief rabbi in Yashwen. During a visit to her family, her parents suggested that she should take me with her. Mother entrusted me to her because she knew I would be treated right.

She was a young, unmarried lady. When I say lady, I really mean it. Miss Amsterdam took an interest in me and treated me like her own child. I was so happy that in a few months I suggested to Sifre's daughter, Anna, who was a year younger than myself, to come to Kovno and share in my happiness. I got her a job similar to mine, only it was with a married couple.

Of course, we had very little time to visit each other, but every Saturday, we met in the park and stayed together until sunset. The stores were opened for business.

The job was not very easy. It was in a nice residential neighborhood where everyone lived in large homes and had servants. Miss Amsterdam and I lived in the rear of the store in one large room that served as kitchen, bedroom and living room. Water was drawn right from a faucet in the kitchen.

The store had to be opened at 6 a.m. to receive bakery and milk products and be ready for the sale of fresh breakfast rolls.

The first unpleasant experience in my new world happened about two months after I started. One morning, a tall woman with a pockmarked face came to the store carrying the customary two baskets. One basket already had a few bags filled with things that she had bought in the marketplace. She started by ordering the best canned goods and other items carried in the store. She told us that she was a cook for one of the nearby estates. The bill came to over three rubles, which is a good sale.

After everything was placed in the basket, she said that she did not have all the money, so if I would come along to help her carry the baskets, her Mrs. would pay me for the purchase. I went along with her.

We came to a large estate with an orchard, where a man was waiting with horse and buggy. The woman grabbed the basket out of my hand, slapped me in the face, cursed me in the bargain, jumped on the buggy and drove off. I was scared and started to cry. There was no one around to tell. Still in tears, I went back to the store and explained. The woman had disappeared, but Miss Amsterdam did not blame me. She took all the fault on herself.

My employer was well-liked, as she really was a well-educated, cultured and very lovable woman. Despite being a rabbi's daughter, she herself was not religious and in fact, very radically inclined. She associated with few people, but her associates were all radicals. Tolstoy was their God.

She was not only my employer but also my teacher. I remained with her for a number of years, until she sold her business and went to St. Petersburg. Mother became ill, and I returned home.

DISSATISFACTION

My youngest brother Charlie left home at the age of thirteen to go to America and live with Max. Abe, who was three years younger than me, stayed at home. Mother, Abe and I struggled along by renting out part of the house. We had a vegetable garden and kept one cow and some chickens.

To be poor in those days was not only an inconvenience, but a disgrace. I hated small-town life with all its discomforts and everyone watching what you did.

After a taste of city life, it was hard to put up with all the inconvenient and unsanitary conditions. Mud in the streets was more than a foot deep in rainy weather and turned to dust in the dry summer.

There was one public bath house, which was only available once a week. Fifty or more women were in one room filled with steam hot enough to suffocate, seated naked on benches, with wooden pails of hot water to wash themselves.

The public bath also served as a dispensary to cure high blood pressure by drawing blood with leeches, which were kept hungry and put on the naked body until they filled up and fell off dead. Very few leeches ever survived to be used again.

Another method to lower blood pressure was to cut the skin with a very sharp instrument. Some little metal cups were placed on the cut that drew out blood in large quantities. It streamed down on the floor of the bathhouse. These operations were not done by doctors or nurses, but just by plain women who earned their living by doing it. Men did the same, attended by men, of course.

It really is hard to believe that people could survive under such conditions. And yet some lived to a very old age.

Child mortality was high, as well as women dying in childbirth. There were no doctors, so children were delivered by midwives who were not trained. Some babies were delivered just by their next-door neighbor. Peasant women gave birth and went out to work in the field on the second or third day (if they did not die while giving birth).

I became dissatisfied with such an existence, grew restless and decided to go to America. By then, it was no longer a disgrace to go to the new world.

(Stanley, you probably remember the story about Mr. Asher, Judge Jacob Asher's Father, who lived in Worcester. He used to tell me that he was married at the age of fourteen. The next day he went out with the boys to play marbles. His Father went after him and gave him a calling down. He was a married man now and could not play any more, either marbles or other games. The oldest daughter is only fifteen years younger than her Father. Her Mother was a few years older. Mr. Asher passed away last year at the age of eighty-nine).[69]

PREPARING FOR THE JOURNEY

From the middle 1880s, there was large-scale emigration, especially of the Jewish people after the pogroms started in Russia.

I scraped together the money needed for the voyage. Mother packed my trousseau into two large wicker baskets with locks.

Every Mother started a trousseau when her daughter was very young, perhaps from the age of three. It consisted of a feather bed and three large pillows. There were perhaps seventy pounds of pure white geese feathers. The stems of every feather were removed by hand, then the feathers were mixed with down, which was also pure white. It takes years to collect seventy or more pounds of feathers, but it is done. I still use some pillows and had enough for my children when they were married.

There were dozens of cotton or linen hand-knitted stockings, but I never could use the stockings in this country. Trousseaus included all sorts of pure linen sheets, towels, pillowcases, hand-embroidered underwear, some charms for good luck and hundreds of other things that I never had any use for.

Mother had loads of copper and silver utensils, which were inherited from generation to generation. Some were sold in secret when hard times came, such as when my second sister was married after Father's death. But there still was plenty, so I took my share with me. Everything was packed in the two baskets that weighed almost 300 pounds.

It was a miracle that I had a home to leave behind. Two days before my departure, a fire broke out three houses away and the whole street burned down. I almost lost my valuable trousseau in the fire.

It did not take long to burn, with all the straw roofs, dry timber and no fire apparatus. Of course, all the men in town came and tried to put out the fire. Since the water had to be drawn from a well, two hours later, half of the town was a heap of ashes. But our house, with all the barns and storehouses remained, to be destroyed fifty years later by Hitler. I still have a picture of our home, taken by a nephew of mine who visited in 1928.

With the two wicker baskets, a large bundle and the necessary money, I left my sick Mother, brother Abe and my home.

◆◆◆◆◆◆◆◆

Jasspon home, Village of Yashwen, Lithuania, c. 1928.
Department of Special Collections, Princeton University Library

HOPE, COURAGE AND AMBITION

Yetta Helen Jasspon joined other European emigrants who were making their way to the New World with few possessions and an abundance of hope. They knew poverty, unemployment, oppression and persecution but rejected the notion that the troubling quartet was their lot in life. They planned to transplant themselves into an economic Paradise, get to work, and make their fortunes.

A typical *S.S. Rhynland* manifest offered snapshots of passengers, some with families, but most traveling alone. In saloon and second cabin classes, the smallest groups were adult female passengers listed as "Wife" or "Lady" and males who declared their occupations as lawyers, teachers, merchants, artists, bookmakers, students and doctors.

In steerage, the largest group consisted of males who identified themselves as laborers, bakers, tailors, capmakers, shoemakers, stonecutters, miners, and gardeners. Women were either married or worked as servants, dressmakers, laundresses or cooks.[70] Yetta's marketable skills were scant. She had worked in a shop but felt confident that she could learn other trades if she were given the chance.

After traveling from their villages and arriving in Antwerp, Belgium, emigrants could expect to sail for between seven and fourteen days. In 1890, the *Rhynland* sailed from Antwerp to New York eight times between March and November. Destination: Castle Garden, New York, gateway to the Golden Land.[71]

◆◆◆◆◆◆◆◆◆

A GOOD SAILOR

I left Yashwen in August 1890 to visit my sister Rebecca in Shavel for a few days. I had no passport, so I was taken over the German border at night. Then I took a train for Bremen. Hundreds of emigrants were passing through Germany in that period. No one troubled you, as long as you could pay your fare. Today, we would be called refugees, but it is practically the same.

In Bremen, I purchased my ticket to New York and waited four days. We stopped in a hotel called Emigranten Haus, which was free. On the fifth day, we were put on a train bound for Antwerp.

We arrived there late in the evening. They also had an Emigranten Haus, very neat and clean. We had ten days more to wait for a liner.

During this time, an agent came around. He asked questions and offered jobs that would begin when we arrived in New York. Families were offered jobs in the cotton mills in Fall River, Massachusetts. The agent even gave tickets for the boat from New York to Fall River. People were instructed not to say anything until they passed through the gates in Castle Garden. Men, mostly Slavs from eastern Europe, were offered jobs in the Pennsylvania coal mines and told of all the prosperity that awaited them. Those that had addresses for relatives or friends in New York were not offered any "help," as they called it.

The reason given for not saying anything about the jobs was that contract labor was forbidden entry into the United States. I think the law had been passed in that year.[72]

After ten days in Antwerp, we finally were taken to the ship, a Red Star liner. The ship was the *Rhynland* or *Rhineland*, and it was not a luxury liner, by any means. We traveled steerage, so each cubic hole had four bunks. There was no window because it was below water level.

The food for the main meal was potatoes cooked with skins and herring. They served tea and bread, too. But who cared about the food when you were young and going to the Golden Land, where a job and everything else awaited you? Most passengers brought along a variety of food stuffs that came in handy. Some passengers were sick the whole trip and stayed in their bunks and lived on tea.

I happened to be a good sailor. I felt good and spent my times on the deck. I came to know every passenger and listened to their plans for what they intended to do after they saved up some capital and became Americanized. Almost all planned to become businessmen sooner or later. No one knew how they would earn the money—they

Emigrants, Castle Garden, June 7, 1890.
Photo by Robert L. Bracklow (1849-1919). Museum of the City of New York

worried more about what they would do with it. No one had any money left after paying for their passage, but they all had hope, courage and ambition. Single girls hoped to marry rich men, of which there were plenty in America. The married men planned to send for their families as soon as they saved up money.

I listened to all, but my own heart was heavy. I knew what I left behind and was uncertain of what awaited me in my new world. I was worried about my Mother and not very optimistic about all these expectations in America.

At 9:30 a.m. on September 22nd, we passed the Statue of Liberty and neared Castle Garden. Finally, the ship stopped.[73]

CHAPTER THREE

New York's Lower East Side
1890–1893

I don't have much hope for changing the world,
but I can try to change myself.

—From *Conversations with Stanley Kunitz*,
ed. Kent P. Ljungquist, interviewer Robert Russell, 1967

JUST GIVE ME A CHANCE

ONCE YETTA DINE started her memoir—"Without my consent, I was brought into the world much too early in the year 1866 ..." —memories flowed easily from her pencil, grateful for the breath of release. The fifty-five-year span since her arrival in New York gave her the opportunity to selectively escape to a happier past: "I started to write and found myself on Henry Street. I have so much to tell about all the people who came into my life on that street."

When she disembarked from the *S.S. Rhynland*, Yetta willfully chose a new beginning and unhooked herself from a life of superstition, censorship and ignorance. However, her new freedom was tempered by one lesson she carried like a heavy bundle: Her father's power and prestige in the community was rewarded with varying amounts of respect, but his death left his wife and children in poverty.

While she may have rued the year in which she was born, three years on New York's Lower East Side were sweet drops in what was to become life's bitter cup. The gift of writing allowed her to remember the energetic, ambitious person she once was. Strange language and new surroundings aside, the young woman's motto was right for the times: "Just give me a chance."

One of the sweetest drops in her cup materialized soon after she arrived. The Educational Alliance opened at 197 East Broadway and offered immigrants a rich brocade of lectures, books and English classes, all free. Politics, philosophy, ethics and social reform were topics that nourished her curious, skeptical mind and shaped her destiny. Spinoza's criticism of organized religions, including Judaism, and his arguments for a democratic form of government had already taken root in her mind in Lithuania. Just as Yetta would exchange European clothes for American ones, she was ready to build an independent, intellectual life.

Educational Alliance exterior, undated.
From the Archives of the YIVO Institute for Jewish Research

WICKER BASKETS AND BUNDLES

Passengers who had addresses of relatives or friends sent telegrams, and they were met outside the gate. Others just took their bundles, got in line for the desk, and gave their names. No visas or passports were required back then, so people walked through the gates.

Those who were given tickets for the coal mines stuck them in their hats. They were picked up by an agent and sent to their destination. The same thing happened with families who went to the cotton mills.

I had an address for my brother-in-law that came a few months before I left. In fact, Aaron Gordon was important because, as dean of the first Jewish yeshiva or shul of higher education in Talmud and theology, Sifre's husband was a highly learned man. He was an ordained rabbi, but never liked it as a profession. My sister had a grocery, or rather, a variety store in our town and supported the family. He spent his time studying and instructing younger students and not being paid for it. But finally, he got that call for the position and came to New York.

I had sent a telegram to his lodging address before reaching Castle Garden. I waited and waited. No one came for me.

I decided it was no use waiting any longer, so I took my two wicker baskets and bundle to the desk. I gave my name and my brother-in-law's, but they did not ask me much. I went out from Castle Garden and looked around but could not decide what to do.

To my surprise, a countryman of mine who was in New York for a couple years had come to meet his sister. He expected her on that steamer. He recognized me, and I told him my plight. He said it was all right, and that I could go with him as soon as he found

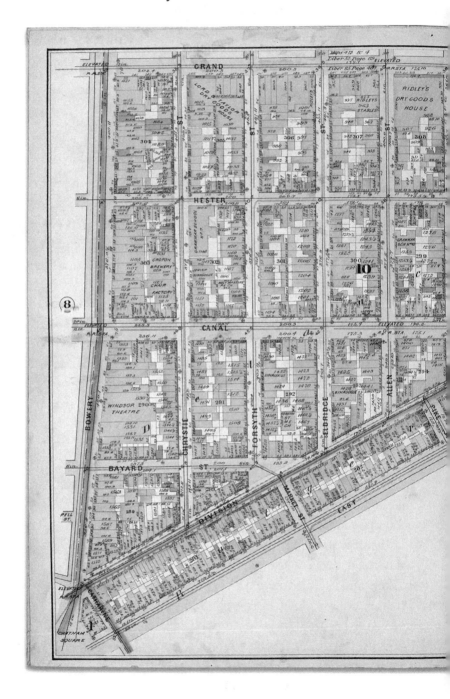

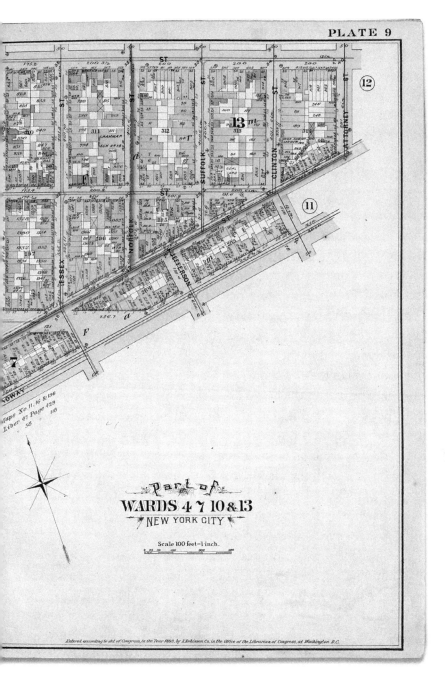

Plate 9: Map bounded by Grand St., Attorney St., E. Broadway, Bowery.
Lionel Pincus and Princess Firyal Map Division, The New York Public Library

his sister. She was still on the steamer looking for her baggage. We waited until she finally came through the gate.

They took me to relatives of theirs at 38 Chrystie Street on the Lower East Side. We climbed four flights of stairs before we reached that haven.

WELCOME

It was already late afternoon when we arrived, and I was hot, tired and hungry. The Mrs. of the establishment made me feel at home, and they all promised to find my brother-in-law. We put my wicker baskets and bundle on the fire escape.

This was the rear part of the house, a five-storey building with four tenements on each floor. Down a long dark hall, there was one sink and toilet for the four families. All the doors were open, and the neighbors were talking to each other, waiting to get the sink or use of the toilet. I knew that I could not stay there, because the four or five of them lived in these two rooms.

The windows of the one room that was kitchen, dining and living room faced the rear of the house on Forsyth Street. Other windows faced a brick wall and had clothes lines, which were drawn by a pulley. This was quite a novelty to me. Clothes lines were connected to the window casing on both sides and drawn by the pulley. There was one line for each tenant. As it was a sunny day, all lines of the five floors were filled with laundry, bedding, dirty quilts with faded patterns, and old worn cotton blankets. The laundry had a lot of infants' articles and household linens.

I examined them with my eyes because it was interesting to recognize familiar articles, just like those in my two wicker baskets. Some of the linens or the ticking of the pillows on the fire escapes were collected by mothers for their daughters' trousseaus. It took years to make up all the familiar hand embroidery and hand-made lace of fine thread. I thought maybe they hung them on the lines to welcome me.

By looking at the laundry, I could guess where their owners came from. The neighborhood was all foreigners, mostly Jewish, as I came to learn later. There were also some Italians, Greeks, Poles and other nationalities. Everyone seemed to know each other and tried to be friendly. I suppose they felt lonely and lost, as all emigrants feel. No matter what kind of a home was left behind, they missed it. It is hard for anyone to be upended and transplanted. Everyone left someone behind to miss and to worry about. It takes a lot of time to adjust.

Curious neighbors came in with all kinds of excuses to survey the new arrival and owner of the baggage on the fire escape. I sat in a chair by the window near the kitchen coal stove, which was covered with newspaper. The dinner was being cooked on top of a two-burner kerosene stove. It smelled good.

When I came in, I was told by the Mrs. that I could have dinner with them and stay until my brother-in-law called for me. She said not to worry and to wait until her husband and a boarder came home from work. After dinner, her husband would go to find my brother-in-law. Everyone tried to be helpful in those days.

All the doors were still open, and the neighbors were talking while they were cooking. The smells and sounds mixed together—the food and the crying children, who were being brought in from the streets. Naturally, the children were tired, hungry and dirty. The women were busy, and for a while, they forgot I was sitting there.

About 7 o'clock, her husband and the boarder arrived. They had noticed my baggage on the fire escape and saw me sitting there. His wife hastily explained how I happened to be there. He greeted me very friendly and wished me luck in the new land of opportunity.

They washed up, and we all had dinner. We talked for a while and I could see that he was of the new generation that had sprung up in Russia, an intellectual. But when he arrived in New York, he became a capmaker and worked in a sweatshop. His wife had to keep a boarder to help meet expenses. They were both nice people and tried hard to make ends meet. The two-room tenement was spotless, and their two lovely children looked nice after they came in from playing in the street.

After dinner, her husband went out to look for my brother-in-law. They came back after ten. My brother-in-law said that he was sorry he was not there to meet me. He had not gotten my cable until he returned to his lodging from the yeshiva.

He was glad to see me and hear from the family. He had a room engaged for me and went out and hired a pushcart for my baggage. We walked to my new home just a couple blocks away. But before I left, I paid for my first meal, twelve cents. The Mrs. did not want to be paid, but I insisted, and she took the twelve cents. I thought it was not enough, but she said that was all her boarder paid her, and she certainly would not charge me anymore. I have never forgotten her.

I'LL FIND MY WAY

When we arrived at my new home, it was almost eleven o'clock at night. I could not see much of my new haven. My bed was made up on a couch in the parlor. The Mrs., her husband and their two children were already sleeping. My brother-in-law promised to come the next day, then he left.

I got up the next morning, refreshed after a night's rest. I met the family and ate my breakfast. This was also a rear apartment, as it is called nowadays, with three rooms and a sink in the kitchen. Everything was spotless. The stove was polished and had bright copper utensils that were brought over. Her two children were nice and clean.

I was impressed with the way everything was in place. She had made room for my clothes, and my baskets were again put on the fire escape.

I wanted to explore New York and exchange my forty-four rubles for American money. The Mrs. was afraid I'd get lost, but I assured her by saying, "I'll find my way."

I marked the number of the house and tried to remember the door of the tenement on the third floor. I walked to Jarmulovsky's Bank on Canal Street. My rubles shrunk into twenty-one dollars and some change. I was sorry that my good Russian rubles made my capital so much less in American dollars—and I wondered how long I could live on it. The price for my room and breakfast and dinner was $3.50 per week, which was not much. But in Russian exchange, it is seven rubles. I felt very sad.

I walked from Canal Street to Allen and finally to Forsyth. One thing I could not understand was this: so many little stores had an Indian outside and the same name: Ice Cream. I thought it was the storekeeper's name. I knew there were a lot of Cohens and Levys, but Ice Cream was an unfamiliar name where I came from.

I had promised I'd be back at noon, so I tried to be on time. I ate lunch and started out again to survey. I was more sure of myself after I had found my way back without any difficulty. This time, I walked as far as Grand Street. I was very much impressed to look at all the nice things in the windows of Ridley's, Lord and Taylor and several other stores. I decided that America was not so bad. I got very tired walking the streets but went home a little more cheerful.

After dinner, my brother-in-law and some other people from our hometown came to see me. I asked them how I could find work if I remained in New York. Everyone was helpful and promised to find a job for me.

I had no idea what kind of work I was suited for. I was not even sure if I would stay in New York. My brother Max lived in Alpena, Michigan, and I thought I might go there.

My youngest brother Charlie was peddling in Westchester County. He would come to New York on Sunday. I decided to wait for him. When he left home, he was a mere child of thirteen and came on half fare. Now he was eighteen.

I spent the two days waiting for Charlie and made up my mind. I would take his advice about what to do, either to remain in New York or go to Max, who I had not seen for thirteen years. I hardly remembered him.

Meanwhile, I did not stay in the house and kept surveying the East Side.

Someone came to see me and took me to a store and, to my surprise, ordered an Ice Cream for both of us. So, I discovered that Ice Cream is frozen cream, not the name of the storekeeper. I was glad that I had not said my mistake to anyone.

The second evening, my brother-in-law came to see me and played a joke on me. I had never seen or tasted a tomato and had no idea what it was. He came in and handed me a large, red tomato saying, "Here is a nice apple for you" and insisted I should try it. When I took a bite, it seemed so horrible that I never wanted to eat one again. It took more than a year before I tried tomatoes and found them to be very tasty.

My brother Charlie came on Saturday night. I did not recognize him at first. He was tall and looked like a full-grown man. My brother-in-law was visiting and told him about the joke with the tomato.

Charlie took me to East Broadway and bought me a jacket. We talked, and he advised me not to go to Alpena. He had been there and said that a small town was no place for me. Besides, he did not like Max's wife. He thought that I would be better off in New York.

On Sunday, one of our townspeople who had settled in Tarrytown came to see me and invited me to visit him for a few days.

We took the Hudson River Day Line that stopped at Tarrytown. I spent a few days there and saw my friends, who were peddlers. Some had a horse and team, while others still had to carry their merchandise in a pack or basket. Their wives kept a couple boarders to help out. None of them looked very prosperous at that time.

I wanted to get back to New York and look for work. My twenty-one dollars was still untouched. I spent the change. I took the boat back to New York and found my way to Forsyth Street. Everyone marveled that I did not get lost.

I still did not know where or what kind of work to look for. A girl who was a relative of the people I visited in Tarrytown told me that she could bring me to where she was working on men's shirts. She was sure that I could learn. She had been working there almost a year and made $3.50 a week. I wondered how I could manage, since I paid that much for my board and room.

The next morning, she called for me at a quarter to seven. They started at seven o'clock, and she said it was not far. She lived with a married sister at 126 Hester Street.

The shop was at 22 Bayard Street, a tenement house where people lived and had six or eight sewing machines. The operators were of both sexes. I still don't know which was strongest, the smell of cooking or perspiration, the noise of the machines or the crying of children. I also heard the operators singing.

When I came in, the Boss surveyed me and said he was willing to give me work under the following agreement: I had to order a sewing machine and make a first payment of five dollars and then three dollars per month. I would work three weeks without pay. After the three weeks, if I proved that I had learned to operate the machine, he would pay me three dollars a week. It was all week work.

I surveyed the place and the inhabitants and decided not to accept this wonderful opportunity. First of all, I did not like the people who worked there, and the place itself was not to my liking. Above all, I did not want to make payments on a machine. Five dollars is ten rubles, a fourth of my capital. And I would have to work three weeks without pay! So, I returned without the job.

Next, someone else visited and offered to take me to a factory where they made men's clothing. The job was as finisher, sewing on buttons. There you didn't have to work without pay, and it was a real factory on Walker Street, not a sweatshop. I promised I would wait until the next Monday, since it was already Thursday. My landlady, Mrs. Deutch, said I made the right decision.

Meanwhile, I found out that there was a school with evening classes on Henry Street, so I went and registered. I still held on to what was left of my money after I paid for one week's board.

Charlie went back to the country, but my brother-in-law came to see me every evening. He had a brother on Delancey Street who was a customer peddler. We were invited there for Saturday dinner. He and his wife had seven or eight children, but their home had more shine of prosperity than any of the other homes I visited so far.

I did not tell them about the jobs I had been offered but told them I expected to go to work the next week.

MY FIRST JOB IN AMERICA

My former teacher in Yashwen heard that I was in New York. On Sunday, he, his wife and child came to see me. We talked for a while. I told him that I had registered at the Henry Street School and about the jobs I was offered. He told me that was not the work he would advise me to do. He went out and came back with the *New Yorker Staats-Zeitung*, a German newspaper that had a lot of ads.[74] We both started to read carefully.

Finally, I found a job that I thought I could do. It was at 11-15 Union Square. He promised to come the next morning and bring me there. He said, "If that one does not materialize, we will cut out other ads, and not to worry, I would never let you go to work in a sweatshop."

He came in the morning, and we went by streetcar to 14th Street, where I landed my first job. The firm's name was Samuels & Leo. Whenever I pass that building today, I always stop to look at the entrance on 15th Street.

The floor lady spoke German, and I was delighted to be able to understand her. The job was hand embroidery, clean piece work, in nice surroundings. The bright colors of the silks and plush fabric helped to cheer me up.

I did not know how much money I earned that day, but I was happy that I did not have to work in a sweatshop under conditions such as I had seen on Bayard Street.[75]

I found my way home by walking from 14th Street along Broadway. I came to my living place in a much happier mood, ate my dinner and went off to night school.

The pupils were mostly foreigners, like myself. Some were here two or three years before they decided to go to night school. I had learned some English at home with the aid of a dictionary by Harkavy that translated Jewish into English. But it did not always help, because many silent letters do not exist in the Russian or German language.[76]

Very few people in the class knew much more than I did, but I did not give up hope that someday I would learn the language. I envied my brother Charlie because he spoke and wrote English very well. He was only thirteen years old when he came over and went right to school in Alpena, Michigan.

I went to work every morning and to school every evening. During my first week, I brought some of my work home to do for a couple of hours after school. I had no idea how much my pay would be.

When I received my envelope on Monday, I looked at the figures. I could not believe my eyes—$9.01. I opened the envelope to see if it was really that much. Yes, it was—nine dollars and one cent. In figures of the Russian exchange, it was a small fortune of eighteen rubles. Who makes that much money? I decided that this was really a good country when a greenhorn could earn that much money the first week of work.

That day, I did not walk home. I took the Broadway car, then actually ran the few blocks to get home early. I told Mrs. Deutch of my fortune. She could not believe it. My pay was almost as much her husband's, who was an operator on caps. He was the second capmaker I knew. The first one worked in a sweatshop on Catharine Street. The poor man was not fit for his job and did not last very long. He became sick and was taken to Welfare Island, where he died about three years later.[77]

Everyone was amazed and could not understand how I did so well the first week. Some of them did not believe me, but I had my envelope and the slip inside for evidence. I was happy and thankful to my former teacher who helped me get the job.

When Charlie came to see me the following Sunday, he was very glad that I did so well.

But I kept admiring the ease with which Charlie spoke English and noticed that he always came in with an American newspaper. He was here only five years and could express himself better in English than in Jewish. It was such a wonder to me. I understand now why he learned so rapidly. He went to school and did not live amongst Jewish people where only Jewish is spoken.

The following week, my pay increased by more than a dollar.

I no longer felt like a stranger in the factory and did well on any work they gave me. The girls who worked in the factory were mostly German or from German-speaking countries, as well as a few Italians. All were friendly to one another. I came to know quite a few of the girls on the floor where I worked.

The factory occupied two floors. The one above had machines that made all kinds of braid and silk and cotton tape. They manufactured everything in the line of trimming for decorators.

The work itself was interesting, and I hoped it would last. The girls told me that there was plenty of work now, but after Christmas there would be no work for a couple of months.

The floor lady asked me if I would like to take some work home for Sunday. I did, and my pay swelled to over twelve dollars. I had no complaints about America.

What I could not understand was why girls had to work in the sweatshops for three or four dollars a week, twelve hours a day, instead of ten hours like the place I worked. On Saturday, it was only four hours. They used to work Sunday all day. Their week was seventy-two hours compared with my fifty-four.

The East Side was full of sweatshops in tenements, where they manufactured muslin underwear, neckties, artificial flowers and hand embroidery under horrible conditions. Some families did not want their children to go out to the factory and brought in work for them to do from daybreak to midnight. More than fifty percent of all goods manufactured in the needle trade, from men's and women's clothing to shirts, caps, even furs were made by sweatshop operators that employed mostly emigrants. Of course, there was a stream of them coming in every day, and they found their way into sweatshops.

New York became infested with tuberculosis under those working conditions. Why they didn't try to help themselves, I could not understand.

I escaped all these hardships, thanks to those that helped me find an easier way to earn my living.

THE DAY WAS NEVER LONG ENOUGH

At times, I felt homesick. I knew Mother was not well, and Abe was waiting to be sent for because there was no future for him at home.

Charlie came into the city every weekend and talked English to me. I tried hard to understand. I quickly learned the names of things used in everyday life.

My brother-in-law sent for his two older daughters, and we were planning to establish a home together. My two nieces, Bertha and Anna, were almost my own age. We were always together at home, so this was a pleasant expectation.

Six weeks went by, and I had enough money to make a fifty percent payment to send for my brother. I hoped that maybe Mother would come over later. We can always make plans but don't know what the future holds in store for us.[78]

It took six weeks to pay the balance on the ticket, but I was happy that I could accomplish that much. Charlie promised to pay for Abe's clothing or whatever was necessary for a newcomer.

I tried to earn a little more by bringing work home to do every evening for a couple of hours after I got home from night school. I kept very busy between working and trying to learn English. The day was never long enough to accomplish what I had in mind to do. I walked home every day from work and read the signs on 14th Street and Broadway.

I started to buy the *New York American* instead of the *Morgen-Journal* or the *New Yorker Staats-Zeitung*, even though I did not understand half of what I was reading.[79] The German-speaking girls in the factory read nothing but German, but I wanted to learn English, so it was English that I must read.

Mr. and Mrs. Deutch never tried to read anything other than the radical Jewish newspaper, although he was a very intelligent man and was in this country more than a year. He still worked in the sweatshop and earned very little. The radical Jewish newspaper was trying to encourage people to organize and demand a living wage. But the people did not try to help themselves.

One day, Mr. Deutch told me someone by the name of Samuel Gompers had organized a cigarmakers' union and that they had gone on strike for higher wages. They also wanted to organize a capmakers' union.[80] It would mean that Mr. Deutch would be out of work if they also went out on strike. How could they survive if his pay stopped? They already lived from hand-to-mouth. He did not know what to do and was worried. Should he join the union or not? A majority of the working class on the East Side were in the same predicament. No one had any reserve to live on for a month or so.

I thought myself very lucky, but of course I had my worries too. The atmosphere I lived in was not to my liking. My only hope was that when my two nieces came over, my home life would be more pleasant with them and my brother-in-law. I had no idea how we could keep house. The girls would have to work because Aaron did not make much at his post in the yeshiva. Just the same, I looked forward to their arrival.

I spent very little on myself. I still was dressed in my European clothes, except for a few things like a hat or a pair of shoes. I had to save for Abe's ticket and manage to have a few dollars, in case my work stopped. The girls said it would be in December, which was not very far off. I tried to hold on to my fortune.

Suddenly, I became rich. My brother Max sent me a check for thirty-five dollars. I took it and fifteen dollars from my savings to deposit in the Bowery Savings Bank, not telling anyone how rich I was. I felt a little more secure, knowing that in case of emergency, I had fifty dollars in the bank and a few dollars in cash that I always carried with me in a very safe place.

If I would have been as careful with money in my later years, I would have been in a much better position financially.

I had absolutely no time for myself during the week, but on Saturday afternoons, I would walk up Grand Street and window shop. I had no desire for all the finery in the windows. I figured even if did possess them, I would not have time or the occasion to wear them, as I had no friends or associates. I did not seem care for the few people I had met.

One Saturday afternoon as I was walking on Grand Street, I decided to explore other streets. I came to 197 East Broadway and the newly-erected building someone had told me about, the Educational Alliance. There was a sign telling about lectures in Jewish or English by Drs. Felix Adler and Henry Pereira Mendes and a list of classes for immigrants. I went inside to inquire, and they gave me the week's program.[81]

I was delighted to see all these free lectures and musical programs. But the question was how could I make time to attend when I had to work overtime or do my night school homework? I simply did not know what to do. Should I give up night school or give up bringing work home? I needed the money and wanted to go to night school, no matter how little I had learned in the past two months. But I decided to try.

I went home, ate my supper and went back to the Educational Alliance. Dr. Felix Adler was scheduled to lecture. I came an hour before time, a habit I still have. Whether it's to see a show or take a train, I always have to wait. Time seems so much longer when you really wait for something, but I have always been that way, and now I'm too old to change. I know I can wait for a train or the show or lecture to start, but they would not wait for me. I cannot remember ever being late for any appointment or missing a train. So, of course, to hear my first lecture I came a whole hour early.

I was impressed with the atmosphere. They had a library with books in Yiddish, Hebrew, Russian and German. Young men and women were reading in a large room. The people as a whole were more to my liking. I went into the lecture room and saw it was

Educational Alliance, library reading room, undated.
Archives of the YIVO Institute for Jewish Research

almost filled, but in those days, it made no difference. Back then, I could hear well, even if I was sitting at the very end. Now I need to come early in order to get a front seat, otherwise I don't hear a word.

Dr. Adler spoke of the opportunities and the hardships that confronted the newcomer in a strange land. In the short time I had been there, I knew how true it was. Some people could never readjust themselves and find a way of life to fit in. If only more immigrants would look for places like the Educational Alliance to get this valuable advice, perhaps they could better themselves. Dr. Adler spoke for an hour, and I wished it would have lasted two more.

I did not hurry to go home to Forsyth Street. Instead, I walked up and down the four floors of the building and looked into every room. I was amazed that all this knowledge could be obtained free, but the obstacle was how to get the time, which was not free.

English classes for adults, undated.
Archives of the YIVO Institute for Jewish Research

When I went home, I told Mr. Deutch of my pleasant discovery. He said he knew about it, but he had no time to attend lectures. He was too tired when he got home to go anywhere. I did not argue with him. I knew it was true, but just the same, I thought he would never get ahead if he kept working at his present job.

I got up early on Sunday and hurried to finish the work that I brought home with me. In the afternoon, I returned to the Educational Alliance to find out about the English classes and decided to try. Perhaps I would not have to waste my time learning 2x2 or 3-2 in night school on Henry Street.

Sure enough, the Educational Alliance teachers had a different system. They called it adult education, and I found it much more interesting. I could learn more in a week than what would take me a year in public school. All the teachers understood the Jewish language and could explain in a simple way. Their classes were made according to what the pupils' knowledge consisted of.

So, I became a pupil at the Educational Alliance, instead of Henry Street School. I liked it much better. First of all, the classes were much smaller, and the pupils were more to my liking. None of them were exactly illiterate. They all knew how to read some language. The teacher was also very helpful and encouraging. I was very pleased with the change.

MARBLE HALLS AND FLOOR

In December, my two nieces Bertha and Anna arrived, and we started looking for a place. There was a shortage of housing on the East Side, as emigrants were coming in every day and families needed a place to live.

Finally, my brother-in-law came one evening with the good news that he rented a two-room tenement in 25 Allen Street. It was on the first floor in the front, where you could look out on all the dirt and pushcarts on the streets and had the pleasure of hearing the noise of the 2nd Avenue elevated train. They bought second-hand furniture and moved in.

I kept putting it off, as I did not like the place. It was worse than the one I was in, but on the other hand, I felt that I would be much happier with my own family than living with strangers who were always in a depressed mood. And my nieces would have been disappointed if I did not live with them. I was always closer to Bertha, although Anna was my own age.

After a couple weeks of hesitation, I moved in. It was hard to arrange a place for our three trousseaus and wicker baskets. Like Mother, my sister Sifre also collected feathers for her three daughters, Bertha, Anna and Sarah. She knitted stockings and made all the linens similar to mine. Our two rooms were filled and terribly crowded. We got rid of some of the baskets and put things in bundles because they required less space.

The three of us slept in one bed, and my brother-in-law had a folding bed in the kitchen. Through Aaron's friend, Bertha had found a job making neckties on Broadway and Third Street. The older one, Anna, learned to operate a sewing machine and worked at home on cotton shirtwaists. She also took care of our two-room tenement and did the cooking.

But our living quarters were unbearable. We could not sleep on account of the noise from the el and the filthy air from the streets. People on the upper floors found it easier to throw their garbage through the windows than bring it down to put in the barrels that were standing in front of the house.

Above all, there were some permanent occupants either in the second-hand furniture or in the walls. We paid the rent, but against our protests, they resided there just the same. We could not remove them and decided we would have to move.

One evening, my brother-in-law came home and told us he had a surprise for us. Someone he knew, a wealthy man, had just erected two tenement houses, Numbers 160 and 162 Henry Street. At that time, it was the aristocratic residential section of the East Side. The block had all brownstone private homes, and these were the first tenement houses to be built. The owner, a Mr. Benjamin Harrison, was an admirer of my brother-in-law who knew him through his position at the yeshiva, where his only son was Aaron's student. Mr. Harrison offered him three rooms on the first floor in the rear for $12.50 a month. We paid nine dollars per month on Allen Street.

On the way to the Educational Alliance, Bertha and I looked at the house. It was on the corner of Jefferson Street, on the south side of the street. We looked into the entrance, because it was too late to see the rooms.

I could not believe it. Was it really possible for us to live in a house of this kind? Marble halls and floor in a nice design, twenty brass letter boxes in the entrance, with a light so you could read the names of the occupants and a bell under each name. I could not believe this was really the house. Compared with all the houses I had seen so far, it looked like a palace.

Bertha also thought that her father must have misunderstood Mr. Harrison, and it could not be possible that he was offered this tenement. Everything was new and shiny; two brass rails were on each side of the four steps to the entrance. The door was locked, but someone came out, and we could see the long hall with the marble floor. We both were very excited about it.

We went to class, but our minds were on 160 Henry Street. That evening, we went straight home after class. We always used to stay for a while, but not this evening.

We told my brother-in-law about the house and asked if it was possible that it was really 160 Henry. He was quite sure it was. He had not seen the house yet, but Mr. Harrison told him that it was a brand-new building at 160 Henry Street, and we could be sure this was the one.

Because Bertha and I worked during the day, we could not get a look at the rooms and had to wait until Saturday. But Aaron would go with Anna the next day. We told him to take it anyway, no matter what the rooms looked like. We would have more room and a beautiful entrance and all private homes on the block, no pushcarts on the streets, and above all, it was right around the corner from our haven, the Educational Alliance. All these advantages, plus a new building without permanent tenants that inhabited and multiplied for a generation or more, like in Allen Street. And not to forget, the el was ten or more blocks away and would not disturb our sleep. We took all this into consideration and thought it was too good to be true.

The following evening when Bertha and I came home, we were told that it was no mistake. Anna described the rooms. There was a sink and stone tub in the kitchen, and something else to our surprise: you could get hot water when the coal stove was in use and real hot water from a faucet in the sink and tub. Each had two faucets, one for hot and one for cold water. In the summer, you could keep ice in the tub to preserve your food.

They had the keys to the front hall and the rooms. Mr. Harrison had not even asked for a month's rent in advance. We were all very happy that night and even forgot the noise of the el.

On our way to class the next day, we stopped again to look at the building, and I marveled how different it looked compared to the Chrystie, Forsyth and Allen Street houses. It was even better than the house on Delancey Street where Mr. Gordon, Aaron's brother, lived. His flat was like a long railroad car with six cubbyholes for rooms, which were kept spotless and sheltered Mr. and Mrs. Gordon and their seven or eight children. Mr. Gordon was a very proud man and master of the establishment. He liked everyone to know how prosperous and accomplished he had become in a short time. I believe he emigrated three years earlier. So, even Uncle Gordon—as Bertha and Anna used to call him—his house could not to compare with 160 Henry Street.

Every evening when we went to class, we stopped to look at the house. The more we looked at it, the more we liked it. We started to study the names on the letter boxes that were already occupied. To our great surprise and joy, we came upon names that were famous at home—people whose books we had read and whose songs we used to sing. We never dreamt that someday we would be sheltered under the same roof. These were names that we admired and really had some influence in my life. (I shall speak of these people later.)

I could not wait until we moved. On Saturday, the three of us went to examine our new home-to-be. With pride, we unlocked the front door and walked the length of the marble hall. Then we opened the door to our own place.

Coming in from the outside on a sunny day, the rooms looked very dark. As we entered the kitchen, there was a room on each side. The only light in the kitchen was from a small window in a skylight, looking out on a very narrow alley. There was also a large window in the partition to the living room which faced the rear of the house from Madison Street. The bedroom had a small square window from the same alley or skylight as the kitchen. The window in the bedroom was very high, in order not to use up wall space.

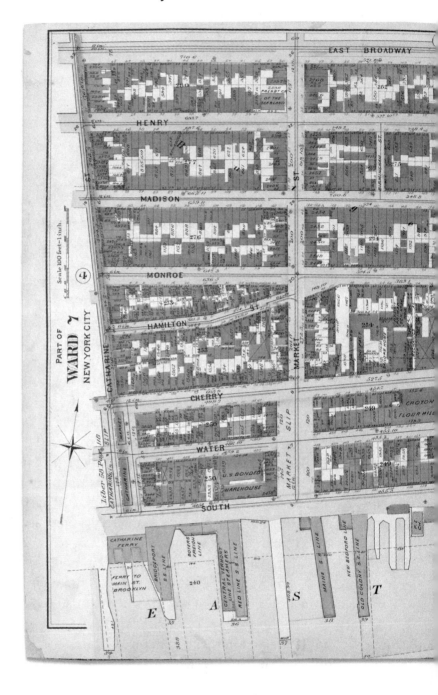

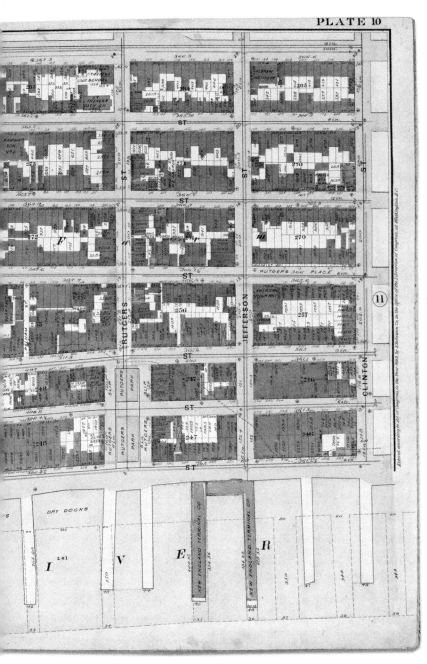

Plate 10: Map bounded by E. Broadway, Clinton St.,
East River, Catharine St.
Lionel Pincus and Princess Fiyal Map Division, The New York Public Library

Everything was new, with nice hardwood floors. There was a new coal stove with the hot water boiler across the top. The sink and tub were on the opposite wall. After we became used to the darkness, it looked much brighter, and we forgot that there was a sun shining. This tenement was deprived of the sun, but none of the other homes I have lived in or visited in New York had much benefit from the sun. Uncle Gordon's living room faced Delancey Street and had the sun for a few hours—that is, if it was allowed to shine in the room. The shades were always down, because the sun would fade the rug and the covers of the furniture. So, it really did not make much difference if we had carpet or furniture that could fade, the shades would be drawn down anyway, like in Uncle Gordon's house.

In the long hall, there was a toilet with a window for the four families. The two front apartments had four rooms. The two rear apartments had three rooms, and each one had a fire escape. Being on the lower floor, the windows had heavy iron bars for protection, so we would be safe.

We looked around for places to keep our trousseaus. We still had a couple of baskets but decided not to worry about it. We would do the best we could. We came out into the sunlit street and kept admiring the entrance.

We went back to Allen Street with a satisfactory report for my brother-in-law.

On Sunday, we all finished our work early and went hunting for affordable furniture. Uncle Gordon was a customer peddler and an authority on household articles. He went with us, and we bought a second-hand living room suite, upholstered with black mohair, which was in style. He assured us that it was a bargain. We went to Hester and Orchard Streets and found some very reasonable decorations. We were all in a happy mood and planned to move on Tuesday, the luckiest day in the week.

Bertha and I went to work on Monday, and on Tuesday we walked from work to our new home.

The bedroom was very small, with just enough room for the

double bed where the three of us would sleep. My brother-in-law would sleep in the parlor on the same folding bed. The furniture was carefully cleaned and sprayed with carbolic acid, to be sure no livestock was moving in with us. We wanted no part of Allen Street. My niece Anna was immaculate and cleaned and polished everything we had. Our living room suite had been delivered the same day. When we arrived, the coal stove had a nice fire and dinner was waiting for us. Sure enough, we had hot water to get washed, which was a wonderful change from our last home.

We did not attend class that evening. We ate dinner and got busy arranging the furniture. We could find places for everything except our three trousseaus. We all wished we had left them in Yashwen. Somehow, we arranged them in the best possible way and hung up our clothes in the one small closet. What could not fit into the closet, we hung on hooks along the bedroom wall.

We were delighted not to have the el noise. Instead, to our surprise, we heard someone singing who was accompanied by a violin. The music came through the window in the alley connected with the next house, 162 Henry. It was built in the same style, except it had two five-room and two four-room apartments on each floor. The music was filled with sweet, familiar tunes. It added a lot to our happiness. Every evening, we listened to the music and tried to find out whose tenor voice it was, and who was playing the violin.

By the end of the week, we discovered that it was Eliakum Zunser, a well-known Lithuanian songwriter who wrote hundreds of songs and composed music that was known all over Russia. Everyone knew that famous composer Zunser from Vilna. Wherever you came from, a remote village or large city, wherever Jewish people lived, they sang his songs. Who would have ever dreamt that someday we would hear this famous man's voice, accompanied by his son on the violin?

Zunser's songs were not merely love songs or melodies to put children to sleep. His songs were a call to his people to awaken and seek something better, to enlighten their minds, to find a better way of life and to throw away the yoke of superstition and oppression. The Russian censors discovered that Zunser's songs said something between the lines. So, he was ordered to leave Russia in twenty-four hours. I think he came the same year as we did. He came with his wife and five children and made his home at 162 Henry Street. We were all happy to be under the same roof and, in the evenings, listen to his sweet voice.

At that time, he was composing a new song called "The Golden Land." Children in the streets began singing it, and in a few weeks, you could hear that song come from every house and shop.

A few weeks later, he composed another called "The Peddler." He called on people to try to better themselves, not remain in the big cities but to go back to the soil. His message was to do something, not to be conspicuous, not to become a burden on the country and to look for useful occupations.

Every word and melody that seeped through our kitchen window from the narrow alley gave me pleasure beyond my ability to describe. And up to this day when I'm alone, I love to sing Zunser's songs to myself. I have no voice to sing and wouldn't want anyone to hear me, but it always gives me pleasure to remember his deep-meaning words and sweet tunes.[82]

His children were trying in recent years to collect his songs and publish them. I was told that they succeeded in collecting over four hundred songs and had them published in book form. I have not seen it, but I shall try to get a copy.

The Henry Street atmosphere was altogether different from either Allen or Forsyth Street. The forty families in the two houses were more of the intellectual class, those who had to leave Russia or other countries in Europe. There also resided some Yiddish authors whose books were well known in Russia. They had to leave because the censors did not like what was written between the lines.

I remember a Yiddish novel that was published in 1873. It was called *The Mare*. All the heavy burdens were piled on the back of the poor starved horse. The book caused a sensation. Everyone wanted to read it and understand what the author was telling readers about the mare and the much-too-heavy load and much-too-little food she was getting. The government got wise, and the book was confiscated. The author Sholem Abramovitsh was told to leave within twenty-four hours.[83] He, too, resided at 162 Henry Street, but in America he was not so popular. Immigrants had very little time to read, and those that spared some of their time for reading were trying to learn English, like me. In later years, some writers found their way in the Yiddish theatres. At that time, they were struggling to make a living. Nevertheless, it did not diminish my admiration and respect for their knowledge.

Writers and composers also spent a lot of time in the Educational Alliance reading room or lecture hall. I was very proud that I was housed under the same roof with these once famous people.

Henry Street, especially the block between Pike and Jefferson, had private homes on both sides of the street, with one family occupying the whole house of four floors. Some had a horse and buggy, and we would watch them go out riding. Their children spoke English, and they all kept servants. The environment gave me more courage and hope.

Our life was very hard, and time was so precious. After work, we barely had time to eat and go off to class, then return and work for an hour or two to make a little more money – my expenses had increased.

I came to know some interesting people and started to discard my European clothes and buy new ones. However, there was always the fear of being out of work.

ALL BEGINNINGS ARE HARD

Shortly after Christmas, the floor lady told us there was not much work, but she would try to divide whatever she had among all the girls, which was fair enough. I asked the girls who had been there for a couple years how much work they got during the slow season, and they told me it was very little. But most of the girls had their parents and lived at home, so they managed somehow. Others told me that they looked for other work during those couple of months. I knew that I could not afford to wait two months or more until the spring season started.

I did not say anything to the floor lady or the girls. I got my pay and walked home on Broadway and looked into each cross street to see if there were any Help Wanted signs for work that I could do.

On lower Broadway, there was a short street named Howard, between Broadway and Center. I saw a sign, Wanted Operators on Shirt Waists, and marked down the number 25. I decided to try the next morning. I never operated a machine, but I knew I could learn if I was given a chance.

I came home a little late but did not tell the reason. I did not want them to know that I had to look for work. My nieces were not making nearly as much as I was. Bertha used to bring home her neckties and work every evening for two hours after school. I earned twice as much as she did. And Anna never earned more than three dollars on the work she brought home, because she had to pay three dollars a month on her machine. So, I decided to try to get another job. If I didn't succeed, I could also work at home but hoped I would not have to do that.

The next morning, I left as usual with my lunch in a bag and went directly to Howard Street. I walked up to the second floor to the M. I. Nathan Magnet Shirtwaist Company. I felt a little nervous. I liked the place because it was light, clean and not overcrowded. There were not too many machines, and the girls all looked cheerful and happy.

When the foreman came over, I told him I was looking for a job. He asked me if I was an experienced operator because they didn't take inexperienced help. I said that I was. He told the floor lady to give me some work and put me at a machine.

The machines were Wheeler and Wilson. I told her in my broken English that I worked on a Singer sewing machine and asked if she would teach me how to thread and operate the Wheeler and Wilson.

She agreed and showed me how to thread it, then gave me the work. I tried and found it was not so hard. I knew I could learn, but she was watching me from a distance. Then she went to the foreman and told him that I knew nothing about operating a sewing machine. But meanwhile, I was sewing the straight seams very slowly, praying the thread would not break because I was not sure if I would remember how to thread it.

I saw the foreman coming, and my heart started beating faster. He was very polite but told me I did not have enough experience, and they could not bother to train me. He spoke German. Evidently my English did not warrant that I would understand him.

I told him that I knew could learn, and he should give me a chance. But he insisted that they couldn't bother, because learners spoiled the material. I kept insisting that I could learn. He was already getting impatient with me. I asked him if all the operators were born operators. If they learned, so could I. If he feared I would spoil the material, then I would be willing to pay for it. I had my pay and a few dollars from last week, so I took out my money and offered it to him. "If I spoil anything, I'll pay for it. I need the job, and you need the help. Why not give me the chance to try?" He still hesitated.

Meanwhile, Mrs. Nathan, the manufacturer's wife, came over to see what we were arguing about. He told her in English. She looked at me and spoke to me in German in a very friendly tone: "You can try. If I find that you can do the work, you can have the job." She handed me back my money, and she herself told me a few points about sewing. I thanked her, and she went back to the cutting table. She was a designer and knew the business.

I worked until lunch hour. No one came over to look at my work. When the machines stopped, the foreman came over, looked at my work and left.

After lunch, Mrs. Nathan came over with her pleasant smile and asked me if I found it hard to catch on to the work. I told her, "All beginnings are hard, but I'm sure I will do as well as all the other girls if I'm only given a chance."

The girls all spoke English. The foreman was a German Jew, and so were Mr. and Mrs. Nathan. I was the only Jewish girl at the machines. Some of the girls went down for a drink at the stand on the corner of Broadway. But I stayed and surveyed the place. I felt lonely and strange among the rest of the girls and was still not sure of my job.

At 12:30, work was resumed, and I forgot my loneliness. I worked carefully and did not hurry but tried to do the work well. It was all piece work, so I didn't try to hurry because I would pick up speed later.

The afternoon passed very fast, and to my surprise, at 5:30 the bell sounded. Work stopped, and I could not understand why so early. I wished we would work until 6:00. I waited for a few minutes and looked in the direction of Mrs. Nathan and the foreman. I still feared they would tell me not to return the next day, but nothing happened, so I left for home.

I walked slowly down Grand Street and looked in all the windows. I did not want to get home too early because no one knew about my new job. I thought I would tell no one until the next week. I had no idea how much I could earn there, but nevertheless, I felt it was a good job, and I was going to like it.

Bertha came in and had brought home some work. She asked me how much work I brought home. She was surprised when I told her none.

After dinner, we both started out for school, and she asked again about work and why I did not meet her on the corner of Broadway and Bond Streets. I could not lie, so I told her about the new job. She felt very sorry that I had left the other place. Maybe I had made a mistake. I should have waited. I was too hasty. And how did I know if I could do as well on new work? I told her that I could always go back to my other work if this job did not prove satisfactory.

I was glad I did not tell her before because she would have discouraged me. I went to work, still not being too sure of myself. I had my work sample and finished the first bundle of six shirtwaists before noon. I brought them to Mrs. Nathan, instead of the foreman. She examined them and said in a friendly way, "O.K., give it to Mr. Wilson. He will give you some more work." He gave me a dozen of the same style.

The job did prove satisfactory. I learned the work in no time. My first week's pay was over nine dollars without overtime, and within four months, I was making samples and paid sixteen dollars by the week, which was a small fortune in those days.

Now I felt sure of my job, as they found no fault with my work. I became more acquainted with the girls and spoke my broken English to them. I worked there until I left New York to be married in Worcester, Massachusetts.

PASSING THROUGH
– on my seventy-ninth birthday

Nobody in the widow's household
ever celebrated anniversaries.
In the secrecy of my room
I would not admit I cared
that my friends were given parties.
Before I left town for school
my birthday went up in smoke
in a fire at City Hall that gutted
the Department of Vital Statistics.
If it weren't for a census report
of a five-year-old White Male
sharing my mother's address
at the Green Street tenement in Worcester
I'd have no documentary proof
that I exist. You are the first,
my dear, to bully me
into these festive occasions.

Sometimes, you say, I wear
an abstracted look that drives you
up the wall, as though it signified
distress or disaffection.
Don't take it so to heart.
Maybe I enjoy not-being as much
as being who I am. Maybe
it's time for me to practice
growing old. The way I look
at it, I'm passing through a phase:
gradually I'm changing to a word.
Whatever you choose to claim
of me is always yours;
nothing is truly mine
except my name. I only
borrowed this dust.

—Stanley Kunitz, *Passing Through:*
The Later Poems, New and Selected

CHAPTER FOUR

A Feast of Losses
1893–1950

In the recurring dream
my mother stands
in her bridal gown
under the burning lilac,
with Bernard Shaw and Bertie
Russell kissing her hands;
the house behind her is in ruins;
she is wearing an owl's face
and makes barking noises.
Her minatory finger points.

—From "The Testing-Tree," Stanley Kunitz, *Passing Through:
The Later Poems, New and Selected*

IN HIS POEM "The Layers," Stanley Kunitz posed a question: "How shall the heart be reconciled/ to its feast of losses?" While her son would use his pen to transform loss into art, Yetta retracted hers. She hoped her son could "patch together" her memoir and "put each pattern where it would fit best." What caused threads of memory to snap and end what had become an exhilarating writer's journey?

Reconstructing the next period of Yetta's life required fabric different from that which she provided. Letters, reports, diaries, newspaper articles, interviews, books and telephone conversations were used to shape narratives about a quintet of individuals with whom she shared homes. Interweaving her story with theirs offered insight into her transformation from hopeful, independent immigrant to bereft, even tragic, woman of reduced circumstances.

SOLOMON KUNITZ, 1893–1905

Look for me, Father, on the roof
of the red brick building
at the foot of Green Street –
that's where we live, you know, on the top floor.

—From "Halley's Comet," Stanley Kunitz, *Passing Through:
The Later Poems, New and Selected*

In 1893, Worcester was a thriving industrial city surrounded by the upheaval of a severe economic depression. But not every business was successful and not everyone welcomed its newest citizens.

George Maynard (1850–1917) was born into a farming family in nearby Paxton and came to Worcester in 1869 to seek a different life.[84] He kept a diary from 1862–1909 and recorded his travails, adventures and poetry, along with the weather and local news.

Maynard's small printing business was barely solvent in 1893. During hard times, he walked to orchards and subsisted on meals of berries and fruits that had fallen to the ground. On July 30th, Maynard observed,

> When I was a boy, matters were very different, and people went where they pleased and did as they pleased, but the great influx of the lawless foreign element into the city has hardened the farmers' hearts and they have declared war to the knife on all "trespassers," whether "roughs" or philosophers under "Penalty of LAW!"[85]

Welcome or not, immigrants continued to come. By 1895, the city was home to 100,000 people, and nearly a third were foreign-born.[86] Irish, French-Canadian, Poles, Ukrainians, English, Scots, Armenians, Finns and Swedes settled in pockets throughout the city. Churches and synagogues dotted the neighborhoods.

Factories attracted workers like dry sponges absorbing water. Chimneys belched smoke; tools, barbed wire, and fencing were products that satisfied a national market and kept the open-hearth blast furnaces active.[87] Production of corsets and all manner of clothing fulfilled the needs of customers near and far.

By 1893, Worcester's east side was both home and workplace to the growing Jewish community, a group skilled in wholesaling and retailing cotton and woolen dry goods and in tailoring and manufacturing clothing.

> The first job of many Jewish immigrant men was to travel around on foot peddling cloth, lace, sewing notions, household goods, or collecting junk or old rags for resale. As they accumulated enough capital, many were able to buy a horse and wagon, and later to establish a store or business.[88]

Worcester-born Alfred G. Isenberg (1891–1983) remembered his family's struggles.

> Many a day we didn't have anything to eat. Although that was temporary, I can remember going to the grocery store, picking up what we needed and saying, "We'll have to pay you later." … I went to Providence Street School … and there were many more Jewish students … about 20 percent … Other kids threw stones at us. And we had trouble playing baseball because kids would bust in and try to break up the game.[89]

Solomon Kunitz was born in 1865 and emigrated in 1887 from Odessa, Ukraine, which was then part of the Russian Empire. He settled in Providence, Rhode Island, where he worked at a gold paint company.[90] In 1893, he traveled forty-five miles north to Worcester and married Yetta Jasspon, a union possibly arranged by her brother Abe, who was working as a cutter in a Worcester wrapper factory.[91]

Twenty-six-year-old Yetta would have been viewed as a good match. She had three years of experience in the New York garment trade and confidence that a business could prosper, if she were given the "chance to try." On July 27, 1893, Yetta and Solomon married.[92]

Solomon Kunitz was destined for the front pages of Worcester's newspapers twice.

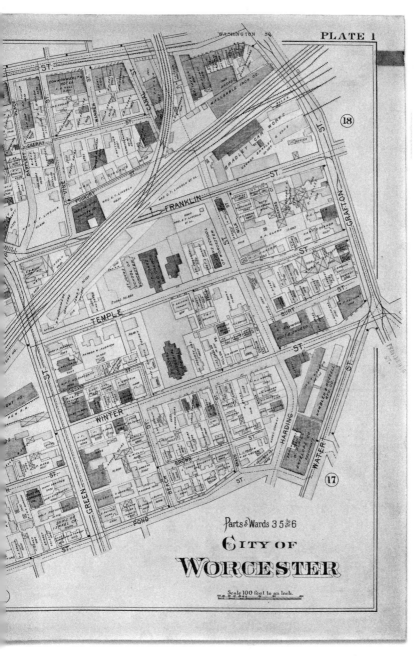

Plate 1. Atlas of the City of Worcester, Massachusetts.
L.J. Richards & Co., Springfield, Massachusetts. 1896.
From the collection of Worcester Historical Museum

103

He started a small women's clothing manufacturing shop at 83 Green Street. Soon, he was able to expand and move into a factory on the corner of Winter and Harding streets. By 1897, The Parisian Wrapper Manufacturing Company was prospering, and Solomon was featured as one of nine men and one woman in the business section of *The Fitchburg Sentinel*.[93,94] He became a member of B'rith Abraham and Sons of Benjamin, Jewish men's fraternal orders which adopted Masonic rituals.[95]

The couple could not know that skeins of loss would unravel, tumble into their path and throw them profoundly off-balance.

On January 26, 1895, Yetta gave birth to Harris, who was named after her father. Eight months later, the boy died from a severe form of gastroenteritis. Sarah Agnes was born on January 25, 1896. Bessie was born on July 20, 1897 but died January 10, 1898 from "spasm of glottis, rickets." The Hebrew word *shakul* translates into "parents who lose children," and the Kunitzes absorbed the heartache of that appellation.[96]

On January 20, 1899, *The Worcester Spy*'s front-page headline declared: "BIG LOSS. Parisian Wrapper Company IS BADLY GUTTED. An Early Morning Blaze on Winter Street." During the night, a mysterious fire started in the basement cutting room of the four-storey brick building. Small pieces of cloth and bolts of fabric "burned like powder." The fire spread upward quickly through a freight elevator shaft, located in the corner of the building.

Fifteen minutes earlier, night watchman James Mars and his dog had passed through the basement and walked into the engine room, where he took a seat. Smelling smoke, Mars opened the door into the basement, and flames blinded him. An escape to the street through the fire-proof door in the basement was his first thought, so he tried again but failed. Despite his badly-burned hands, he used his stool to break the engine room window and climb out. After scaling the fence that surrounded the factory, he cried out to a passer-by to send in an alarm.

When firefighters arrived, the building was fully ablaze. It took

Yetta Helen Jasspon Kunitz, c. 1895.
Collection of Gretchen Kunitz, M.D.

them over an hour to put down the fire. One firefighter was injured, and the watchman's dog perished.

A *Spy* reporter went to 54 Providence Street and woke Solomon Kunitz and his family. When told of the fire, he "was greatly over-come." Kunitz told the reporter that his insurance policy worth $50,000 covered the "building, stock and machinery." Anticipating the busiest season of the year, new fabrics had been purchased, making the loss greater than the coverage.

Three months earlier, he had taken on two partners from Boston and made improvements to the factory, including $2,000 in the office area. Kunitz stated,

> I had the best factory for the manufacture of wrappers in the country ... with 225 machines of the latest design ... At the pres-ent time there have been about 300 girls employed here ... [with orders for] between $50,000 and $60,000 ahead.

1899 advertisement for The Parisian Wrapper
Manufacturing Company, Worcester City Directory.
Worcester Public Library

The safe and till were intact, but the machinery was a total loss.
The article stated that "the large amount of extra-fine stock, which
he had on hand ready for shipment, made the loss seem almost irrep-
arable." Some wrappers and dresses had been rescued and brought
to Asa Goddard's stockroom in a neighboring building.

What ignited the fire? No oil was stored in the basement, so the boiler was ruled out. The mystery remained unsolved.[97]

In the months following, Yetta became pregnant again, but delivered a stillborn male on October 12, 1899.[98]

Family and neighbors must have provided some comfort and aid to the unfortunate couple. Brother Abe and his wife Dora, whom he had married in 1897, and their infant son, Harold, lived next door on Providence Street. In 1897, Aaron and Sifre's third daughter Sarah had emigrated and married Louis Levitan, a wrapper cutter; they lived two blocks away at 10½ Clarkson Street with their son Harold. Brother Charlie married Bessie Levien in 1902, started their family and opened a clothing store in Fitchburg, about twenty-five miles north of Worcester.[99]

Solomon Kunitz's business never recovered completely. The 1900 census shows him, Yetta, four-year-old Sarah, fifteen-year-old niece Celia Kunitz and servant Annie Johnson at 58 Providence Street. His occupation is still listed as "wrapper manufacturer," and his Mason membership card for that year stated "manufacturer."[100] Death continued to plague Solomon and Yetta. Daughter Rebecca, who was born on February 28, 1901, died five weeks later from "convulsions, pertussis."

A baby girl, Sophia Alysson, arrived on April 10, 1902.

That same year, the city directory's real estate record provides a snapshot of the Kunitzes' possible solution to recovery. Using the remaining fire insurance payout as collateral, they became landlords. They took out mortgages for 133 Green, 3 Ash, 73 Harrison and 58 and 60 Providence streets, adding to 32 Ellsworth and 8 and 10 Spruce Street properties that Solomon had purchased earlier. In 1903, the city directory shows the Kunitzes living at 58 Providence Street, but Solomon had no employment address.[101] By 1904, Solomon was back to work, managing a tobacco shop at 46 Madison Street, where his wife was a clerk.[102] At the end of the year, they moved to 133 Green Street, and Yetta Kunitz became pregnant for the seventh time.

On June 3, 1905, a *Worcester Daily Telegram* article on page fourteen read: "SWALLOWS CARBOLIC. Solomon Kunitz Ends His Life in Elm Park."

The account began with caretaker Walter Comerford's interview.

I was working near the pond when a boy came along and said there was a man a little ways back who was acting queer. I went back and found the man, and I smelled something queer about him. I knew it wasn't liquor. I suppose it was the carbolic acid they said he had been taking.

The boy said he saw him take something from a little bottle and pour it into a cup at the drinking fountain close by. Then he went along the path about fifty feet and threw himself down in the shrubbery beside the path.

When I got to him, he was lying on his right side with his right arm stretched out. He was in the bushes there and was just breathing. I saw he was dying, and I ran to the telephone and called the police station.

Solomon Kunitz, verso "Solomon Kunitz, c. 1903."
Department of Special Collections, Princeton University Library

The Captain sent Officer Silas D. Hemenway and driver George A. Baker with the ambulance, and by that time the man was dead, as far as we could see. The officer telephoned back to the police station and the captain told him to take the body to Athy's undertaking rooms.

The man was not a familiar figure around the park, and I do not remember having seen him previously. The first thing I did, after notifying the police, was to take away the cup which had been used for the carbolic acid from the fountain where it had hung when it was used by Kunitz, so there would be no one else using it.[103]

Later the bottle which had contained the acid was found in shallow water at the edge of the pond, where Kunitz had thrown it. The deed was done nearly opposite Cedar street and not far from where I was working at the time.

The reporter found a June 1st copy of *The Jewish Daily News* on a walk near the body. It bore the subscriber's name and address: "S. Kunitz, 133 Green street." Kunitz had walked the mile and a half from home to Elm Park carrying his sole means of identification.

The Evening Post's second edition front-page story, published on June 2nd, and the *Worcester Daily Telegram* article acknowledged the forty-four-year-old as "widely known in Worcester" and "one of the best-known Hebrew residents in the city." Yetta Kunitz was quoted directly, saying that her husband "had been ill for the last three years and had slept little. Last night he was restless. He left the house about 11 o'clock this morning, saying he was not feeling well." The *Post* cited temporary insanity brought on by ill health as the cause of his suicide.[104]

The *Post*'s reporter described Solomon Kunitz's surviving family: "his wife, who is in delicate condition, and two children." Both accounts mentioned his business background:

[He] *formerly* conducted a news stand in Madison square and previous to that was in the wrapper manufacturing business on Winter street [*author's emphasis*].

Could the use of past tense when referring to his Madison square job have meant that Solomon was unemployed again at the time of his suicide? Long-term sleeplessness and despair are not difficult to comprehend when placed alongside his losses and the future support of three-year-old Sophia, nine-year-old Sarah and Yetta, who was seven months into another pregnancy.

How might these grief-and-anxiety-filled years have affected Yetta? No written documents exist to offer answers. In 1990, Peter Stitt asked Stanley Kunitz what he knew about the suicide.

> The only person I could talk to was my older sister [Sarah, whose] … memories were limited. I tried to pump her for information, but she had little to offer. The detail I remember most clearly relates to my father's funeral. At the cemetery, when my mother became hysterical and tried to leap into the grave, our family physician— whose name was Dr. Nightingale, all so mythic—restrained her and said, "Be quiet! Don't forget, you have a lot to do with this." Now that's my sister's story, I do not know how accurate.[105]

Elm Park, 1905.
From the collection of Worcester Historical Museum

Solomon Kunitz gravesite, Hope Cemetery, Worcester, Massachusetts.
Photo by John Gaumond, 2009

The suicide delivered a blow not easily absorbed by the close-knit community. When Yetta Kunitz gave birth to her son on July 29, 1905, she named him Solomon S.[106]

She packed away her late husband's belongings, along with insight into his dark ending, and prepared herself to raise three children.

Yetta could control one aspect of Solomon's death. As front-page news, it was likely a point of discussion throughout the city and especially in her neighborhood. But not in her home. Perhaps she believed in the superstition that talking about the suicide would endanger her surviving children. Openness about their father's suicide would make her responsible for handing the legacy of a father's "temporary insanity" to their children. Pouring this newest grief into her bitter cup, Yetta mixed it with the deaths of their four siblings and decreed silence.

Stanley Kunitz, 1907, born Solomon S. Kunitz.
Department of Special Collections, Princeton University Library

While Yetta's decision may have robbed her son of his father's memory, it would reward him with his most enduring themes. In poems such as "Father and Son" and "The Testing-Tree," he would pursue a lost father and confront a mother whose "minatory finger point[ed]" the way to self-knowledge and poetry.

Family secrets fuel curiosity and fan the fires of imagination. In a 1972 interview, Kunitz guessed,

> The dress manufacturing business they'd started together was going bankrupt; but there must have been another woman, too, or mother wouldn't have made the subject taboo.[107]

He could have been referring first to the financial disaster of the Parisian Wrapper Manufacturing Company fire; his second conjecture could have been a case of projection, brought on by guilt over his own infidelities.[108]

Mark Dine, 1906–1925

> My name is Solomon Levi,
> the desert is my home,
> my mother's breast was thorny,
> and father I had none.

—From "An Old Cracked Tune," Stanley Kunitz, *The Collected Poems*

Faced with managing the support of nine-year-old Sarah, three-year-old Sophia and her infant son, Yetta struggled to pay her mortgages and collect rents from her tenants. She was soon back to work as a clerk at a dry goods store at 123 Green Street. Her children were left in the care of others, a circumstance she would later describe as their being orphaned. Kunitz offered a comment about his mother during those days:

> When she came home in the evening, she was tired and easily vexed, impatient with my moodiness. She was not one to demonstrate affection physically-in fact, I don't recall ever being kissed by her during my childhood.[109]

Kunitz's poem "The Magic Curtain" opens with the scene:

> At breakfast mother sipped her buttermilk,
> her mind already on her shop,
> unrolling gingham by the yard,
> stitching her dresses for the Boston trade.

In 1906, Mark Dine, a widower ten years Yetta's senior, emigrated from Kovno, Lithuania, to Boston with three sons: Max Dain and Herman settled close to Boston, while he and a third son, Mitchell, moved to Worcester.[110] Dine worked as a clerk in a dry goods store and as a salesman at a men's furnishings store.

A family member introduced Dine to Yetta Kunitz, and they were married on November 4, 1910.[111] Perhaps the pieces of her life could be stitched together to create a brighter life and a period of relative stability for her and her three children. It should be noted that the

1910 census, which had been taken in May, recorded the presence of four-year-old Solomon; he would be turning five in July and entering first grade in the fall. It is possible that his being renamed Stanley (Jasspon Kunitz) occurred during this period to deflect recollections of his father's front-page suicide with its diagnosis of temporary insanity, thereby unburdening the five-year-old of a given name stained with tragedy.

Real estate records reflect a way in which the couple could have managed to open their new business, The Dine Manufacturing Company at 69 Water Street. Yetta H. Dine sold her properties.[112] Soon, they moved the business to 65 Water Street, where Yetta was manager and stepson Mitchell was the salesman.

Childcare was a challenge met with the aid of relatives, servants, and friends. Nine-year-old Stanley was too young to stay alone in the summer while his mother and stepfather worked. In 1906, Yetta's former neighbors, Jacob and Annie Albert, had opened the Hebrew Inn in Quinapoxet, a village of textile mills and farms eleven miles north of Worcester. By 1913, the Alberts moved and rented out their farm and boarding house. The farm in Quinapoxet provided an ideal solution for the Dines, as well as fresh air and inspiration for Stanley Kunitz's future poems.[113]

> That was the summer I practiced
> sleight-of-hand and fell asleep
> over my picture-books of magic.
> Toward dusk, at crossings
> and at farmhouse gates,
> under the solitary iron trees
> I stood on the rim of the buggy wheel
> and raised my enchanter's wand,
> with its tip of orange flame,
> to the gas mantles in their cages,
> touching them, one by one,
> till the whole countryside bloomed.

—From "Lamplighter: 1914," Stanley Kunitz, *Passing Through: The Later Poems, New and Selected*

The Kunitz/Dine household was part of Worcester's Jewish community. In 1906, after purchasing a bond for five dollars, Yetta Kunitz was listed as a shareholder of the Congregation Shaarai Thorah, a new synagogue that opened in 1906 at 32 Providence Street.[114] Next door was the German shul where her son would celebrate his bar mitzvah in 1918. It was "very formal. Everyone wore jackets and dressed up. On Simchat Torah ..., they gave out Hersey bars ... so the kids liked going there."[115]

Kunitz clarified the Kunitz-Dine position on Judaism and assimilation. Worcester's east side was the bedrock of its Jewish population; his upbringing emphasized the ethical, rather than the religious, tradition. Further, his mother's admiration for brother Charlie's facility with the English language translated into their monolingual household: "I never heard Russian or any foreign language spoken in our household during my childhood."[116]

Mark Dine's sons were thriving in America. Max Dain was a

Left to right: Stanley Kunitz, unidentified man (possibly Abe Jasspon), Yetta Dine, Sophia Kunitz, Sarah Kunitz, unidentified man (possibly Mark Dine), 46½ Providence Street, c. 1915.
Collection of Gretchen Kunitz, M.D.

pharmacist in Cambridge, and Herman Dine graduated from Harvard in 1916, after which he would begin a career in municipal finances. Mitchell and his wife, Jennie, became an integral part of Yetta and Mark's family and business.[117] Sarah had graduated in 1912 from English High School, which prepared students for entry into the business world. Her income as a secretary added to the family's stability.[118]

By 1918, Yetta Dine and Mollie Siff, a friend whose husband Jacob owned a woolen clothing store in the neighborhood, were eyeing property in an undeveloped section of Vernon Hill called Academy Terrace. Within walking distance of both workplaces, Woodford Street beckoned with two-family homes and the feeling of country living. The house would be a step up from three-decker houses and tenements both couples had known.

In March 1919, Dworman Brothers on Providence Street pulled a building permit for 4 Woodford Street; water came onto the property in May. The grand, three-storey stucco house shot upward into the summer sky. The Dine's first-floor plan mirrored the Siff's on the second: front room, dining room, a library with French doors which could double as a bedroom, a pantry adjoining the kitchen, two bedrooms and bathroom. The third floor had six rooms—four storage rooms to be divided between the co-owners and two set aside for a tenant, "the income therefrom to go into the common fund" to be used for upkeep of the house.

And luxury of luxuries: a backyard for a garden and fruit trees! Yetta and Mollie signed the mortgage on December 16th and became co-owners of the tenth house on Woodford Street.[119]

Yetta's appreciation for her new home must have brought back sweet memories of her move to Henry Street. The house's stucco and wood exterior blended Craftsman, Spanish Mission and bungalow styles, and its grandeur was in the details. Large square pillars supported porches on three storeys; diamond-shaped geometric stucco decorations drew the eye upward to quatrefoil windows under the house's three peaks.

Inside, oak and ash floors gleamed, and pine and oak woodwork glowed. Stained-glass windows graced the front room and dining room, which boasted a built-in mirrored display unit, complete with drawers for linen storage. More delight awaited Yetta and Mollie in the wainscoted kitchens and pantries, which were anchored with soapstone sinks. A modern bathroom featured white hexagonal floor tiles and a built-in tub, complete with shower. The back-hall floor drains anticipated weighty ice chests.

A door swung open to the backyard and woods beyond.[120] The house and neighborhood telegraphed to the community: the Dines and the Siffs are successful business people.

To fourteen-year-old Stanley, the back door was a gateway to nature, now that he was old enough to stay alone when school was out. While his mother and stepfather were at work, he could walk

Quatrefoil detail, 4 Woodford Street.
Photo by John Gaumond, 2019

the four-mile round trip to the library on Elm Street or hike in the woods and pretend to be an Indian scout. The boy collected images and invented fables for future poems, such as "The Testing-Tree."[121]

Yetta's pride was centered on her shy, brilliant, book-loving son, who had his own ideas about a future.

> I knew that I was going to be a poet ... from a very early age. I can picture telling my mother ... I thought she would be shocked... "I always felt you would do something like that ... Sonny, how are you going to earn your living?" That's a mother's natural thought. I'll never forget that. I said, "I'll find a way."[122]

Sophia graduated from Classical High School in June. Her yearbook sketch revealed a plan "to fit herself for a literary occupation, after graduation, by taking a secretarial course." It seems fair to wonder where Sophia's literary dreams would have taken her if the months just ahead were kinder to her ambition.

More excitement bubbled in the new house because Sarah was engaged to be married the following November to Percy Baker of Somerville. With the holiday bustle and activity surrounding the move, fourteen-year-old Stanley was sent to Cambridge to spend

114   *THE AFTERMATH*

SOPHIA ALYSSON KUNITZ
"Sophie"
Born, April 10, 1902, Worcester, Mass.
Ledge Street School.

Sophia has been very sociable while a member of our class, and will be well remembered by those of '19. She has found time to attend nearly all of the social functions of the school, and made many friends by her pleasant smile. "Sophie" did not neglect her studies, and maintained a very satisfactory standard in each class. She plans to fit herself for a literary occupation, after graduation, by taking a secretarial course. The best wishes of the class go with her.
*"A little mischief now and then,
Is relished by the best of men."*

Sophia Alysson Kunitz, 1919. *The Aftermath of the Class of Nineteen Nineteen of the Worcester Classical High School.*
From the collection of Worcester Historical Museum

c. 1919

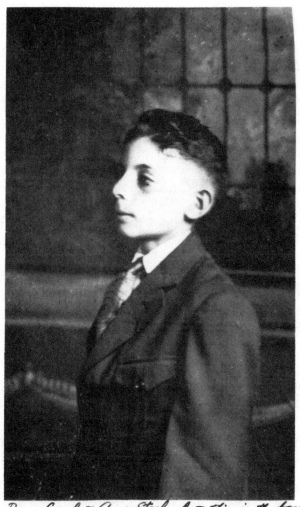

Dear Carol, & Greg Stockmal — this is the boy
who lived in (y)our house. at 4 Woodford St.
                              Blessings;
                              Stanley Kunitz
8/27/86

Stanley J. Kunitz, c. 1918.
The Stanley Kunitz-Stockmal Collection,
Clark University, Worcester, Massachusetts

New Year's Eve with his stepbrother, Max, wife Beatrice and their sons Albert, seven, and Norman, two.[123] The night was so memorable that it would later provide Kunitz with inspiration for a fictional piece, which he submitted to his Harvard professor.

> There is a night that is burned indelibly in my consciousness. It is New Year's Eve and the snow is falling. (Perhaps the falling of the snow is only a trick of memory.) Through an open window from the street drifts a woman's tipsy laughter that fades into the maudlin voices and the hoarse bray of horns. A boy ... he is fourteen ... kneels by his bed alone in a narrow room and for the first time in his life really prays out of the depths of his being, simply and fervently in a child's way of prayer. Then he climbs into bed and with a perfect act of faith closes his eyes. In the middle of the night he is awakened by a loud terrible cry from the next room. He sits up in bed, knowing what has happened, but there are no tears in his eyes. Something has hardened inside his taut young body. Suddenly, the dark of night takes on a rhythm, words breed in the dark and climb like bats up the blackened wall ... He hears "There is no God."
>
> There was a time when the thought of death used to terrify me. I would struggle in bed not to fall asleep, because I was afraid to deliver myself to the dark ... The cult of spiritualism is trivial and in the hands of charlatans. Therefore, I have resigned myself to death, since there is nothing else to do. I do not mean to say that I shall submit abjectly to dissolution. Not at all. I pray that I shall always love life so ardently as never to be glad to die. [Sartre: "I can't go on. I'll go on."][124]

The dire truth was that fourteen days after the mortgage had been signed, his "new father had died of a heart attack when he was hanging curtains in the new house."[125]

Kunitz recalled this time of his life in a 1977 letter to Herman Dine's granddaughter, Carol.

> My recollection is that my stepfather Mark Dine—that sweet and gentle man—I knew Mr. Dine for too brief a period ... was the only father I ever had—how dear he was to me! And when he died, I was devastated ... After I lost my stepfather, I settled back

Mark Dine's gravesite, Hope Cemetery, Worcester, Massachusetts.
Photo by John Gaumond, 2009

into being a solitary Kunitz. That was the only interlude when I had a sense of family.[126]

As the young boy shifted away from relatives, the same people provided solace for Yetta because they required her energy, help and perseverance. Rabbi Jesse Bienenfeld married Sarah and Percy Baker in the ballroom of Worcester's Bancroft Hotel on November 20th. The couple lived in Somerville, where Percy worked in the family hardware store. The first grandson, Stanton, arrived in 1923.[127]

In 1922, when Sophia married insurance salesman Alfred Isenberg, they lived at 4 Woodford Street. The Isenbergs moved to an apartment on Worcester's west side after their son Slater was

STANLEY JASSPON KUNITZ
"Sonnie" *"Stan"*
Born, July 29, 1905, Worcester, Mass.
Ledge Street Grammar School

Athlete as well as student of first rank is our "Sonnie". Not only is he a good baseball and basketball performer, but he was the racket wielder in Classical last year. "Stan" is a first honor student with a handsome collection of A's, a member of every class debating team and of two Amherst Cup teams, the captain of the successful 1922 Declaiming team, the president of the C. H. S. Debating Assembly, and Editor-in-Chief of *The Argus* are a few of the honors "Stan" has collected at Classical. We must go far to find another such orator as he. "Sonnie" goes to Harvard, where nought will stop his conquests.

"His silver tongue rocked the mob as upon a stormy sea."

Stanley J. Kunitz, 1922.
The Aftermath of the Class of Nineteen Twenty-Two of the Worcester Classical High School.
From the collection of Worcester Historical Museum

born in 1925.[128] Here was a second grandson and source of happiness for Yetta.

More reasons to be proud often sprang from her son's accomplishments. Kunitz was 1922 Classical High School's valedictorian and voted Class Scholar, graduating with "a handsome collection of A's"; he would be attending Harvard College on full scholarship.[129]

As sweet a victory as attending Harvard was, "Sonnie" or "Stan," as he was called, would feel a double sting:

> Remember this was the period when there was a two percent quota for Jews at Harvard. One felt (especially for a scholarship student, which I was) that to be both poor and Jewish at Harvard was to be outside the pale.[130]

After her second husband's death, Yetta Dine struggled to manage the Dine Manufacturing Company, which morphed and relocated into The Dine and Freidman Dress Manufacturing Company at 194

Stanley Jasspon Kunitz, 1926. Yearbook photograph
from 1926 Harvard Class Album.
Department of Special Collections, Princeton University Library

Front Street. Kunitz assessed her skills and shortcomings:

> She was extraordinarily competent ... but she was not a very good
> business woman. And she was always expanding. She never fired
> anybody. And during the bad years, she always kept her staff
> completely under her. The result was that anytime there was an
> economic decline, my mother went bankrupt.[131]

In April 1925, when Kunitz was finishing his junior year at
Harvard, his mother could not pay her portion of the mortgage on
4 Woodford Street. She signed over her half of the property to co-
owner, Mollie Siff.[132]

Kunitz's 1944 second book of poems, *Passport to the War*, fea-
tures "Father and Son," a dreamscape where a son pursues his
father's ghost: "How should I tell him my fable and the fears,/
How bridge the chasm in a casual tone,/ Saying, 'The house, the
stucco one you built,/ We lost ...'". The house exerted a permanent
hold on Kunitz, who would memorialize 4 Woodford Street and

the neighborhood in "Three Floors," "The Portrait," "The Magic Curtain," "Halley's Comet," and "My Mother's Pears."

Kunitz's shame could not have equaled that of his mother's. Business lost. House lost. Her independence threatened. But she still had her family and could be useful.

SOPHIA ISENBERG, 1926–1933

When she lost 4 Woodford Street in 1925, Yetta's living arrangements developed a permanent wobble. In Worcester, she lived with her stepson Mitchell Dine and his wife Jennie at 29 Woodford and her brother Abe across town in his apartment on Pleasant Street. She stayed with her daughter Sophia Isenberg in their Pleasant Street apartment, then in their homes on Midland and Coolidge streets. Slater Isenberg remembered his grandmother: "She was a guest in our home for about three years ... she was always well-dressed, even though she stayed in the house." He recalled being chased home from school by bullies and seeing her standing on the porch, "with a heavy object, perhaps a frying pan, in her hand."[133] By 1927, she lived alternately between Sophia and Sarah in Somerville, Massachusetts.[134]

Two more sweet drops fell into her bitter cup when grandson Lawrence Baker was born in 1926. Three years later, Kunitz congratulated Alfred and Sophia on their "new born babe" Conrad noting that he now had a "quartet of nephews."[135] For Yetta, it meant that she could be useful in raising her grandsons, spinning threads would tie them to their "bube."[136] It also meant that she traveled the thirty-five miles between Worcester and Somerville during this period, with occasional visits to her niece Sarah in Tarrytown.

Another highlight of Yetta's life was revealed in a set of letters from her son, written in 1927 while he was finishing his master's degree at Harvard University. Weighing her losses against her belief in Zionism, a visit to Palestine offered relief wrapped in a stellar experience. [137]

Letters reflect her twenty-two-year-old son's reaction to her journey.

> February 9, 1927 … You will be glad to know that I received
> a couple more A's for grades. Well, mother, you have a pleas-
> ant holiday before you – and you deserve it one thousand times
> over. Be merry. Enjoy yourself. Please go with a light heart. You
> have been sad long enough.
> February 19, 1927 … this letter will have to serve for my
> voice when you move out of the harbor … You know that I

Yetta Dine, right, with an unidentified companion on a voyage
to Palestine, c. 1927. The ship's manifest listed 52 Powder House
Boulevard in Somerville, Massachusetts, as her permanent address. At
the time, she made her home between daughters Sarah and Sophia.
Department of Special Collections, Princeton University Library

have wanted very much to go abroad, but I am honestly gladder at your going than I should be at my own. You have worked hard all your life; you have had little pleasure; it is good to think that you will be having some happy hours now ...

There are some things I want to say to you as you leave: I want you to feel how grateful I am to you for all that you have done for me—all that you have sacrificed. I will do everything in my power to make you happy ... I'm young—I'll have my chance to travel. Now, it is a hard road that I must climb; it will be many years, perhaps, before I accomplish anything worth the struggle. But I have confidence in myself. I think that you will have reason to be proud of me some day.

March 15, 1927 ... I'm going to NY next month to look for a job ... I'm glad to hear that you had a pleasant voyage and that you are enjoying the change of atmosphere and scenery. To see how the other half of the world lives is to learn a great deal about yourself... I shall not return to college [for a Ph.D.] next year, regardless of opportunities ... I spoke to 'the Captain' about a column in the *Telegram* ... I am not really enthusiastic about being in Worcester, as you know. Let me know how you find the Holy Land.

April 7, 1927 ... your letter from Tel Aviv. You certainly are leading a gay life. When you get back to the States, your children probably won't recognize you. You'll want to be wearing your party dresses all the time and go dancing at the night-clubs or see the latest show in town. I shall be weary and exhausted from escorting you to all your social affairs ... Don't think about coming home until your last cent's gone. Such holidays don't come every month of the year.[138]

After Kunitz's honor-laden undergraduate and graduate work, he expected to be asked to join the department. He described the outcome:

When I inquired about it, the word came back from the English faculty that I couldn't hope to teach there because "Anglo-Saxons would resent being taught English by a Jew."[139]

In 1926, Kunitz had clipped an editorial from *Liberty: A Weekly for the Whole Family* titled "Who should go to college?" which indicted "effete Eastern ones," such as Harvard, for their admissions restrictions against

> foreign groups (especially the Jews). [Colleges deemed it] necessary for the preservation of certain traditions and for the protection of the "parent American stock" ... Harvard ... has proposed examining men as to their mental, physical, social, and even financial fitness before admitting them to the fellowship of the university.

Harvard had awarded "1,625 degrees, and seven men were picked for highest scholastic achievement ..." The editor listed the names, Stanley J. Kunitz among them, and nudged readers to "analyze the names and ... find that four of the seven 'summa cum laude' men of Harvard, '26, are of the so-called "foreign groups." The next argument considered the overall high percentage of students of "foreign stock" who garnered colleges' highest honors.

> The probable meaning is that these boys of "foreign" stock know why they are attending college, and are willing to work and sacrifice pleasures and luxuries in order to acquire the knowledge they seek ... they regard college as an opportunity, a great privilege, and not as a four-year residence in a country club.[140]

Harvard's rejection left Kunitz with a bitter taste for his alma mater and was a source of disappointment for his mother, who would wait decades before seeing her son's name on a faculty door.

After receiving his master's degree, Kunitz continued to work in Worcester at the *Telegram* as "assistant Sunday editor... [who] wrote a literary column and ... some features."[141] His nom de plume was Mathilda Eureka, but when writing about newsworthy events, he had no by-line. A folder of clippings exposed his angst over anonymity: he inscribed "MINE" across them.[142]

While stability and security had escaped her, Yetta hoped to see her children settled happily with spouses and raising children who were poised for exemplary educations.

Her daughters seemed to have fulfilled her wishes. By 1930, Sarah and Percy left Somerville and moved with their two boys to 1815 Riverside Drive in New York, where Percy was an insurance salesman. The census listed mother-in-law Yetta Dine and "author/ writer" Stanley residing with them.

Son-in-law Alfred not only headed an insurance agency in downtown Worcester but was inspired by *The Boston Jewish Advocate* to join forces with colleagues to found a small, local newspaper, *The Jewish Civic Leader*.[143] Sophia became an active and prominent member of Worcester's Jewish community and joined several women's organizations.[144]

Yetta watched her son slip from idealistic youth into responsible adulthood. His decision to start out with less financial stability still left her enough bragging rights. His poems and literary criticism were being published in leading journals, such as *The Dial, Poetry, The Nation,* and *The Saturday Review of Literature*.[145]

In June 1928, he was awarded a residency to Yaddo, a 400-acre artists' retreat in Saratoga Springs, New York. He wrote to his mother about the "idyllic life."

> This is the most magnificent place imaginable, fit for a king, and full of wise and pleasant persons ... I hope you don't have too much trouble with your teeth and that you are as happy as I am for the present.

It was a place "with poets and novelists and painters, artists all of them, interested in the things of the spirit and worshipping beauty above all other things."[146]

The twenty-three-year-old had found Paradise, complete with Eve.

When Kunitz joined a dozen other artists and writers that summer, poet Helen Pearce was among them. She was "a great beauty," and they soon began their love affair.[147]

In June 1929, Kunitz managed to secure funds for a trip to Italy and France with Helen, although letters to his family made no mention of her. Mid-ocean, he wrote euphorically to his mother about

Helen Pearce, Italy, 1929.
Department of Special Collections, Princeton University Library

his "year abroad—this one will be very important for me-and maybe for English literature." In September, the contract for his first book of poems, *Intellectual Things,* caught up with him—500 copies would be printed, and he would receive ten percent royalties. It was scheduled for publication the following February. The sixty-three-page hard-cover volume would sell for two dollars.

Kunitz regaled his mother with details of European life as a solitary traveler. He was in Nice, France, staying in a boarding house

Stanley Kunitz, Italy, 1929–1930.
Department of Special Collections, Princeton University Library

searching for a house, which he then found in nearby Vence. Kunitz had fallen in love with France, a haven of cheap food and accommodations. His novel writing was slow going, but he was studying Italian for his trip to Fiesole, outside of Florence.[148]

He wrote to Sophia and Alfred, congratulating them on the birth of their son Conrad and made a promise about when he would return to Italy: "I'll take one of your sons with me." He reported, "Living is cheap here, and I like the loneliness." The next month, his letter to Sarah brimmed with details about the sumptuous life that could be lived on "$1500 a year," signing it "Stanley, your little brother."[149]

Kunitz responded to a letter from his mother:

> You reproach me for not writing ... it is absolutely necessary for me to work in a serene, untroubled atmosphere. That's why I fled

from New York … [All you have ever done] was worry about me ever since I can remember. That doesn't help me in the least. It has made your life miserable.

He wrote to her about his financial situation: He had heard from reference book publisher H.W. Wilson that a job in New York was "always open … But I'm not thinking about going back to my enemy, the time-clock, yet."

From Fiesole: "My money will hold out till the spring, I guess … 500 copies of *Intellectual Things* won't bring in a lot of money."

In March, he planned to leave Italy for Paris, then return to the United States. His career choice as a writer would grant him what he wanted: "The only success I care about is the success of saying what I mean to say." One can imagine Yetta's feelings when she read of her son's priorities and lack of interest in the "superficial benefits" of money.

He shared his plans, still not making any reference to Helen Pearce:

> When I'm back in the States, I shall look for a place in the country (but not too far from the city) where I can be quiet and work, perhaps with one or two friends of mine. I've sold several poems lately. Nowadays (believe it or not!) editors ask me for poems![150]

Kunitz returned to glowing reviews of *Intellectual Things* in publications, such as *The Nation* and his first place of employment, *The Worcester Daily Telegram*.[151] The book's dedication read: "To Helen Pearce."[152] His editorial work at H.W. Wilson began, but the twenty-five-year-old's tug-of-war with money continued.

On July 7, 1931, he wrote:

> I had practically decided on the Mansfield [Connecticut] farm … $4000. The owner will take a first mortgage and accept a $600 payment. For the rest, payable $400 a year … How much do you think I can raise on the [life] insurance now? (Unfortunately, a payment is due next month).[153]

Yetta, who was staying with Sophia at 90 Coolidge Street in

Worcester, received a two-word telegram dated July 16, 1931. Her son was "MARRIED TODAY" at City Hall in New York City.[154]

Five days later, Kunitz wrote a fuller explanation to his mother. He had married Helen Pearce in a five-minute ceremony and "didn't even have time to tell Sarah about it because we left in such a hurry." Now he and his bride were on their farm "tearing down wallpaper—the roofer is on the roof ... As soon as we get the place in shape, I'll drive you up to see the bride and groom and their magnificent(?) estate." He added that he had let his insurance policy lapse and asked his mother to fill out forms and send them with his enclosed money order. "I may have to borrow that money from Mrs. Gabilowitz in a few weeks."[155]

On July 23rd, the Kunitzes, "husband and wife of New York City," went to Mansfield's town hall and signed the $3,400 mortgage for Wormwood Hill, an eighty-acre farm.[156]

On August 5th, Pearce described her new life to Genevieve Taggard: Stanley traveled to his job at H.W. Wilson's in New York for a few days every month, where his collection of literary biographies was due to be published.

> *Intellectual Things* is on the reserve list at the library and [had] an advertisement in *The Publishers Weekly.* I haven't much to report about us. Stanley is asked everywhere for poems ... As for myself, I am hopeless. I am undergoing so much change and so much repudiation of values (literary). Ideas I once held, and I see no sign of coalescence.[157]

Kunitz's first reference book for H.W. Wilson, *Living Authors: A Book of Biographies,* was published in 1931. Shunning the non-literary nature of the work, he traded his earlier nom de plume, Mathilda Eureka, for Dilly Tante. When asked about this period of his literary life, Kunitz answered:

> ... I had to earn a living. After college I went to work for a publisher in New York and soon discovered that I wasn't geared for an office existence. So, I fled to a farm in Connecticut, where I

Wormwood Hill farmhouse, Mansfield, Connecticut, 1932.
Department of Special Collections, Princeton University Library

produced a crop of herbs, flowers, and reference books. And, perennially, poems.[158]

A letter from Kunitz to his mother revealed the couple's money struggles:

> Please try to mail the money order to me by Thursday, since I'll be leaving for the city Sunday or Monday. If you can't get it out by that time, you'd better hold it until I see you, although the other arrangement would be preferable, since I don't want to leave Helen without any cash at all.[159]

The stress of cobbling together a married life with that of farmer and poet was taking its toll. Kunitz's notebook entry read,

> My head is full of poems. But they are all fragments ... Why does my hand lie dead on the page? I think that I am not lonely enough ... I think I should have made a better hermit than a husband.[160]

Yetta and the Isenbergs visited the Mansfield farm, which was fifty-five miles from Worcester. Kunitz's nephew Slater remembered his uncle as "brilliant" but not one to socialize. "He would leave after saying hello." Isenberg recalled that there were children at the farm when they visited; perhaps one was Helen's nine-year old daughter, Lee, from her first marriage to Donald Downer.[161]

While Yetta worried about her son's financial straits, another tragedy was about to cloak her family in sorrow.

In 1932, Alfred and Sophia were at their summer home sixteen miles away in Princeton, Massachusetts. Late morning on August 24th, Sophia died from "furunculosis pyaemia," a rapidly progressing blood infection, caused by abscesses, such as boils, in soft tissue. She was thirty years old.[162]

On August 27th, Kunitz made another entry into his notebook: "The first rain is falling tonight on my sister's grave."[163]

Slater, who was seven years old, recalled that his grandmother "stayed on after Mother died" to take care of him and his two-year-old brother Conrad.[164]

In 1933, Alfred married Blema Alpert, a widow with two children, Robert, twelve, and Sonya, eight.[165]

Another door closed behind grief-stricken Yetta. Her permanent residence was now with Sarah, Percy, and their teenage sons Stanton and Larry, or "Buddy," as she called him.

SARAH BAKER, 1933–1944

The Bakers had moved the short distance from their apartment on Riverside Drive to a six-storey building at 34 Hillside Avenue in the Fort George section of upper Manhattan. Percy was a sales supervisor at an electrical appliance store, and Sarah, who had won an international typing medal in the 1913 New York Business Show, was a secretary at the Anderson Art Gallery.[166]

The next seven years in Yetta's life were relatively stable. With Sarah at work, she could make herself useful to the Baker household.

Left to right: Slater Isenberg, Yetta Dine, Conrad Isenberg, c. 1933.
Department of Special Collections, Princeton University Library

She drew her energy from loving and being needed by them. Her affections were focused on her dwindling family: Sarah, Stanley and four grandsons, although she would see less of Slater and Conrad in Worcester now that they had a new stepmother.

Whether or not Yetta was informed or merely suspected, her son's money troubles continued, and his marriage was foundering. In June 1935, Kunitz wrote to Genevieve Taggard, who was teaching at Bennington College in Vermont. He asked for help in securing a position: "assistant in poetry ... if it's not too late, would it be possible to have me considered for this post? ... salary doesn't matter." He arranged a meeting with Taggard at H.W. Wilson's New York offices adding, "I think I should tell you that Helen would not be with me."[167] Kunitz did not get an offer for the position.

That same year, the Kunitzes sold their Mansfield farm and purchased a fourteen-acre farm on Lurgan Road in New Hope, Pennsylvania, an artists' enclave seventy-two miles southwest of Manhattan.[168]

In 1936, Helen Kunitz is listed without her husband as a passenger on the *S.S. Vulcania*, sailing from Naples, Italy into New York.[169]

When Stanley Kunitz was in his nineties, he described the end of their marriage: "One April day, with no warning, Helen Pearce disappeared from the farm without a trace."[170] Kunitz and Pearce were divorced in 1937.[171]

Eleanor Evans Danysh became Yetta's new daughter-in-law on November 21, 1939. Kunitz and his bride resided at the New Hope farm and on East 24th Street in Manhattan.[172]

Nine months later, Death paid another visit to the family, delivering a blow almost too difficult to imagine. After three weeks under her doctor's care, on August 31, 1940, Sarah Baker died of breast cancer. She was forty-four years old. Her husband Percy, seventeen-year-old Stanton, fourteen-year-old Buddy, and her mother were left to mourn her. Sarah was buried in Westchester Hills Cemetery.[173]

As she had done after Sophia's death, Yetta stayed to help care for her grandsons.

Looking ahead to her own ending, Yetta made the $60 deposit to reserve a grave in Westchester Hills Cemetery. After paying the $40 balance, she took an envelope, addressed it "To Stanley and Eleanor Kunitz" and enclosed a life insurance policy and plot documents. Included was a letter, which amounted to her last will and testament.

February 14, 1944

My dear Son,

If anything should happen to me suddenly, I want you to know that I do not fear death. I have lived a long life, but not a very pleasant one.

I'm thankful to you and Eleanor for my support. You certainly have done your share.

You will find a bank book. I don't know how much of it will be left when my time comes. When I deposited the money in this bank, I made it out that you can get it by identifying that you are my Son Stanley J. Kunitz. I try to get along on what I get from the government. In case of emergencies, I did not have to trouble you.

There is also the deed for my plot in the cemetery, next to Sarah. It is all paid for.

Also enclosed is the paid-up policy which will cover all necessary expenses.

I have done the best I knew how to in all my troubles and kept my courage to the best of my knowledge.

All I pray and hope for is that I should not become a helpless burden on anyone. I'm thankful to the Levitans because they are very good to me.

You should not worry. You have both done your duty. The money in the bank belongs to you and no one else.

Your mother, Yetta H. Dine

500 Lurgan Road, Upper Makefield Township, Pennsylvania.
Department of Special Collections, Princeton University Library

P.S. Sarah's medal is in the dresser. Keep it for the boys.
The wedding ring belongs to Slater Isenberg. It was Sophia's. I
promised to keep it for him.[174]

When Percy Baker married Lily Goldberg in July 1943, Yetta
moved in with niece Sarah Levitan's daughter Rosilyn.[175]

In 1976, Kunitz gathered remnants of his grief to write "My
Sisters." The last stanza of an early draft reads: "Rest, rest ... Sarah
and Sophia, wherever they put you down."[176]

MY SISTERS

Who whispered, souls have shapes?
So has the wind, I say.
But I don't know,
I only feel things blow.

I had two sisters once
with long black hair
who walked apart from me
and wrote the history of tears.
Their story's faded with their names,
but the candlelight they carried,
like dancers in a dream,
still flickers on their gowns
as they bend over me
to comfort my night-fears.

Let nothing grieve you,
Sarah and Sophia.
Shush, shush, my dears,
now and forever.

—Stanley Kunitz, *Passing Through:*
The Later Poems, New and Selected

◆◆◆◆◆◆◆◆

ROSILYN LEVITAN, 1944–1951

What have we done to them that what they are
Shrinks from the touch of what they hoped to be?

—From "Night Letter," Stanley Kunitz, *The Collected Poems*

The move to live with Rosilyn Levitan in Tarrytown cemented Yetta
Dine's status as a guest in a relative's home. Her son and grandsons'
comings and goings remained the hub of her life. During this time,
her son asked her to write her memoir.

Family events threw light into some corners of Yetta's life: Stanton
Baker married Lucille Spiro in December 1946.[177] Slater Isenberg
graduated in 1947 from Yale University.[178] Buddy married Jacqueline
Benzell, sister of opera singer, Mimi Benzell, in April 1950. Her
grandsons and their wives remained faithful by visiting Tarrytown
or by writing.[179]

Her son's peripatetic lifestyle continued to vex Yetta. They were
still not settled according to her definition: steady employment and
a single address. Fresh in her memory was the year following his
stint in the army. He had been awarded the 1945 Guggenheim fel-
lowship in creative writing, and he and Eleanor used the $2,500
to move to Seton Ranch in New Mexico, where he could write in
peace and travel. He shared his lust for life with a former colleague
in Worcester:

> My wife and I live on a 2500-acre estate of naturalist Ernest
> Thompson Seton. We have had homes in Mansfield, Connecticut,
> and New Hope, Pennsylvania. In August, we return east to
> Bennington, where I have a professorship in English.[180]

For Kunitz, each move was a badge of distinction. His displaced
mother was more skeptical.

The Kunitzes sold the fourteen-acre farm on Lurgan Road in
New Hope in 1946.[181] From 1946–49, they lived in Vermont, where
Kunitz was a professor at Bennington College, a position he acquired

Stanton Baker and Yetta Dine. In an August 14, 1998 letter to Stanley
Kunitz, Stanton wrote: "The picture with me was taken in January
1947—probably in Tarrytown—where Lucille and I would visit her.
This would have been one month after our marriage in December 1946."
Department of Special Collections, Princeton University Library

140

through his friendship with poet Theodore Roethke. He explained, "When Ted was fired from Bennington ... after a breakdown, he got me the job to succeed him ..."[182]

Babies were arriving, which meant work for Yetta—knitting and crocheting outfits. The family marveled at her skill and artistry. Her first great-grandson, Stuart, was born to Stanton and Lucille. In February 1950, Yetta's first and only granddaughter Gretchen was born to her son and his wife. Her knitting needles sprang into motion with each birth.[183]

The 1950 fall semester found Kunitz teaching at the New School for Social Research in New York. His intention to be free from academic constraints remained intact. He preferred to teach on his "own terms, which was never to accept tenure, always to be on an annual contract ... still an outsider."[184] He chose a life of low-paying adjunct professorships, fellowships, editing reference books for H.W. Wilson, and teaching summer writing institutes.

Negotiations began for one venture that would provide work for both new parents. Potsdam State Teachers College was planning a summer program, "Workshop in the Arts" at White Pine Camp at Paul Smith College's facilities. Kunitz would lecture in creative writing and Eleanor would teach a stage arts course. They planned to bring along their "extremely active" daughter Gretchen. The Kunitzes signed contracts stipulating that they would be paid $600 each for their six-week courses.[185]

In June 1950, Yetta wrote to her daughter-in-law and "darling Gretchen," asking if her son had found a house and a new job for the fall and noting that they had been moving around "plenty the last few years." She added her opinion:

> I don't think Gretchen will want you to be changing living quarters too often, and both Stanley and yourself will find it more difficult to move around with your darling little daughter ... If everything goes well, I'll see all in September. For me it seems a long time to wait.[186]

Eleanor and Stanley Kunitz taking turns holding
their daughter Gretchen, 1950.
Department of Special Collections, Princeton University Library

The needle of her own yearnings and frustrations pierced a line
straight to the heart of her relationship with her son.

CHAPTER FIVE

Mount Vernon, New York
1951

Your mother, whom the mirror-world has claimed,
Plucks at the telltale hairs with violent hand
And thinks time backward to a brassy song,
Rolling the grape of hysteria under her tongue.

—From "The Tutored Child," Stanley Kunitz, *Passport to the War*

JOURNEY'S END

The new year in Tarrytown began with a letter from grandson Slater Isenberg: "Glad to hear that you are having a much pleasanter winter than the previous two." He was in the United States Navy Reserve in Washington, D.C., searching for a teaching job, and having passed his doctoral comprehensive exams, looking for the "right approach" to his dissertation topic.[187]

Larry Baker's wife Jacqueline wrote in early February, thanking "Bube" for letters to her and her mother.

> We were indeed sorry that you weren't feeling well ... I'm sure you are placing the blame properly, as winter is always bad with all the cold weather, snow and ice. Another few months and we have spring again ... I'm glad that you have tickets for Mimi's performance ... I think that this will be the first time you will hear Mimi sing, isn't that right? ... Larry is still going to school two nights a week, and goes bowling another night, so the days fly by.[188]

Yetta's health continued to decline. Her stroke likely occurred in late February or early March, after which she was moved to the Westchester Convalescent and Nursing Home. Stanton Baker's wife, Lucille, recalled that "they [Rosilyn and Nathan Moses] couldn't take care of her anymore."[189]

She sat in her room, with a pencil poised over the twenty-five-cent spiral notebook. Like a dutiful student, she printed her name on its brown cardboard cover: "MRS Y. H. DINE." Now eighty-four years old, she was a shadow of the woman she was in 1945, when writing her memoir gave her renewed energy and purpose. On the other hand, the notebook fulfilled a need—a place to collect her thoughts, dark as they could be.

She opened to a page near the middle: "Wednesday March 7th." This would be her habit—open the notebook, find a blank page and, if she were interrupted or feeling ill or tired, fold back the metal spiral and resume mid-sentence another day. It was an undisciplined approach, but at least she was writing.

Deterioration of her handwriting was a blow to the inveterate letter-writer. Some days, she struggled to stay on the lines, multiplied the arcade formations in her m's, n's and added e's and m's to words, such as "seeem" and "Imn"; she rarely crossed her t's. A combination of damage to her motor system, possible worsening vision, bouts of asthma and encroaching deafness added to her woes.

The notebook functioned as a diary, although at times, it shifted into a letter to her son, a farewell speech to family and friends, or an agonized plea to God for release from a life bereft of independence, usefulness and connection.

Even then, she clung to the idea that her writing would be published.

She pulled at threads of happiness and mixed memories with hope and imagination. She even designed a plan to rebuild a life of self-sufficiency and purpose.

When she felt well enough, she participated in the rest home's activities, such as playing cards and visiting the Mount Vernon

Saturday June

Today is the worst day I ever had. I hope I don't survive for an this day I'm still hopping Stanley my only surviving child and Eleanor whom I love more than any thing in this world I pray and hope she keeps well she is such a lovely good soul. and made my son so happy she deserves all the good in the world

The last hours or maybe the last days of my life is full with sorrow that I cause Stanley and Eleanor so much trouble but my hope is it will be over soon perhaps I get another stroke and this time they let me Die as I have no more desire to live help me almighty God Just let me Die to free my only surviving child from such a terrible worry, let me Die so he can live a normal useful life, without worry about an old usseless Skeleton He has a lot to offer to the literary world with his briliant mind if is only free from worry but what can I do to help him I wish and want to Die but I'm not strong enough to make an end to my life I always fear all bring sorry and troble to others I don't fear for myself but I fear for others so I have to concult myself with prayers that I could Die a natural Death without involving others God help

Yetta Dine's diary, page 33.
Collection of Gretchen Kunitz, M.D.

145

Public Library. An overdue book notice reflected her reading tastes: Aldous Huxley's collection of short fiction *Mortal Coils* and, not surprisingly, *A Second Treasury of the World's Great Letters.*[190]

Her thoughts turned to Spinoza and Fredrich Nietzsche, as she tried to grasp why the fabric of her life had frayed to the point of disintegration. Her idiosyncratic embrace of a blended Spinozian/Nietzschean philosophy underlined her long-held skepticism and profound despair. Both men's ideas challenged traditional views of organized religion and advocated self-reliance, as opposed to dependence on a personal God or immortal soul for moral guidance. Her choice of philosophers left her without consolation, as she pounded at heaven's gate and demanded the attention of an unresponsive God. Yetta would have welcomed a discussion with Professor Felix Adler, who lectured at the Educational Alliance and was known for his views on euthanasia.

She tried unsuccessfully to push aside thoughts about her myriad discomforts or the decision to place her in a rest home. Her wish not to become "a helpless burden on anyone" was useless, because her son and daughter-in-law were bearing the cost.

Perceived and real separation from family and friends weighed her down with loneliness. As soon as Buddy and Jacquie, Stanton and Lucille, or Stanley and Eleanor and their children left, she wondered how many days or weeks would pass until another visit. The next best thing would need to be either writing and receiving letters or taking infrequent and costly long-distance telephone calls. The remainder of her hours were spent thinking about her hapless existence.

Even as misery soaked her to the core, she extracted a few drops of sweetness. Buddy and Jacquie were expecting. Yetta was unsure how she could manage the work of knitting outfits, her traditional gift. Most days, she was either tired, in pain, or both. Letters from family and friends, placed chronologically among her nine entries, offered relief from her intense unhappiness.

◆◆◆◆◆◆◆◆

THE DIARY

My ancestors step from my American bones.
There's mother in a woven shawl, and that
No doubt, is father picking up his pack
For the return voyage through those dreadful years
Into the winter of the raging eye.

—From "Reflection by a Mailbox," Stanley Kunitz,
The Collected Poems

WEDNESDAY, MARCH 7—At last, I think I have reached journey's end. I was invited today to play bridge at a club for older men and women. I have enjoyed the game in the past and had a real good time all day. I met nice people, so my last day of life was pleasant.

It was an effort and very tiresome to get dressed, but the nurses helped me. Just the same, I felt much better when we arrived at the clubhouse.

We came back to the home in time for dinner, but I had no desire to eat. I was sick all night and sure that I was at the end.

THURSDAY, MARCH 8—Today, I was in my room all day, just awaiting the end. But who knows how long I will have to wait? I'm suffering great discomfort. My trouble now is my asthma. Evidently, the Almighty listened to my prayer not to die of abdominal cancer. I have seen so much suffering from that dreadful illness.

Whatever it is, I know this much, that my end is near, and I'm leaving unfinished work. I need two weeks more to finish the job I started a few days ago. I would very much like to finish writing the last chapter of my life's journey. I also would like to finish a set I started for Buddy's baby, but I'm not anxious to prolong my life.

I want to be through with life. I'm just tired of living, so I have to leave work unfinished.

I hope Stanley and Eleanor will visit me this evening. I want to thank them for all they have done for me. I know tomorrow will be too late. If I were more careful about time the last two weeks, I would have finished my job.

I suppose my constant suffering had a lot to do with it. I just could not concentrate on anything, so I lost count with the race against time.

Now, it is too late. Before closing the last chapter, I want to thank everyone for their kindness to me. Special thanks to Mr. and Mrs. Malken, who have given so much of their time. They certainly were a great help to me in all my troubles. I have not forgotten all they have done for the two boys when Sarah passed away. I do hope they will be rewarded for all their good deeds, of which they have done many! May God bless you and reward you for your kindness. I know it makes you happy to do the noble work you have always done for others.

I have several things I would like to write down, but it is too late now. My time is up.

SATURDAY MORNING, MARCH 10—I'm called and have to leave soon, so my work remains unfinished. I'm sorry that I could not finish this last chapter of my journey's end. Forgive me, my dear son, in that I have failed you at the end. I did not do this intentionally. I just became too sick to do anything.

I also want to apologize to my dear grandson Buddy and his darling wife Jacquie. I have disappointed you. I could not finish the set I started for your baby. I did not think time would run out on me. Every doctor who examined me said that I would last many months.

I really did not try to prolong my life. I'm sick of life and want to be through with it. I have suffered too much. You will all forgive me that I have failed you. I meant well.

I looked forward to seeing Jacquie and Buddy's baby. Buddy himself is still my darling baby. I have to leave you all. I hope you all take good care of your health and live long, happy lives. You know, my dear ones, how I love you all. You are the sweet drops in the bitter cup of my struggling. Can anyone imagine the thrill I get when darling Stuart comes in and says, "Hello, Bube"?[191] I hope he will be a pleasure and comfort to you for all your life, as my dear son and his talented wife are to me.

I'm sorry that I could not see you all in the last moments of my life, to bless you and thank you for all the kindnesses and sacrifices you made for me. I know what a burden I have been on all of you. May the Almighty reward you.

As I'm sitting here and awaiting my death, they asked me if they should call you to come and say good-by. But I decided not to ask you to come. I want to save you the ordeal of watching me die. I have witnessed so many of my loved ones depart, and I know how it affects one's health, most especially a young person's. So, I say good-by to all of you, my dears. May God bless you all with health and happiness. Keep well and take care of yourselves.

Thanks again to all my good friends. Your visits meant so much to me. I felt so lonesome being ill amongst strangers, although everyone here was wonderful to me. Yet, I longed to see a familiar face. What a relief it was when a nurse came in to tell me that I had company. Thanks again and again.

So, life's journey is coming to an end.

My dear son, I hope you will be able to get some idea of this piece of raw material I'm leaving to you. If you can do something with it, good and well. If it is too much of a job, just put it in the wastebasket. It might not be worth the labor you would have to put into it. You can add whatever you want from your own imagination. You know what my life was. I'm wondering now if it was worth the struggle for almost eighty-five years.

SATURDAY, APRIL 28—I'm now at journey's end, or at the end of my rope. But today, I feel much better. Stanley, Jacquie, Stanton and Buddy came to see me and promised for sure to take me to Tarrytown next Sunday. It will be a long week for me, but this is the best they can do. I have to be satisfied, wait again, count the days, and even the hours.

I hope when I settle down and have peace of mind, I will be able to really concentrate and write the last chapter of my long, unhappy life.

On the last lap of my journey's end, I landed in Mount Vernon at the Westchester Convalescent and Nursing Home, thanks to my dear son and his talented and understanding wife. The first day I came here, I made up my mind to make the best of the situation. My health has not changed much.

Of course, I don't know how long I will last. I have no great desire to get well. I feel I have lived long enough. My work is done, and I have absolutely nothing to expect of life. I feel I have outlived my usefulness. So, why go on living a useless life with nothing to look forward to except death itself? I want to be relieved of both hope and fear of the daily struggle of life, of pain and sleepless nights. I think I have had all I want of life.

◆◆◆◆◆◆◆◆

Usefulness comes in all sizes: Friend Betsy asked for her help: "Israel was wondering if you can remember the year and month he arrived in this country." Ethel Blumner had seen Rosilyn:

> She told us she was up to visit you and you are getting along fine. We'll try to be up ... enclosed are hair nets you need. [Next time, I] promise to send combs. Mother feels terrible she hasn't been up to visit you ...

A letter arrived from Mrs. A.H. Malken, her friend from the days when she lived with Sarah.[192] People were thinking of her, albeit not enough to ward off the chill of loneliness.

◆◆◆◆◆◆◆◆

SATURDAY, APRIL 28[193]—This nursing home is a former private residence. It is well-furnished and well-administrated by a young Dr.

Cohen, with a staff of five nurses who care for the thirty to forty boarders. They work hard to make us very comfortable. The food is excellent, prepared well and balanced. Everything is home-cooked, and nothing is canned. Soups are served. It's like real home cooking, made on the premises and served three times a day.

It is a blessing, a place like this for older people—much better than living with children or living in a furnished room, like most old people have to do. It is even better than living in a hotel.

When I first arrived here, I spoke to myself, which is an old habit of mine. I do this if I want to convince myself of something. I said, "Now, Mrs. Dine, you came here, so be thankful for the opportunity. You have to try to be satisfied."

So, I tried to find out about the people who have lived here for some time. Then I said to myself, "Mrs. Dine, you are no better than any of the thirty women and five men who make their home here. Be happy that you were lucky to find a home that provides comfortable living quarters with good food and agreeable companionship. Just learn to be happy. Forget the past and don't worry about the future." This is a philosophy I adopted long ago.

The future that I worried about and feared all my life is already the past. My tomorrows are already yesterdays. I live from day to day. Of course, I know I'm living on borrowed time, so I try not waste it on useless worrying. I'm waiting for death to free me from physical pain, uncertain hope and fear, and regrets for the past. There is no other cure for me. Only death can free me.

I don't fear death. I never did fear death, not any more than I feared sleep, even in my childhood days when I came face to face with death. In fact, I was even sorry then that I survived.

I was twelve years old when I was taken by sled to Kovno for my first job, shortly after my father's death in 1878. It was in early March, but still very cold. From Yashwen, my birthplace, to Kovno, it was six Russian miles, approximately forty-two American miles by road.

But the roads were very bad. Big mountains of frozen snow made it impossible for the horses to draw the heavy cargo. So, they traveled on the frozen river, which is smoother and shorter. But it was very dangerous. In some places, holes had been cut in the ice for fishing.

Our cargo consisted of several sacks of grain, a crate of geese, a crate of chickens and some boxes of eggs. I was perched on top of the cargo, wrapped in my father's sheepskin coat and comforters, with heavy woolen stockings and mittens to keep my feet and hands from freezing. But the March wind penetrated all the heavy covering and made me very uncomfortable.

Six miles from our town to where the journey began on the Nevėžis River is a town called Labūnava. We left Yashwen at 4 p.m. and started our journey on the river about 6:30. It became very cold after the sun went down. The chickens started to protest and made a lot of noise, but the geese were quiet, as if they did not mind the cold.

The driver jumped off the sled every few minutes to take some vodka from the two bottles he brought along. Sometimes, he walked alongside the horses.

Suddenly, we heard a crack. The horses had reached a small hole, and the ice broke all around it. The horses went down, pulling the heavy cargo with them. The geese, chickens, driver and I got nice cold baths under the ice.

An alarm was sent out in the village. In a few minutes, help came. It was not an easy task to pull two horses with all the cargo from under the ice. Everything was frozen stiff. When we reached the surface, the chickens and geese looked as if they were made of glass.

We were all taken to a farmhouse, where they tried to dry our clothes. We started to take off the frozen clothing, but it was so stiff that it took hours to pull everything apart. It took all day to have any of it dry enough to wear. Such was my first experience leaving home.

We arrived in Kovno about 10 p.m. My employer was waiting for us. Her mother was there, too, and we all got busy preparing a nice hot meal and getting the rooms warm by retaining the precious heat from the fire.

Mrs. Amsterdam closed the chimney, so in a few minutes, the

room was filled with coal gas, and I started to feel dizzy. I went to bed, but when I tried to get up in the morning, I felt sick.

We both slept in the same bed. She told me to stay in bed until I felt better, and she went out. When I tried to get up, I fainted and fell on the floor.

When she returned and looked through a small pane of glass in the door, she saw me on the floor. She became alarmed and went for a doctor. When she arrived with the doctor, they opened the door to let in some fresh air and put me back in bed.

The doctor said it was a narrow escape. In thirty minutes, I would have been dead. So, what would have been lost if I had died then? It would have saved me seventy years of suffering and all kinds of disappointments.

I am bitter and do too much complaining. I did have a few sweet drops in my bitter cup. The sweetest memories are not the five months of traveling through all the historical countries in the Middle East, where I met all kinds of people - people who made history.

For the last fifteen years, my pleasure has been in seeing my orphaned grandchildren grow up to be useful citizens, of which I have the right to be proud.

I will never forget the day when Buddy came to Tarrytown in his car and said, "Come on, Bube, I'll take you to Bennington College to see Uncle Sonny."

So, we drove to Albany and then to Troy to see Rensselaer Polytechnic Institute, where Buddy graduated from and became an instructor at the age of nineteen. He took us through the administration building where all the faculty have their offices. I read on one of the doors: Lawrence Herbert Baker, Instructor of Mechanical Engineering. I could hardly believe my eyes. My little Buddy, already an instructor at a big college at that early age. Of course, my pride was mixed with grief and pain that my poor Sarah did not live to see it.

From Rochester, we drove to Vermont where Stanley and Eleanor were waiting for us on the Bennington campus.

Stanley took us to the second floor of the administration building and pointed out the first door in the row of offices. I read with pleasure: Stanley Kunitz, Professor of Literature.

So, I did get a few sweet drops in my bitter cup. Perhaps it was worth my suffering. My grandsons are very devoted to me, and we really are close friends. They see me often and confide in me about whatever confronts them. Lucille, Stanton's wife and Jacquie, Buddy's wife, are more like daughters to me. They manage to visit or write every week. They call me Bube, and when my beautiful little great-grandson comes in, he always greets me with "Hello, Bube!" I'm expecting another great-grandchild in the near future, I think late in July. I'm looking forward to the event. I hope and pray everything will come along in a normal way.[194]

I have lived through all these troubles and seen Stanton and Buddy married and established in comfortable homes with good jobs. So, I'm getting some reward for the struggles of my past.

If only I was well enough to enjoy the little pleasures that the Almighty granted me. But here I am, broken in health and spirit. I have no desire to go on living. I want to be through with life. I'm just worn out from the constant pain and sleepless nights and look forward to being freed by death. There is no other hope for me. I'm beyond repair and not anxious to get well, even if I could. What good is it to try to prolong a miserable, painful life? What is in store for me - more suffering? I hope and pray that the Almighty will not let me suffer too much longer.

I have no courage to do away with myself. I have to wait until the Almighty will put an end to my suffering with a painless death.

The law is more merciful to animals than to us human beings. When an animal gets sick or is too old, science ends its life with a painless death.

But they let humans suffer. Can't we have the same privilege as our animals? What good is it, this useless suffering? I think a law should be amended similar to the prevention of cruelty to animals. In hopeless and incurable cases, science should be permitted to put an end to suffering with a painless death.

What good is a broken life? It would be a blessing to make an end to such a life and free the sufferer from his or her suffering. It would free the unfortunate family or society from having to care for such a person. Why try to prolong a miserable life that has no value to anyone? We are all here to contribute something to the big household, as I call the world. Every person becomes an asset, but when one becomes hopeless and helpless, he or she becomes a liability to our large establishment.[195]

I would rather welcome death than keep on suffering. For what purpose should a life like mine be saved or prolonged? No one will miss me. They all can get along without me. I have outlived my usefulness, so I'm ready, just waiting for the last call, hoping it will come soon. I have lived longer than I ever wanted or expected.

I'm almost eighty-five. It's time for me to exit this world that I was brought into without my consent. I appeal to science to make an end to my suffering life, to give me something that will make me go to sleep forever. Life is not worth the suffering, not to me or millions of others like myself.

There was a time long, long ago when life was very precious to me, not for my own sake or for the pleasure of life, but for my orphan children's sake. They needed me then. There was no one else to care for them, so I tried hard to survive all the hardship I was confronted with. I felt that I brought children into the world, so I must try to live to take care of them. I tried to overcome my difficulties. Life was my precious possession. In later years, when I lost my Sophie who passed away at the age of thirty, I felt maybe I could be some help to the two little orphans she left. In all my tragic life, when one tragedy after another struck me, I tried to survive, in case I could be of any help to the family for which I was responsible.

Now, thank heavens, no one needs me. They are all grown up, so I can die in peace and feel that my passing will not affect anyone. That is why I'm not fighting for life and not trying to get well. I have no desire to live, so why go on suffering day and night? I have no courage to do away with myself. But I do wish there was a law that science could put me out of my misery, without involving the lives of others and without bringing more suffering or hardship on those who care for me.

May God be merciful and end my suffering. It must be easier to die when one does not fear death. They say many people live not for the love of life, but for the fear of death. In my case, I neither fear death, nor do I love life. In fact, I'm looking forward to death to free me of the fear of what may confront me in the future in whatever time is allotted to me. Who can tell how long that will take?

Meanwhile, I have to suffer and make the best of it, since there is no other way out. We are all well cared for here, fed and made comfortable in every other way. Some days, I become restless and would like to go somewhere to break up the monotony of a life of doing nothing. When I left Tarrytown on my last lap for journey's end, I did not prepare myself.

I would like to go there to get my summer dresses and other little commodities which I need badly. If I want to go out, even for a walk, no one seems to think it is important. So, they don't take me. I have had many promises, but so far, I'm still waiting and hoping and looking forward from day to day that someone at last will call for me to take me to Tarrytown. I also need some medicine from my chest, which I should have brought with me when I first came here. I have suffered a lot on account of that, and now I have to wait day after day until someone remembers that they promised to call for me.

I also need some change. I have not got even one dime to use the telephone, so I'm cut off from everyone, God knows for how long. My hope is for this weekend. My dear son promised to call for me. Roz Levitan has also promised to call for me, but promising does not cost anything. They probably mean well but forget soon after. If I could use the telephone, I would remind them. Perhaps that would help, but I'm cut off from everyone and have to wait until they remind themselves and will at last remember to call for me.

I have not seen my grandsons in over a week. How I would love to see them and their wives. I love Lucille and Jacquie and darling Stuart, my great-grandson. Since my days are numbered, I would like to see them all as much as possible. I have been living on borrowed time for some months, sitting here and waiting for the last call of my journey's end. The last lap of the journey seems very slow, although we are very comfortable here, no complaints whatever.

My only worry is that it is too much of a burden on my son. It takes half of their income for my upkeep. It hurts me to think that both Stanley and Eleanor have to work so hard and spend so much on me, but what can I do? I have no other way. That is why I am so tired of life. If I were well, I still could earn a living. I could get a job in a factory and do sewing on any kind of machine. But I'm not even able to look for a job, because it means traveling to New York by bus, train and subway. I'm not able to do that. I'm still trying to find out if there is any factory here in Mount Vernon or in the nearby towns I could reach by bus.

◆◆◆◆◆◆◆◆

Anna K. Smith was a friend and faithful writer whose letters were filled with friendly chatter and concern—"[I] heard that you did not feel well." In another letter, she counseled her: "You have been such a good friend to me … think about the pleasant times you had in life and the useful things you did."

That same day, a letter from Lucille and Stanton arrived, with pictures of son Stuart. Family news was followed by a promise: "We'll get a ride and drive up to see you in the very near future."

Louise Volpe, who was possibly a relative on her mother's side, referred to a telephone call, when she was "happy to hear [Yetta's] voice."[196]

Meanwhile, the Kunitzes, including baby Gretchen, were at home on Jones Street in New York making final preparations for the 1951 summer program in Potsdam. Their teaching commitments meant that Yetta could look forward to one less set of visitors.

◆◆◆◆◆◆◆◆

6444 Fleecydale Road, Carversville, Pennsylvania, 1952.
Collection of Gretchen Kunitz, M.D.

Eleanor Kunitz, with Gretchen and family pet, Bonnie, 1952.
Collection of Gretchen Kunitz, M.D.

SATURDAY AFTERNOON, JUNE 7—God Almighty, I'm confused and despondent. I can't live, and I don't die. What shall I do? I'm not courageous enough to do away with my life. I just keep on praying that God should help me die. I'm tired, confused and discouraged. I want to talk to either Stanley or Eleanor. I asked Dr. Cohen to call them on the phone.

I even don't know if they returned from New Hope.

◆◆◆◆◆◆◆◆

After five years of not owning a home in the New Hope area, the Kunitzes were planning to return there. The announcement must have sent Yetta reeling because their drive to Mount Vernon would stretch to nearly 100 miles.

Kunitz wrote to Helen Hosner, Department of Music at Potsdam:

> We found another country place, that we like even better than the one we lost, a few miles up-river from New Hope. It seems perfect for Gretchen and us old folks ... though howinhell we're going to pay for it is another story. Our moving date is November 28th.[197,198]

Yetta's despair continued to unspool on the pages, yet she came up with what might seem like a preposterous idea.

◆◆◆◆◆◆◆◆

What shall I do? I'm without money to get telephone connections. Of course, it is all my own fault. I don't know what to do.

Just this moment, I think and think and make plans to try to live by myself. But I'm so helpless. I know my only solution is death, but I can't die. Nietzsche was perfectly right when he wrote that the sweetest thing in life is death. No hope without fear.[199] I know of no pleasure without pain, so I only live and suffer. I want to die. God Almighty, help me.

Just don't let me lose my mind or reason. I want my only surviving child to remember me as I always was, with a good sound mind.

Waiting, waiting all day to hear from Stanley. But no luck, so I'm doomed. If I can find a way to have the courage to do it.

I will wait. Tomorrow is Sunday. Perhaps I'll hear from him. What can I do? I must tell him of my last plans. Since I cannot die, I have to do something with my life or for my life.

If only Stanley and Eleanor will agree with my last plan, which runs through my confused worn-out brain. If I have to go on living, I'd like to do this. Of course, it might sound crazy to Eleanor and Stanley. Without their consent, I cannot do anything.

If they could arrange for me to be transferred to a New York institution, I would like to enroll for the winter term in some college to take a course in creative writing. I learn very easily. Perhaps I could make something of myself. My stories are interesting, but I need some training on how to approach a story. I'm willing and anxious to learn, if the opportunity is given to me. But it is worthwhile to try.

I never had any training in anything. Whatever I did, I had to learn by myself. When I began to work, I started the same way, not having taken one lesson. I wasted my time and material by sewing things without a system. Had I gone to school and learned the right way, I could have done a better job. Even today, I would have been able to look for a job as a designer.

But now I have decided if I'm going to write, which I intend to do, I must learn some rules about writing. I hope my son will help me. I will work hard. It will be good for my health to have something worthwhile to think about, instead of always thinking about how to die. My idea is that no one is ever too old to learn, if one has the desire to learn. I was always anxious to learn, but unfortunately never had the chance to get any schooling in anything.

This is my last and only hope and opportunity. I must not fail. With God's and my son's help and encouragement, I want them to see what a little old skeleton can do. If I fail in this, I hope at least by living in New York, I'll find a way to support myself. My health will improve in New York. I can find a factory job in the work I do well. I'm sure my problem now is to be able to get in a place not far from the manufacturing center. Traveling is the hardest job for me. I need to be on the bus line. I hope my son will be able to get me transferred to the 87th Street project.

My poor son. All the trouble I cause you. But if we are successful, I will not trouble you anymore, and you will have the satisfaction of knowing that you helped your desperate Mother to be independent. My God, help us. I promise I'll try not to fail. You cannot imagine how happy I would be if I could support myself. I always wanted to work and support myself, but in Tarrytown it was impossible and commuting to New York was also impossible.

But I hope now that I will be able to do it. With your consent and God's help, my health should not fail me. At present, I feel ...

◆◆◆◆◆◆◆◆

Yetta's words drifted off the page into the air.

On June 21st, another letter from Louise Volpe arrived, with news and a pledge: "I will never forget your kindness to me." It inspired the despondent Yetta, who turned it over and started to draft a poem.

> Back to the lands of yesterday
> Back to friends of yore
> Back through the dark and weary
> ways to life light and health
> and hope once more
> Back to the land of beginning
> again where broken dreams
> come true and the skies are always blue[200]

The back of a February letter from Larry and Jacquie offered a place to write a second draft when the urge to work on it returned. But, instead of lifting her spirits, despair crushed them.

> Back to the lands of Yesterday
> Back to friends of Yore
> Back through the dark and
> dreary ways to life

health and hope once more
Back to hearts that
wait for me, warmed
from the Sun above
Back from the lands
of yesterday's dream
to a new life of hope
light and health again

◆◆◆◆◆◆◆◆

I dream of a new life, but I know it cannot be. I'm too far gone. My physical health is not so hopeless, but my spirit is low. I know my position. I'm only trying to fool myself. I know there is no hope for me. My only hope is in death, the only thing left for me to look forward to. I pray and hope it will come soon [201]

MONDAY, JUNE 24—It is the second day of a holiday. The doctor called me this morning to tell me they are having services downstairs, if I wanted to come down and join in prayer.[202] Never did I pray so earnestly. All my life, my prayer was for the same thing that I have been praying for since I began. I always pray to God for the only thing I hope and desire, death, the sweetest thing in life, according to Nietzsche's philosophy.

Anyhow, I have been very despondent since Stanley and Eleanor went away to their new home in New Hope, Pennsylvania. I don't even have an address to communicate with them, so here I'm left with all my hopeless plans and don't know where to turn.

God Almighty, be merciful. What shall I do? I cannot go on living, even for another day. I'm such trouble to the only person I have left in my life, my only dear son. Why do you have to suffer on my account? I want to die, and I must die in order for you, darling Eleanor and your innocent little baby to be able to live in peace and comfort. I have no right to ruin your life. I'm ready to die. My time is up, but you must live your useful life to create future poetry and literature. Just forget me and live your life in happiness. Do the things you like to do without being disturbed over an old skeleton who has outlived her usefulness. I'm no good for anything anymore.

I never could accomplish anything according to my plans or empty dreams. I would have loved to try out my last plan to enroll in some college for six months and try again to rebuild my broken unsuccessful life. I had the chance to try, but that meant dragging in my son into it, which I have no right to do, even if he would consent to my crazy idea.

I do want to speak to both Eleanor and Stanley. Perhaps they could help me make my home in a New York institution. Meanwhile, I could try to get a job and be self-supporting. I know I can do that if I only could get the chance to try.

I have to find a way either to live or to die. God, please guide me in the right direction. I don't want to be more of a tragedy to my dear son and grandsons. I must try the best way out, but I also have no right to make trouble for the institution, to disturb the whole household by trying to take my own life. Everyone has been great to me. Why make trouble for them?

I must try to find a way to get to New York to look for a job, and later on, I might be able to fulfill my other plan to enroll in some college. But I need to work fast. Time is running out on me. First of all, I must ask Stanton and Buddy to give me a couple of dollars, so I can go to New York or perhaps to Tarrytown.

SATURDAY, JUNE [30]—Today is the worst day I ever had. I hope I don't survive for another day. I'm still hoping to see Stanley, my only surviving child and Eleanor, whom I love more than anything in this world. I pray and hope she keeps well. She is such a lovely, good soul and has made my son so happy. She deserves all the good in the world.

The last hours, or maybe the last days of my life, are filled with sorrow that I caused Stanley and Eleanor so much trouble. My hope is that it will be over soon. Perhaps I will have another stroke and this time they will let me die, as I have no more desire to live. Help me, Almighty God, just let me die and free my only surviving child from such terrible worry. Let me die, so he can live a normal useful life, without worrying about an old useless skeleton. He has a lot to offer to the literary world with his brilliant mind, if it's only free from worry. But what can I do to help him? I want to die, but I'm not strong enough to make an end to my life.

I always feared that I'd bring sorrow and trouble to others. I don't fear for myself, but I fear for others, so I have to content myself with prayers that I should die a natural death, without involving others. God help me not to live. Help me to die. Why did they not let me die when I first got sick? It would have been all over and forgotten.

Ever since I was a child, I was always unhappy and had nothing to hold on to life. I studied Spinoza's philosophy when I was twelve years old and I lost my God, though Spinoza did not deny the existence of a God. But he did not believe in a personal God. He said there was no personal God that has to do with the destiny of Man. Whatever befalls a human being is either by his own fault or by other men. So, I was left without a God and without hope in all my troubles.

I always blamed myself, because I could not believe what I was going through was God's will. I needed a personal God to pray to and to think it was his will, and that it was not my fault. I did the best I knew how to, I never wanted to do wrong to anyone, and I trusted everyone. So, people took advantage of me and brought me to my present state.

My second philosopher who helped me to my ruin was Nietzsche. He said nothing was worth the struggle for life. No hope without fear, no pleasure without pain, that the sweetest thing in life is death. So, I have wanted to die ever since I was fourteen years old. I still believe that his philosophy has a lot of good. How happy I would be if I just could die a natural death since I have nothing to live for.

I love my only surviving child and my dear Eleanor and their lovely little Gretchen. Yet, I cannot struggle to live to enjoy the pleasure of my beloved ones. My dear grandsons, who I'm so proud of, I have to say good-by to all of you. My lovely Stuart and the expectation of seeing Buddy's child. I'm willing to give up all this heavenly pleasure in death in order to free you all and not to have to bother you with my broken life. I know you all love me and don't want me to die. You are all trying to help me, but it is too late, I fear.

Just a few days ago, I still had hope and started to nurse an idea to enroll in a creative writing course and try to save what is left of my life, but that failed, as have all my other hopes. Stanley had to go away to his new home and without him, I cannot move. Without funds and with a broken body and confused mind, someone has to help me out until I can help myself. I must wait for dear Eleanor. She is the only one who can help me. She is calm and understanding.

I have to keep busy. A job would be the best medicine for me. Who can help me get a job in a factory among people? Work does not scare me. I always was happier when I worked. I cannot live an idle life. I have to forget about my health. I really feel much better physically, but my spirit is at a low ebb. If I can brace up and make myself presentable, I could be saved from destroying my own life.

Please help me, whoever can do anything to restore me back as a human being. I will cooperate and try to do whatever I'm told to do. I know I'm lost. I have nothing to lose and perhaps much to gain. Where there is life, there is still hope, not much hope in my case, but I must try for Stanley and Eleanor's sake, and also for Buddy and Stanton. I know they would be happy to see me on my feet again.

I'm at the crossroad. Now it depends on what turn I take with the help of God and my dear children, who I caused so much trouble. They are all willing to help me, if there is only a way out.

I have to try to calm down.

THURSDAY, JULY 12—

> Back to the lands of yesterdays
> Is a solace just divine.
> Back to friends of yore,
> Back through the dark and weary ways
> Where hearts of friends are awaiting me,

Warmed by the Sun above.
Back to life, light and health once, once more
And to the land of beginning again
Where broken dreams come true,
Where skies are always blue.

—Y.H. Dine. July 12.51

A flicker of hope is again awakened in me.

I buried my pride and wrote to Rosilyn that I want to come back to her. There is where my only hope of survival is. I hope she will be kind enough to give me one more chance. I'm tired of this idle, lazy life. I must do something to keep me occupied. I really feel physically well enough to be able to work. I have two good jobs promised right here in Mount Vernon, work that I know well if I could only get started. I know I can do both well.

All beginnings are hard and especially in my case. I need someone to take me down to the factory, but I have no one I could depend upon. They promised to go with me, but the promises are never kept, so here I am.

That is my difficulty—to be dependent on other people who are not willing to help. I don't know what will be. Stanley and Eleanor are coming back August 15th. Another month to wait. Each day seems like a year, but I'm helpless. I have to learn to be calm and wait, but I'm made desperate by disappointment. Yet I'm still hopeful that something will turn up to lift my spirits and give me courage to go on living and hoping.

◆◆◆◆◆◆◆◆

Yetta Dine's diary could not hold the full weight of her frustration, so it seeped into her letters. Her brother Charlie's daughter, Agatha Schneller, in Astoria, Long Island, responded: "I won't lecture you about being discouraged. You're far more sensible than I am!"[203]

A letter from Slater Isenberg in D.C. began: "I will do my best to get to New York to see you." He acknowledged the biggest family news—"Jacquie and Larry had twins." Slater's "academic and government expertise" landed him "temp work at the American Political Science Association."[204]

A postcard arrived from Eleanor in Potsdam, a snapshot of brevity and brightness—she was busy teaching and rehearsing a play.[205]

In August, Yetta must have sent a letter of complaint to her son, because she received a typewritten response from him. His salutation was followed by a colon, signaling that he meant business.

August 22, 1951

Dear Mother:

We have just received your letter, and I am going to be severe with you in the hope that you will stop being so unnecessarily and so painfully hysterical about your situation. If you would try to calm down long enough to reflect on the efforts we have made in your behalf and are still making, I don't think you will mention the word "abandoned" again. In a world so full of misery and poverty and hatred and real tragedy you might reasonably consider yourself fortunate to have those who love you and cherish you and who are doing everything within their power to see that in your age you are properly housed and nourished and taken care of. There are millions upon millions who would consider themselves blessed beyond their dreams to exchange places with you right now. Nobody is looking for gratitude, but a little sense of proportion would be greatly appreciated. You have intelligence and character and courage—these are virtues that in your long life you have had plenty of occasion to demonstrate; nothing would make Eleanor and me happier now than to perceive in you some evidence of that serenity which is reputed to be the mark of wisdom in the old.

There is no specific complaint of yours that cannot be remedied—except, of course, old age itself, that universal malady, which unfortunately I can do nothing about! As I told you before I left for Potsdam, if you don't like the home where you are staying—and it's quite clear that you don't—we can try another place on our return. Riverdale is a distinct possibility. There is also, still, the Home for the Aged in New York.

I'm not sure yet what the answer will be, but rest assured that SOMETHING WILL BE DONE.

There is absolutely no reason for you to be so disturbed about the date of our return. We have made clear to you several times in our correspondence that we plan to be back in NY somewhere around the first of September. The reason I am not giving you a more definite date is that we do not have a more definite date. And our reasons for not rushing back to the hot city are simple enough: (1) we subleased our apartment on Jones St. for the summer and cannot get back into it until September; (2) we need a short vacation after our strenuous session of teaching at Potsdam. I shall drive out to Mt. Vernon to see you the day after we return. I do not understand why you say that the boys have neglected you. Buddy writes to me, on the contrary, that they have been visiting you weekly and that you look fine and are improved in health generally.

Please remember above all that the one thing nobody can give you is peace—peace of the heart and peace of the mind. Only you yourself can create it within you.

All our love, Stanley[206]

Ever-faithful Anna K. Smith wrote:

My dear Mrs. Dine ... congratulations on the birth of your two great grandchildren... [I am] glad that your grandchildren are so good to you ... I am enclosing a dollar for stationery and stamps.[207]

Yetta's habit of saving correspondence stopped in late September, a probable result of further deterioration of her health and spirits. Woeful news came at the end of December. Her youngest brother Charlie had passed away.

On February 5, 1952, Yetta was transferred to the Home for Aged and Infirm Hebrews of New York, 121 West 105th Street, where she died on March 31, 1952.[208]

Sad as her son and daughter-in-law must have been, the burden of rest home bills disappeared. Another sort of freedom was granted to her son: Yetta could join the ghost of Solomon in his poems.

CHAPTER SIX

Family Ties

It's a blessing to be born gifted. But it won't
be enough if you lack the character to endure.

—From *Conversations with Stanley Kunitz*, ed. Kent P. Ljungquist,
interviewer Candace DeVries Olesen, 1972

I HAD NO FAMILY

When twenty-four-year-old Stanley Kunitz wrote to his mother about the importance of his year abroad, he made a grand pronouncement: "This one will be very important for me-and maybe for English literature." One such mark of recognition came in 1961, when he returned to Worcester for the first time since his sister Sophia's funeral in 1932.[209] Clark University would be conferring an honorary doctorate of letters for proving himself "to be a master of the highly-compressed, highly-polished lyric ... [and] in recognition of his contributions to modern literature."[210] He was asked to provide a list of people to invite, which he did: Daniel Rich, Director of the Worcester Art Museum; Classical High School English teacher Martin Post and debating and declaiming teams coach Perry S. Howe; stepbrother Mitchell Dine and his wife Jennie at 29 Woodford Street and Sophia's husband Alfred G. Isenberg, whose address was missing from Kunitz's reply to the university.[211]

Jennie Dine wrote to Kunitz, saying that she and Mitchell would not be able to attend the ceremony because they had moved from Worcester and retired to Florida.[212] Despite Isenberg's prominence

Stanley Kunitz, 100th Birthday Celebration, Fine Arts Work Center,
Provincetown, Massachusetts, July 2005.
Photo by John Gaumond

in the community and the ease with which his address could have
been secured, an omission occurred which wounded him deeply.
He wrote to Kunitz:

> We were at the Clark ceremonies, but were never invited or we
> never received any invitation. I was so disappointed and angered
> at not hearing from you that I could have broken steel bars.
> However, from now on, we are going to be a bit closer.

There is no response from Kunitz in which he defended himself.
Another undated Isenberg memo reminded Kunitz

> wherein we all share the pleasure, especially your mother, [n]ever
> forget, Stanley, that you are a Jew and every honor you earn is a
> credit to your people.

Here was an admonishment from Isenberg to his brother-in-law, who at this point in his life had worked "to de-emphasize that heritage."[213]

Isenberg wrote again:

> ... I know I wrote you a sarcastic letter quite a while ago and then felt it was justifiable. What I can't understand is why you have forgotten all of us here. I am not aware of any act on my part to cause this friction and I am very much disturbed about this. If I don't hear from you soon, one of these days I'm going to call you and find out. AI

This time Kunitz answered:

> ... my attitude of apartness has not been motivated by any sense of personal grievance or any feeling of ill-will. All that needs to be said is that after my mother's death, and partly because of the strains caused by her illness, I went through a bad time. One of

Stanley Kunitz and daughter Gretchen Kunitz, 100th Birthday Celebration, Fine Arts Work Center, Provincetown, Massachusetts, July 2005.
Photo by John Gaumond

the conclusions I came to, in that dark period, was that I had no family—none, at least to which I could turn on a basis of natural sympathy or affection. Right or wrong, this conclusion gave me strength: it permitted me to be reborn.

With this honest exchange, the brothers-in-law eventually made peace.[214] Their renewed closeness came in the form of Kunitz's telephone calls to Isenberg. He was seeking information about Worcester, and Kunitz could not have turned to a better source.[215] The timing of their long-distance conversations coincided with his writing "An Old Cracked Tune," "The Portrait," "The Magic Curtain," "Three Floors" and "The Testing-Tree." These poems, which are set on Worcester's east side, appeared in *The Testing-Tree*, published in 1971.

Kunitz's "attitude of apartness" was years in the making. In an interview, an analysis of his mother's necessary absence from home echoed her definition of "orphan."

> In the aftermath of the Industrial Revolution, parents are detached from the dwelling place and doomed to spend their days in the marketplace. The child is left alone or in the custody of strangers. So, isolation, separation, loneliness, and deprivation are multiplied … How can we make ourselves whole when we are separated from our source?[216]

Kunitz had withdrawn from family into books. He garnered admiration from his high school teachers and classmates by excelling in his studies, helping to win the Amherst Cup Debates and becoming editor-in-chief of the school newspaper, *The Argus*. He played baseball, basketball and tennis.[217] Kunitz's arena for identity, attention and affection was school, not family, except to bask in his mother's somber glow.

The taproot of his struggle for identity was his given name, Solomon. In "Passing Through," written to celebrate his seventy-ninth birthday, Kunitz drew this self-portrait: "If it weren't for a census report/ of a five-year-old White Male," he would "have no documentary proof" of his existence. To further heighten the drama of his early life, he invented the fiery destruction of his city hall birth records.

> Kunitz's word choice, in what is otherwise a celebratory poem of love and survival, also embraced his recurring themes of identity and loss. While Kunitz revealed personal history in poems and interviews, he apparently chose to hold on to the secret of his given name. The poem ends, "nothing is truly mine/except my name. I only/ borrowed this dust."[218]

When Kunitz won the 1959 Pulitzer Prize for poetry, his Uncle Charlie's son, Harold Jasspon, was interviewed:

> Mr. Jasspon never knew Kunitz too well, since he's considerably younger than his literary cousin. However, his older sister and brother used to see quite a bit of Kunitz. The Jasspons lived in Fitchburg and Kunitz lived in Worcester ... Mr. Jasspon saw him about five years ago at a family reunion. "He's always quiet," Mr. Jasspon says. "I used to read some of his poetry. It's pretty good."[219]

Kunitz admitted to step-cousin Carol Dine that after Mark Dine's death, he lost the only sense of family he ever had. In 1985, when he returned to Worcester for a week-long poetry festival in his honor, Jan Gottesman, a reporter for *The Jewish Chronicle-Leader*, asked, "Do you have any ties here in Worcester now?" He answered, "Personal ties? No. Except my new friends among the poets who have been extraordinarily hospitable to me."[220]

The next day, Fate stepped in and provided the chance meeting with Carol and Greg Stockmal, who welcomed Kunitz into his boyhood home for the first time in six decades. He soon sent them a 1918 photograph of himself, writing "this is the boy who lived in (y) our house at 4 Woodford St."[221] While it was true that release from his boyhood trauma was granted through writing specific poems, ghosts were permanently laid to rest when he opened the door to this twenty-year friendship and regained honorary possession of

Stanley Kunitz reading at the Stanley Kunitz Poetry Festival,
October 13–17, 1985.
Worcester Historical Museum, *Worcester Telegram & Gazette* Collection

the house. Kunitz acknowledged his debt to the couple in lines from
1989's "My Mother's Pears," which he dedicated to them.

> Plump, green-gold, Worcester's pride,
>   transported through autumn skies
>   in a box marked Handle With Care.
>
> sleep eighteen Bartlett pears,
>   hand-picked and polished and packed
>   for deposit at my door,
>
> each in its crinkled nest
>   with a stub of stem attached
>   and a single bright leaf like a flag.
>
> A smaller than usual crop,
>   but still enough to share with me,
>   as always at harvest time.

Those strangers are my friends
whose kindness blesses the house
my mother built at the edge of town

beyond the last trolley-stop
when the century was young, and she
proposed, for her children's sake,

to marry again, not knowing how soon
the windows would grow dark
and the velvet drapes come down.

—From "My Mother's Pears," Stanley Kunitz, *Passing Through: The Later Poems, New and Selected*

Kunitz's mentorship of young poets gave them what he did not have: support and encouragement.

I felt very isolated as a young person, the son of immigrants, growing up in Worcester, Massachusetts, early in the century. In that period there was no possibility of conversation or even contact with older poets. In fact, I didn't know another soul with whom I could share my interests. Eventually, after my Harvard years, I gravitated to New York, the magnet city for the arts, where I found an editorial job and began to send out my poems. Among the first periodicals to publish me were *Poetry, The Dial, The Nation, The New Republic*, and *Commonweal*, but I was too busy and too shy to make friends easily, so I still felt like an outsider.

My life changed when, soon after its opening, Yaddo invited me to be a guest, much to my surprise. In that small summer group … I was the child among elders. That was my entry, really, into the world of arts and letters.[222]

Kunitz had chosen the right profession if he preferred a solitary life. He explained his retreat to farm life in Mansfield, Connecticut, and New Hope, Pennsylvania.

… I lived in the country and did my editorial work by mail,

because I wanted to be free...I really didn't feel I could live...in the city-at a time when I needed to be solitary and to work out my own destiny.[223]

Further, he admired poets who, like himself, retained their individual voices and "could not be lumped as a school."

Another choice he made was to remain on the periphery of campus life, but the trade-off for adjunct instructor status was low pay. "When I fell into teaching, it was not with any desire to become a permanent member of the academic community. To this day, I have never accepted tenure."[224]

Kunitz built an alternative community, a tribe of his "true affections," a description he used in "The Layers." He said, "My association with other writers and artists, particularly younger poets, remains ... one of the happiest chapters in my story."[225]

◆◆◆◆◆◆◆◆

MOTHER AND SON

In the year of my mother's blood, when I was born,
She buried my innocent head in a field, because the earth
Was sleepy with the winter.

—From "Poem," Stanley Kunitz, *Intellectual Things*

The theme that brought attention to Kunitz's poetry was the lost father. He mythologized Solomon and "followed him, and now down sandy road/ Whiter than bone-dust, through the sweet/ Curdle of fields ..." ("Father and Son"). He searched for evidence of his existence in a "wardrobe trunk/ whose lock a boy could pick..." ("Three Floors"). He rescued his name in "An Old Cracked Tune."

However, when asked the identity of "the parent" he "denied" in "The Illumination," Kunitz said,

It could only have been my mother since she was a living symbol of the ties of blood that chafed me, the possessiveness and constraints inherent in the family structure, whereas my father had escaped

176

into the wilderness of mythology. The words of mine you quote should not be taken literally. They relate to a symbol more than to a person. Intuitively I knew that a soul has to leave before it can fly free. My mother had known that, too, when she fled the Old World in her youth, to seek a new life on these shores...there is a law of return written in our destiny. Sooner or later we need to go back and reclaim the abandoned territory of our heritage.[226]

In "My Mother's Pears," he credited her for urging his poetic return to boyhood: "'Make room/ for the roots!' my mother cries,/ 'Dig the hole deeper.'"

Kunitz continued to struggle with their shared history. Not one to shy away from introspection, he kept a diary in which he recorded his dreams:

Wednesday, March 9—J and I walking on a beach. France. My mother approaches us. She has just arrived. Frail and tired. She begs to be with us for the weekend. I say no—we have things to do. We walk off, leaving her alone. Around the bend, [I] suddenly realize how dependent and helpless she must feel, in this foreign land, [a] country whose language she is utterly ignorant [of], and probably with all her money gone—which she would have been too proud to mention. We whisk back to the place of our encounter, but my mother is gone.[227]

After reading an essay in *Time* magazine, Kunitz drew a line along the margin of one paragraph, tore out the page and saved it:

In the popular, and distorted view ... Mom is either asexual and saintly or a devouring harridan who lives vicariously through her son and whose traumatizing influence is responsible for "everything that goes wrong ..." Such skewed portraits deny the richness and intensity of the connection ... "the tie is stronger than that between father and son and father and daughter. Fathers can mitigate or reinforce a mother's views, but she is the life-giver and, even in today's changing society, still the chief nurturing figure in the family. The bond is also more complex than the one between mother and daughter. For a woman, a son offers the best chance to know the mysterious male existence."[228]

RECONCILIATION

All my mistakes,
from my earliest
bedtimes,
rose against me:
the parent I denied,
the friends I failed,
the hearts I spoiled,

—From "The Illumination," Stanley Kunitz, *The Collected Poems*

Leslie Kelen confronted Kunitz about his relationship with his mother and pointed out that it took him half his life to forgive her for withholding what she knew about Solomon.

> ... I felt deprived of a father and deprived of a soft, maternal presence. And since she was so strong-willed and capable, I had to fight for my own survival ... That was the contest of our early years. She loved me and encouraged me in every way. But she was unable to demonstrate affection. She had lost that capacity through all the tragic circumstances of her life. It was only after her death that I began to rethink my feelings about her and to realize what an extraordinary human being she was and what she had done for me ... So, gradually, my image of her changed. It's a complicated portrait I now have of her. It isn't that I was completely mistaken about her. It was that I have recreated her now in terms of a new understanding. She has become part of my legend.[229]

On May 14, 2006, ten weeks before his 101st birthday, Stanley Jasspon Kunitz died. It was Mother's Day.

◆◆◆◆◆◆◆◆

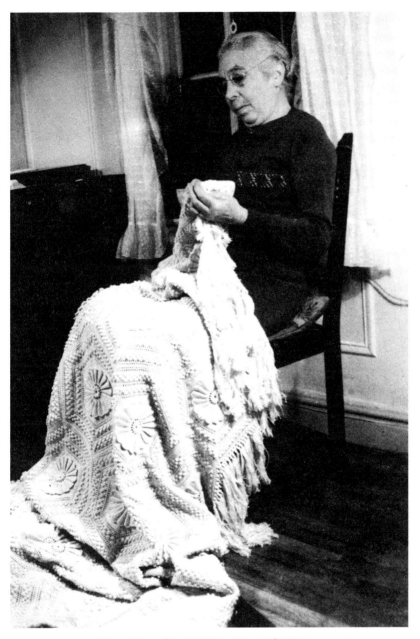

Yetta Dine, late 1930s, Riverside Drive.
Department of Special Collections, Princeton University Library

SYMPATHETIC VIBRATIONS

Demonstrations in the streets.
I am there not there,
ever uneasy in a crowd.
But you belong,
flaunting your home-made
insubordinate flag.
Why should I be surprised?
We come of a flinty maverick line.

—From "Journal for My Daughter," Stanley Kunitz, *Passing Through:
The Later Poems, New and Selected*

One day, Kunitz was invited to sit in on a college poetry class, and a student asked him what he meant in a certain poem. He responded,

> Excuse me ... but I didn't come to explain the poem. I came to listen and perhaps to join in your discussion ... You see, it isn't *my* poem now. It's published. It belongs as much to you as to me.[230]

Can personal connections bring a poem to life, as he wished? In 1980, Kunitz accepted an honorary degree from Worcester State College and gave a reading at the Worcester Public Library. Reporter Amy Zuckerman was there on assignment. After hearing Kunitz read "Journal for My Daughter," she wrote, "Sitting there in the hush of the Saxe Room, I remember wondering, 'How could he know?' hoping Kunitz had read those lines for me."[231]

While Yetta Dine's perceived uselessness contributed to her unhappy end, her death freed her son to make her useful once more. In "Three Floors," brown-eyed Yetta is transformed into a watchful (or prying) mother, who was "a crack of light/ and a gray eye peeping." Kunitz's color choice for her eyes was a telling reference to a goddess—gray-eyed Athena, patron of seamstresses and goddess of war (in this case, a life-long mother-son battle of wills). Was Yetta a muse? Yes, if a muse is a human being who inspires the creation of art but whose integrity can be lost in the bargain. This time, Fate made the muse double back to provoke us and add layers of knowledge and dissonance to her son's poems.

In her introduction to *The Lives of the Muses: Nine Women and the Artists They Inspired*, Francine Prose wrote:

> Each [muse] was a product of her time, and each moved outside and beyond it, either through personal courage, originality, and determination, or through her mysterious role in the process that turns experience into art.[232]

THE POEMS

Excerpts from poems that are threaded throughout present Stanley Kunitz's artistic transformation of family members, especially the mother figure inhabiting the lines either alone or with the lost father.

Written shortly after his mother died, "The Summing-Up" felt as honest a poem as Kunitz could have written in relation to this book.[233]

THE SUMMING-UP

When young I scribbled, boasting, on my wall,
No Love, No Property, No Wages.
In youth's good time I somehow bought them all,
And cheap, you'd think, for maybe a hundred pages.

Now in my prime, disburdened of my gear,
My trophies ransomed, broken, lost,
I carve again on the lintel of the year
My sign: MOBILITY – and damn the cost!

—Stanley Kunitz, *The Collected Poems*

◆◆◆◆◆◆◆◆◆

ABOUT "THE PORTRAIT"

Yetta's poetic persona is a braid of reality and art that stretches long into readers' perceptions. In May 2018, while waiting for an elevator in the New York Public Library, I talked with a couple from San Bernardino, California. They were retired educators who were on a pilgrimage to see the Schwarzman Building's architecture. When the husband asked me why I was there, I said I was doing research on the mother of poet Stanley Kunitz. He lit up, exclaiming, "I know his poems! She's the mother who slaps him when he finds his dead father's picture!"

I answered, "Yes, that's what the mother in the poem does."

In Kunitz's poem, "The Portrait," the speaker looks back on his boyhood and remembers his secretive, angry, unforgiving mother slapping him "hard" when shown the picture of his father he found in an attic trunk. An October 1969 draft includes these words: "...and slapped me hard, / inconsolably sobbing"[234]

Consider the effect of keeping the earlier line. How does the phrase "inconsolably sobbing" contribute to our perception of the mother? Would a sobbing mother have pulled attention away from the shock and humiliation of her slap, which the sixty-four-year-old speaker feels "still burning" his cheek?

Stanley Kunitz said,

> I really didn't know too much about [my father's death]. It floated in the air during my childhood. I never had any specific infor-
> mation. I didn't know the exact details until I happened to be in Worcester, reading. I went over to the city hall and asked for my father's death certificate and there it was.[235] Age thirty-nine. Death by suicide. Carbolic acid. It would have torn his guts out. Strong stuff. I'm not sure how I learned he did it in a park. Maybe my older sister told me. That scene always haunted me. There's a reference to it in a poem called "The Hemorrhage." He becomes the fallen king, a Christ figure. My original title was "The Man in the Park."[236]

As if verifying the truth of the event, including his mother's slap, Kunitz said, "Her anger was directed at him, not at me. She wanted to expunge his memory. No mention of him every crossed her lips."[237]

Readers are positioned to be sympathetic to the speaker's (and Kunitz's) plight and moved by the poem's content, with its direct reference to his personal history: his father Solomon Kunitz's suicide on June 2, 1905 and his own birth on July 29th.[238, 239]

Did Yetta really slap her son? Rather than argue the truth of the event, the larger question is one of motive. What would drive a mother to act this way? Perhaps the Yetta Dine rendered on these pages helps complicate easy answers.

While Kunitz's poems allowed his father to escape into legend, his relationship with his mother was more grounded and complex. Raised by her and older sisters Sarah and Sophia, he described the mother-son relationship:

My mother has become closer to me in recent years. I understand her more than I did in the beginning. There were two strong wills in that household, hers and mine, so that our natural tensions were magnified. We held each other at a distance. She was the most competent woman I have ever known—I respected that. But it took years—after her death ...—for me to be touched by the beauty and bravery of her spirit ...

She obliterated every trace of [my father]. In her very last years, at my request, she began writing her memoirs. It is a remarkable document, which I will someday use in one form or other. She is fresh and vital writing about her childhood in Russia. And her emigration to this country. And her work as an operator in the sweatshops of New York's Lower East Side. About everything until she moved to Worcester. Until she met my father. Then she froze and wrote no more.[240]

◆◆◆◆◆◆◆◆

Stanley Kunitz created a narrative which would not detract from his legend—a son haunted by the suicide of his father and angered by his mother's stubborn silence about the event.

> The people made a ring
> Around the man in the park.
> He was our banished king
> Of blames and staunchless flows,
> Exhibitor of the dark
> Abominable rose;

From "The Hemorrhage" Stanley Kunitz, *The Collected Poems*

Why does it matter? When placed on the scales of biographical and critical analysis, Yetta Dine's biography/memoir acts as a counterbalance to Stanley Kunitz's dramatic lyric poetry and interviews.[241]

Now a larger and more intricate, but perhaps less comfortable garment has been created.

Worcester, Massachusetts
2016

They slip through narrow cervices
and, suddenly blown tall,
glide into my cave of phantoms,
unwelcome guests, but not
unloved, dark emissaries
of the two-faced god.

—From "The Unquiet Ones," Stanley Kunitz,
Passing Through: The Later Poems, New and Selected

SEARCH AND RESCUE

Today, a drive through Worcester's east side in search of places where Stanley Kunitz and his family lived would bring you to four addresses: 133 Green Street where he was born is a parking lot; 79 Green Street, a mixed use building where he lived from 1912–13 was altered and is now a commercial building; 46½ Providence Street, his home from 1914–1919 is a weed-choked vacant lot.[242] The fourth address, a three-storey stucco house, was Kunitz's home from 1919 until 1925. It not only survived a wrecking ball but has been faithfully restored by Carol and Gregory Stockmal, who bought the run-down property in 1979 without knowing its literary history.

The Stockmals' cherished twenty-year friendship with Stanley Kunitz began with a chance meeting on October 17, 1985, as they were returning from apple-picking. They found him standing in the street with his third wife, artist and poet Elise Asher, and an entourage of poets. Everyone was gazing up at their home, the one Kunitz had searched for unsuccessfully on previous visits to Worcester.[243] On this, the final day of the Stanley Kunitz Poetry Festival, his quest would end. The Stockmals invited everyone into the house, which was festooned with drop cloths and furnished with scaffolding.

A month later, Kunitz wrote to the Stockmals: "There was no mistaking, the moment I stepped inside, that this was indeed the house of my childhood, the one I still dream about."[244] That first meeting between the Stockmals and Kunitz transformed lives. Greg overheard Kunitz talking about the tree that he and his mother had planted in the back yard. It had "the most delicious pears you've ever tasted," he said. Greg "started chuckling a little bit." Kunitz asked, "What's so funny?" He answered, "The tree is still there and it does have the most delicious pears you've ever tasted."[245]

The exchange inspired the Stockmals to send Kunitz and Asher a yearly gift: "Bartlett pears, / hand-picked and polished and packed/ for deposit at my door." In 1989, Kunitz sent a draft of "My Mother's Pears" to the Stockmals, along with a letter dedicating the poem to them. The speaker declares, "Those strangers are my friends/ whose kindness blesses the house/ my mother built at the edge of town//..."[246]

The Princeton archives contain what I believe to be the first draft, handwritten, dated "Nov. 1989 ... It has become an autumn ritual,/ the delivery at my door/ on the wings of express mail/ of a box of Bartlett pears, each naked in Styrofoam [pencil cross out 'naked in Styrofoam] in its Styrofoam nest/ with a stub of stem attached/ and a single leaf,/ Thanks to [cross out 'sent by'] the gracious couple/ whose bounty of joy and love/ restored the house my mother built/ seventy years ago/ [in Wor crossed out] / on Woodford Street in Worcester, Massachusetts."

Then there is a break in space and Kunitz posed a question: "Why is there so much heartbreak in this gift from the gracious couple?"[247] Kunitz was paying a price for delving into the past.

4 Woodford Street, Worcester, Massachusetts, 2019.
Photo by John Gaumond

Following Greg Stockmal's death from a heart attack in December 2008, Carol made the decision to continue building the legacy of Stanley Kunitz in Worcester, which would also honor her husband's devotion to him. At a meeting with her and the Worcester County Poetry Association in March 2009, I volunteered to continue doing research and train docents to conduct tours of the house. Further legacy-building on Carol's part included the October donation of The Stanley Kunitz-Stockmal Collection of correspondence and memorabilia to Clark University's Archives and Special Collections.[248] In 2010, 4 Woodford Street was designated as a Literary Landmark™ by the American Library Association.[249] In 2019, the 100th anniversary of 4 Woodford Street's construction, the Worcester Historical Commission and Preservation Worcester presented the Worcester Preservation Stewardship Award to Carol Stockmal in honor of her and Greg's dedication and commitment to preserving the property and Stanley Kunitz's legacy in Worcester.[250]

As I began to glean information from residential and business directories, property records, birth, death and marriage certificates, newspaper archives and on-line data bases, I realized that I had stepped into a major project. In 2012, I visited Princeton University's archives and read through sections of 115 linear feet of the Stanley Kunitz papers. My essay "The House on Woodford Street: Memory and Imagination in the Poems of Stanley Kunitz" appeared in the 2012 issue of *The Worcester Review*, a journal published by the Worcester County Poetry Association.

By 2014, the original docent outline had more than doubled in size to become a 161-page reference guide.[251] My library grew and bulging crates of documents reflected the liveliness of my interest in the life and poems of Stanley Kunitz.

A main source was Kunitz himself. He was a frequent and garrulous interviewee whose appeal rested in his vast knowledge of poetry and descriptions of a long life in twentieth-century arts and letters. While biographical details were plentiful, I soon found that they were not always accurate.

When I received my copy of his 1905 birth certificate at Worcester's City Hall, his birth name startled me: Solomon S. Kunitz. The first line from his poem "An Old Cracked Tune" leapt into my brain and took on special meaning: "My name is Solomon Levi." Kunitz had danced around his given name during interviews, never admitting that it was his.

Kunitz said,

> The poem had its origin in a scurrilous street song remembered from my youth. The butt of the song's mockery was a stereotypically avaricious and conniving Jewish tailor. The very first line —the one I appropriated—went: "My name is Solomon Levi." It didn't occur to me until later that Solomon was my father's given name, and that he was a Levite, a descendant of the priestly house of Levi. When the line from that odious song popped into my head, I wondered, "Can I redeem it?" And so, I wrote the poem.[252]

In 1992, Chris Busa asked him directly about why he appropriated the first line of the song, "My name is Solomon Levi." He answered,

> It was an extraordinary coincidence. My father's name was Solomon ... In Jewish tradition the given name and lineage are passed on from father to son. Why I should have remembered the name of Solomon Levi and virtually nothing else from the song, except its nasty tone, is of some significance. It's taken me years to understand why I had to write that poem ... Sometimes you don't know at the time of writing how central a poem is. The effort, above all, is to discover, step by step, the spirit that answers to your name, to discover it and reveal it. In the workings of time you gradually fasten on a dozen or so poems, a small cluster bonded to one another and to your most secret self.[253]

"An Old Cracked Tune" can be thought of as Kunitz's anthem. Following "my mother's breast was thorny, / and father I had none," his final stanza is victorious: "I dance, for the joy of surviving, / on the edge of the road." He told Bill Moyers,

> I hoped to restore [Solomon's] dignity by identifying with him.

Gregory Stockmal, Stanley Kunitz, Carol Stockmal, verso "Sept. 2004
Stanley Kunitz @ 99 years old." Provincetown, Massachusetts.
Photo by Genine Lentine, Collection of Carol Stockmal

Like him, the poet in our society is a marginal character, dancing
on the edge of the road, not in the middle where the heavy traffic
flows. Maybe one of the secrets of survival is to learn *where* to
dance.[254]

A solitary folder in Princeton's archives labeled "My Mother's
Story" contained one set of drafts for the Prefatory Note written in
preparation for the 1985 publication of *Next-to-Last Things: New
Poems and Essays.*

Handwritten on legal pad paper, Kunitz struggled to express his
thoughts:

One of my mother's gifts to me during my adolescent years was
a green and gold set of the works of Leo Tolstoy in Translation
… I still recall how I pondered over his opening commentary on
the nature of families [in *Anna Karenina*]. "Happy families," he
wrote, "are all alike; every unhappy family is unhappy in its own

way." I was happy in a way to discover that being in a fatherless household in Worcester, Massachusetts with a mother and two older sisters distinguished me from the rest of my schoolmates and qualified me as a member of an unhappy family with a working mother who was absent most of the day and two older sisters who had more than sufficient problems of their own. It took me years before I could say in one of my poems: "We learn, as the thread plays out, that we belong/ less to what flatters us than to what scars."

He [Tolstoy] was telling me that I needn't be so moody about living in a fatherless house. In other words (if one dares to risk sounding impolite), unhappy families are more interesting, distinctive, and basically more "creative" than their boring opposites.[255]

Kunitz's drafts gelled to become the Prefatory Note that precedes "My Mother's Story" in *Next-to-Last Things*.

But where were the rest of his drafts and the original memoir?

MOVING CLOSER

In fall 2016, I taught a course in Worcester for senior learners that focused on several Kunitz poems rooted in his birth city. Interest was high because one session was hosted by Carol Stockmal in the poet's boyhood home.

As we discussed Kunitz's poems and interviews, the group demanded to know more about the unaffectionate, unforgiving Yetta Dine. While the poems presented a one-dimensional and artistically expedient version of "mother," I wondered if there was more to learn about her. The nine-page chapter in *Next to Last Things: New Poems and Essays* could be the key to unlocking the door to her full memoir. I needed to locate the original, if it still existed.

I met Yetta's granddaughter, Gretchen Kunitz, M.D. in 2010, at the Literary Landmark™ dedication of 4 Woodford Street. She is literary co-executor of her father's estate, so we had further contact when I sought permission to publish essays about him and his poetry.

In October 2016, I sent a message to Dr. Kunitz in California asking if the entire memoir existed and if it had been transcribed. She wrote: "In terms of my grandmother's [memoir], I do have the original. To my knowledge only a few excerpts were transcribed by my dad ... I would be delighted if you decide to give it a try."[256]

After her father's death in 2006, Dr. Kunitz found the memoir, along with related letters and documents, in a large manila envelope. She sent me the package, which also included four drafts of "My Mother's Story" from Next-to-Last-Things. Here were the documents missing from the Princeton collection. And much more.

Among the drafts of "My Mother's Story," there was a page of Kunitz's notes with the heading "Notebook." I asked Dr. Kunitz to see if she could locate it. She looked again and found her grandmother's 1951 diary and more documents.

With her permission and cooperation, the project began. While this was not an example of discovering a lost manuscript, it could be regarded as one of search and rescue.

My goal was to inventory, transcribe, photocopy and scan all documents, then protect the contents in archival material and return the collection to Dr. Kunitz. My hope was that she would place her grandmother's papers in an archive, where it would be available to researchers.

Once I began transcribing the letters, memoir and diary, the strength of Yetta's writing excited me, and this book began to take shape in my mind. I could edit her spelling and punctuation, then write sections which filled in gaps, such as her life in Worcester.

Before this could happen, specific challenges rose to greet me.

CHALLENGES

Yetta Dine wrote her memoir in pencil on unlined drawing paper. The decades and storage conditions were not kind to the inexpensive paper; the writing had faded, and pages were browned and in brittle, fragile condition. In some cases, edges had fallen away. Fortunately, very little text was missing.

13.

My Father resumed business after the revolution but earning was hard on account of his ill health, and cares of Capitol, but he still maintain to be the rulles of the community. Certain business he understood was more for the sake of Authority than for the profit derived. For instance as Collector of taxes. The Jewish Communities had to pay a certain lump sume, which was derived in the following way. A tax was put on the slaughter of cattle and Poltry according to the Jewish ritual, which all Jewish of york in those days. Bids would be sent to the Government for the privilege of coleeting this tax. The Government would set a minimune, and the Bidding went up, the highest Bidder got the Contract for all Jewish of that district. It was paid in advence for a year, since I re member Until his death he held that privilege. to sel the ticket for the slaughter, which was 50 Copees for a steer or Cow, 30 Copees for lamb Sheep Goats and calf. 7 c. for Geese and turkey 3 c. for chickens and Ducks. Sometime the income would not cover the price of the contract but there was a prestige to own that privilege or Contract, which came direct from St Petersburg but the Auction as you would call it here was held in Kovno the Capitol of the Province. Some bribing had to be done, my Father new all the Government ojealls and knew who to bribe. Any business done with the Government had to bribed.

A page from Yetta Dine's memoir.
Collection of Gretchen Kunitz M.D.

Yetta was a seamstress, a trade which she had learned in the Lower East Side garment factories after her 1890 arrival from Lithuania. Her handwriting demonstrated the same control used to run a seam on a sewing machine. Every page was crammed edge-to-edge, a horror vacui of straight lines and words.

In 1951, she took up a notebook and resumed writing under different circumstances. The mercurial qualities of her handwriting suggest the effects of myriad illnesses and depression. Beyond its physical characteristics, the diary was saturated with sadness, despair, frustration and loneliness. While her perseverance should be regarded as remarkable, transcribing her diary became a heartbreaking experience.

Two other threads needed to be untangled. Where and when did Yetta write her memoir?

In Kunitz's Prefatory Note to "My Mother's Story," he wrote that she was in a Mount Vernon rest home in 1951, where she wrote her memoir.[257] An exchange of letters from 1951 confirmed her return address was there at the Westchester Convalescent Home.

However, letters from Yetta in the 1940s through 1950 bear the return address of 74 S. Broadway, Tarrytown, New York, Apt. 110.[258]

The Princeton archives also contain a set of seven letters written between 1924 and 1926 from "Rosilyn L." to Harvard student Kunitz with the salutations, "Dear cousin and Cousin Stan." Rosilyn wrote about his mother's visits to her and her mother, Sarah Levitan; Yetta was "Rosilyn L.'s" great-aunt; the return address was 74 S. Broadway St., Tarrytown.[259]

The 1925 New York State Census and an article in the May 21, 1937 issue of *The Daily News*, Tarrytown, N.Y. show the address to be that of Louis and Sarah (Gordon) Levitan, who was Yetta's niece.[260]

By 1905, the Levitans had moved from Worcester to Tarrytown where they finished raising their children, Harold, Florence, Rosilyn and Benjamin. By 1940, Rosilyn remained at the Tarrytown address after her father died and Sarah moved to Michigan City, Indiana.[261]

The Tarrytown 1924 and 1926 return address matched the two envelopes postmarked February and March 1945 that Kunitz had stored with the original memoir.

When did Yetta write her memoir? The answer began with two envelopes and three letters from the collection. One might argue that envelopes can be separated from their contents. However, specific events support the postmarked February and March 1945 envelopes as being authentically paired with the undated letters; the address for Kunitz was 247 Delaware Ave., S.W., Washington, D.C.

Stanley Kunitz was in the United States Army from January 11, 1943, until August 9, 1945. The Princeton archives contain a letter from Kunitz postmarked January 5, 1943, with a return address of New Hope, Pennsylvania. He wrote that his application to be classified as a conscientious objector had been rejected, and he would be assigned non-combatant duty. His wife, Eleanor, would "rent the farm and find a job in D.C."[262]

The three letters' salutations all read "Dear Stanley and Elenor" [sic], indicating her daughter-in-law's presence in Washington, D.C. In addition to mentioning her son's request to write down her memories, one letter contains information crucial to identifying the year. Yetta referred to the loss of her younger brother Abe Jasspon, which is listed in the Massachusetts Death Index as 1945.[263]

Yetta's letters make references to the wartime deployment of three grandsons, Slater Isenberg, Buddy (Lawrence) Baker and Stanton Baker. Her comments coincide with letters and photographs dated during World War II in the Princeton collection.[264]

Given the evidence, the memoir was written in 1945, not in 1951, and in Tarrytown where she resided with her great-niece Rosilyn Levitan, not a Mount Vernon rest home, as Kunitz claimed in his Prefatory Note and subsequent interviews. In 1951, she did pick up a spiral notebook and made a final, agonized attempt to complete her legacy in the form of a diary.

A question lingers. Why did Kunitz continue his loose handling of facts in interviews? A self-proclaimed legend-builder, Kunitz consciously constructed his own public persona. In his Prefatory Note, his mother's story is quickly digested: She was bored with her existence in a rest home, so he told her to write her memoir. When the more complicated truth is told, the story becomes hers, not his. Yetta was not bored—she was sad and worried for reasons that invited a more complete explanation.

Kunitz was not the first or last person to conceal whole truths from interviewers. Consider "An Old Cracked Tune." He could have said, "Oh, by the way, my given name was Solomon ..." Would the truth have diminished the mystery of the poem? I believe that he thought so. Biographical truths silence literary critics, who stay in the abstract world of theory, searching for another way to decode text. The New Criticism shuns use of biography as a means of engaging with literature. A worse consequence from Kunitz's point of view would be that readers might read the poem and think, "Well, that's poetic license" (a.k.a. fabrication) and be distracted from the artistic truth of the poem.

Kunitz deliberately organized and stored his mother's papers but withheld them from public collections. Even she questioned the enterprise and "wonder[ed] who would be interested to know or whoever would waste the time to read it." What kept him from destroying his mother's papers? Was it love and respect for her? Guilt over not taking her in and putting her in a rest home? An acknowledgement that her unabridged memoir was worthy of eventual publication?

I believe that Kunitz recognized their value, even if meant their discovery would step (however lightly) on his legend. He took the risk that the collection would be inadvertently discarded after his death. Perhaps he trusted Fate to step in. Which it did.

◆◆◆◆◆◆◆◆◆

ABOUT YETTA DINE'S WRITING

Direct contact with Yetta's writing had a mesmerizing effect on me. Every page pulsed with an unfiltered, authentic voice. Her vocabulary reflected the reading habits of a highly literate, curious, and skeptical thinker, albeit with non-standard spelling and punctuation. She wrote with a seamstress's eye, artfully positioning sewing metaphors to make her points. Her appreciation for a writer's work was clear—she knew her limitations but wanted to be given a chance to show what she could do. That impulse would hold until her final months in a rest home. Her style is seamless, cinematic and full of energy.

She admitted that her memoir was non-chronological: "I'm writing the way I would be telling my experience" and stressed that it was "not fiction" but "all facts". Her writing style is closer to a dramatic monologue where one memory lights up another. Because she was an expert storyteller, her pages develop into a complex, multifaceted self-portrait, full of opinions and observations. She started life in a Lithuanian village, then emigrated to New York's Lower East Side, where she tasted the sweet success of employment and independence as she acquired a seamstress's skills and absorbed the garment industry's business practices.

Yetta's use of punctuation was highly individualized. Commas and periods appear as almost identical marks; sometimes she put them in the middle of sentences, as if she had rested her pencil to collect her thoughts. Periods were missing from the ends of many paragraphs. For parenthetical thoughts, she sometimes marked the first half of a parentheses as a forward slash, without closing it off at the end. Pages were filled with text, top to bottom, margin to margin, necessitating skilled use of hyphenated words at the ends of lines.

Her cursive handwriting was in the European style, an observation made by Babette Gehnrich, Paper Conservator at the American Antiquarian Society in Worcester, Massachusetts.[265] Grammar and spelling were both idiosyncratic and typical of a writer whose second

Stanley Kunitz at the Worcester Historical Museum, 39 Salisbury Street,
Water Street: World Within a World exhibition, January 10, 1984.
Worcester Historical Museum, *Worcester Telegram & Gazette* Collection

language was English: Pronouns do not always agree with nouns
("this boys") and her spelling is phonetic ("ware" for were). She
capitalized "Brother in law" and "Son," and "Foreman," but not
the first words of sentences or names of months.

A notable physical characteristic of the memoir was the way in
which she attached additional pages to others - she used dressmaker
pins instead of paper clips. She not only wrote what she knew but
reached for familiar tools around her.

While she recognized her own grammatic limitations, Yetta's writ-
ing proved that she was a talented writer who was comfortable using
literary devices, such as adages ("Love thy neighbor as thyself; One
life gone, another arrived") and metaphors to clarify what her son,
the editor, needed to do: "you can add the collar and trimming ...
patch together what I'm sending you and put each pattern where it
would fit best."

There are erasures and corrections throughout the memoir, indicating that she took care to review her work. Stories and observations flow, and she appears not to have taken a breath from her Dickensian first sentence, "Without my consent, I was brought into the world in the year 1866," until she left New York in 1893 to be married in Worcester, Massachusetts.[266]

However, Yetta's 1951 diary pages showed no sign of corrections. She mustered all her strength and forced her hand to do the work of her flagging spirit.

HIS MOTHER'S STORY

When I put out the light
I hear them stir, dissatisfied,
in their separate places,
in death as in life
remote from each other,
having no conversation
except in the common ground
of their son's mind.

—From "The Unquiet Ones," Stanley Kunitz, *Passing Through: The Later Poems, New and Selected*

Early in 1983, the Worcester Historical Museum was preparing the catalog for *Water Street: World Within a World,* an exhibition which focused on the city's thriving Jewish district during the late 19th and early 20th centuries. Yetta had been manager of Dine Manufacturing Company, so it was not surprising that the museum contacted Worcester's native son and asked him to participate.

Curator Norma Feingold wrote to Kunitz because Assumption College professor and Worcester County Poetry Association cofounder Michael True had told her about "a wonderful memoir of [his] mother's." She asked, "Would you be willing to share that with us in some way?" Kunitz confirmed the existence of the memoir:

TO THE GOLDEN LAND
From the memories of Yetta Helen Dine (1866-1952)
Prefatory Note

to

𝕴When I was asked a few years ago/write about ᴍʏxxᴏʀɪɢɪɴxxx myself, I *felt impelled*

to ᴏᴘᴇʀᴋ bᴇgᴀᴎ my ʀᴀᴘᴏʀᴋxᴡɪᴋᴋxᴋᴋᴀxxxx narrati₱ɵ with a report on my origins:

in 1905

"It was not an auspicious beginning. A few weeks before my birth my

father, of whom I know practically nothing aside from his name, killed

himself. The ostensibly prosperous dress-manufacturing business in Worcester,

Massachusetts, that my parents operated was discovered to be bankrupt. My

mother, not yet forty, with three children to support, opened a dry-goods

shop and sewed garments in the back room. Out of pride and honor she drⱥve

herself to pay off her inheritance of debts, though she had no legal obliga

tion to do so. She was a woman of formidable will, staunch heart, and razor-

sharp intelligence, whose only school was the sweatshops of New York, to

which she had come alone as a young woman from her native Lithuania. After

a few years of widowhood she owned a substantial enterprise again, feeding

her designs to a capacious loft humming with machines. She must have been

one of the first women to run a large-scale business in this country.

"My mother had little time to give to her family, and my older sisters

seemed somehow detached from my secret life. When I was eight, I was presented

with a stepfather, Mark Dine, a gentle and scholarly man who was no help

at all to my mother in her business, but who showed me the ways of tender —

ness and affection. His death six years later left me desolate. Both

my sisters married and died young. My mother survived these onslaughts,

as well as another bankruptcy--precipiated by her reluctance to discharge

any of her employees in a time of depression--and lived alertly to the age

ᴏₗ ᵢₕₜy-six, articulate to the last on the errors of capitalism and the

tragedy oₗ ₑₓᵢₛtence."

Typewritten page 1 from final draft of Kunitz's "My Mother's Story."
Collection of Gretchen Kunitz, M.D.

[It was] written by my mother in her last year. It is one of the most vivid and poignant accounts that I know of dealing with the immigrant experience and eventually I plan to edit it for publication.[267]

Eventually.

It is likely that this request was his motivation for retrieving his mother's manuscript to begin the editing process she had longed for in 1945. A seven-paragraph excerpt and 1930s photograph of her were featured in the 1983–84 exhibition catalog.[268]

Kunitz's editing finally produced his nine-page essay, "My Mother's Story," which he then placed in his 1985 collection *Next to Last Things: New Poems and Essays* and is reprinted in this book's appendix. He found the material useful once more in 2003 when "Stanley Kunitz on Paul Celan and the Poetry of the Holocaust," appeared in *Crossroads #58*. In it, four paragraphs were excerpted from the Lithuanian section of his mother's memoir. To my knowledge, these three instances are the only times excerpts have been published.

It is difficult to know if Yetta would have deferred to her son's handling of her memoir and diary. In 1945, she had given him permission to edit her writing as he saw fit. He proceeded to deconstruct the richly textured, colorful, sometimes quirky-looking garment she left behind and reassembled pieces into a serviceable frock. His paragraphs are polished, and the narrative is pared down: She left her village, sailed across the Atlantic and entered the stage of New York's Lower East Side, which was teeming with immigrants seeking work and a better life. Yetta Helen Jasspon emerged as a stereotypical solitary, resourceful, heroic immigrant, which is only a partial truth, as her own writing has shown. Resourceful and heroic, yes. Solitary, no. Her unedited letters, memoir and diary reveal a curious, pragmatic, cynical, intelligent, and resilient woman with strong family ties. In the edited versions, Kunitz honored his mother's wish to become an author, albeit three decades after her death. However, her full character, experiences and distinct writing voice were dimmed. Until now.

Docents at the Stanley Kunitz Boyhood Home tell a story at the end of the tour, and it is a fitting way to close this book. Briefly, poet Marie Howe found a heart-shaped stone washed up on a Provincetown beach, which she gave to Kunitz. He brought it to the Stockmals and wanted to bury it at the base of the pear tree that he and his mother had planted in the garden when the house was being built.

After Greg dug the hole and they buried the stone, Kunitz said, "Wait a minute. I have to do my ritual." Carol recalled, "He seemed to be making silent incantations, as if giving a blessing." The significance of this event was not lost on one of the guests, Aubyn Freed, who attended a house tour in 2014. His daughter Jennifer sent me an email, which began by citing a verse from the Bible followed by his interpretation:

> Ezekiel 36:26 "I will give you a new heart and put a new spirit in you; I will remove from you your heart of stone and give you a heart of flesh."
>
> Stanley's mother removed every trace of her husband after his suicide. The symbolism of Stanley's burying a heart of stone next to the living tree is this: He associated his mother as giver of life and self to her children, and he was burying bitter memories, perhaps with another biblical reference to Proverbs 3:18 in the background: "Wisdom is a tree of life to those who embrace her."[269]

Stanley Kunitz struggled to untangle his relationship with his mother, shuttling between truth and legend. As Yetta wished, these pages "patch together" her cloth and his to make one garment worthy of our contemplation.

Family Trees

Please note that these are not genealogically complete family trees. Rather, they reflect relationships found in this book.

"Now I felt sure of my job, as they found no fault with my work. I became more acquainted with the girls and spoke my broken English to them. I worked there until I left New York to be married in Worcester Massachusetts." —Yetta Dine

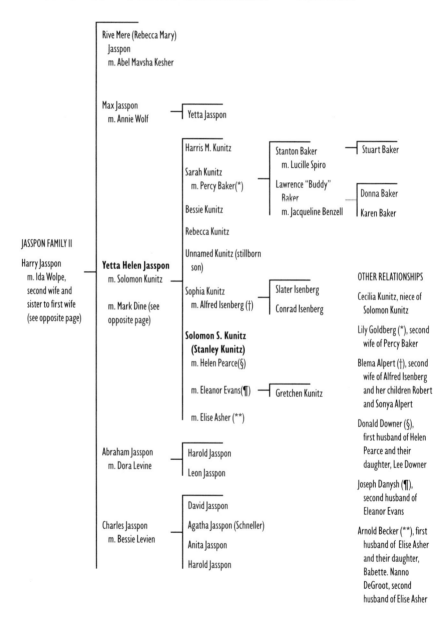

"Father came to Yashwen in 1846, when he married Mother's older sister, who died six years later, leaving one child. Mother took care of the child, and in a year or so, was married to Father. She was sixteen, and the child who was my oldest sister was six. Her name was Sifre. I was the fourth, with two brothers younger than myself." —Yetta Dine

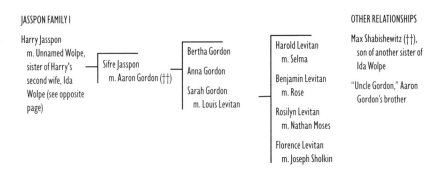

"My recollection is that my stepfather Mark Dine—that sweet and gentle man—I knew Mr. Dine for too brief a period … was the only father I ever had—how dear he was to me! And when he died, I was devastated … After I lost my stepfather, I settled back into being a solitary Kunitz. That was the only interlude when I had a sense of family." —Stanley Kunitz

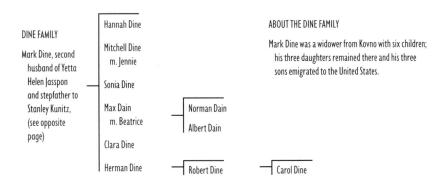

EVIDENCE SUPPORTS STANLEY KUNITZ'S INTEREST IN HIS
MOTHER'S MEMOIR AND DIARY GREW FROM CURATOR NORMA
FEINGOLD'S REQUEST IN 1983 TO HAVE SEVERAL PARAGRAPHS
INCLUDED IN THE WORCESTER HISTORICAL MUSEUM'S
EXHIBITION CATALOGUE FOR *WATER STREET: A WORLD
WITHIN A WORLD*. ONCE KUNITZ REENGAGED WITH HIS
MOTHER'S WRITING, HE DECIDED TO EXPAND AND EDIT IT AS
A NINE-PAGE CHAPTER IN HIS UPCOMING BOOK OF POEMS AND
ESSAYS, *NEXT-TO-LAST THINGS*, PUBLISHED IN 1985.

Appendix

Stanley Kunitz, "My Mother's Story," reprinted from *Next-to-Last Things: New Poems and Essays* – pp. 74–82, with permission from The Literary Estate of Stanley J. Kunitz.

MY MOTHER'S STORY
(YETTA HELEN DINE: 1866–1952)

PREFATORY NOTE: When I was asked a few years ago to write about myself, I felt impelled to deliver a straightforward report on my origins:

> It was not an auspicious beginning. A few weeks before my birth in 1905 my father, of whom I know practically nothing aside from his name, killed himself. The ostensibly prosperous dress-manufacturing business in Worcester, Massachusetts, that my parents operated was discovered to be bankrupt. My mother, not yet forty, with three children to support, opened a dry-goods shop and sewed garments in the back room. Out of pride and honor she drove herself to pay off her inheritance of debts, though she had no legal obligation to do so. She was a woman of formidable will, staunch heart, and razor-sharp intelligence, whose only school was the sweatshops of New York, to which she had come alone as a young woman from her native Lithuania. After a few years of widowhood she owned a substantial enterprise again, feeding her designs to a capacious loft humming with machines. She must have been one of the first women to run a large-scale business in this country.

My mother had little time to give to her family, and my older sisters seemed somehow detached from my secret life. When I was eight, I was presented with a stepfather, Mark Dine, a gentle and scholarly man who was no help at all to my mother in her business, but who showed me the ways of tenderness and affection. His death six years later left me desolate. Both my sisters married and died young. My mother survived these onslaughts, as well as another bankruptcy—precipitated by her reluctance to discharge any of her employees in a time of depression—and lived alertly to the age of eighty-six, articulate to the last on the errors of capitalism and the tragedy of existence.

The account that follows derives from notes written in longhand by my mother in 1951, when she was eighty-five. The previous year she had suffered a stroke that left her weakened but not disabled, with a mind as nimble as ever and a memory, even of old street addresses, that can only be described as extraordinary. She was accustomed to an active and productive life and bitterly resented her confinement to a nursing home in Mount Vernon, New York. On one of my visits, when she complained about the wasteful indolence of her days, I suggested that she occupy herself with putting down on paper for me the untold story of her life. This she did in the months that followed with intense concentration and excitement until she came to the year of her arrival in Worcester and her fateful marriage to Solomon Kunitz, my father—events still too painful for her to recall – after which she wrote no more. —S.K.

◆◆◆◆◆◆◆◆

Without my consent I was brought into the world in the year 1866, much too early and in the wrong place as if I had any choice in the matter. It was a Godforsaken village of three hundred families in Lithuania in the province of Kovno. My name at birth was Yetta Helen Jasspon. We were one of about a hundred Jewish families in Yashwen. The rest of the population consisted of Lithuanians and Poles, with a sprinkling of Germans.

My father was a descendant of Sephardic Jews who had left Spain in the sixteenth century. He and his family were proud of their Spanish origin. In fact, their adopted surname Jasspon, in Russian "Yaspan," means "I'm Spanish." Ever since I can remember he was in poor health, as the result of an incident that happened before I was born, when he was strung from a tree by a band of Polish troopers during a pogrom and almost died of hanging before he was rescued. If my mother had not appeared on the scene, waving a letter of safe-conduct from Count Radziwill, he would surely have perished. At that time the Poles and the Russians were fighting for possession of the land. My father was caught in the middle, since he was a grain merchant, whose chief customers were army horses, regardless of their nationality. He also owned several lime-pits, which were under contract to the Russian government for use in the construction of buildings and railroads. He was a learned man, who loved to give orders, and his orders were law. We all feared our lord and master and would never dare to contradict or disobey him. He had come to Yashwen from Vilna in 1846 to marry my mother's older sister, who died six years later, leaving him with one daughter. A year or so later her married my mother, who bore him five children, of whom I was the fourth.

My mother's family, named Wolpe, had lived in Yashwen for six or seven generations; she and I were both born in the same house. The Wolpes were a large clan, who had settled all over Poland and near the German border. My great-great-grandfather on my mother's side was reputed to be the wisest man of his time. He was very pious and could perform miracles. People came from miles around to receive his blessing. As for miracles, the only one that ever convinced me was that he lived to the age of a hundred and one. My mother was good-natured, warm-hearted, and hard-working, and she was my father's slave. In those days every woman was her husband's slave.

Compared with most of the people in the village, we were relatively well-off. Our house had chimneys and was built of square-cut logs, the walls were plastered, and the floors were made of wood, not clay. The three rooms were comfortably heated by a tile stove. For cooking and baking we had a large Dutch oven, made of brick.

Under the kitchen was a storage cellar for vegetables and adjoining it were several outbuildings that served as barns and warehouses for grain. We kept cows and horses, a couple of goats, and of course chickens. Why anyone bothered with chickens I don't know, for you could buy eggs then for ten kopecks a dozen. The house was full of Russian and German books. My father also had a large library of Hebrew literature, displayed on shelves where nobody could miss seeing them. The oldest of these books he treasured dearly, for they had been brought from Spain by his ancestors.

Most of the villagers, ten or twelve to a family, lived in a single room heated by a clay oven, on top of which as many as possible slept at night, while the chickens clucked underneath. Those who couldn't be accommodated on top of the stove slept on benches along the walls. Every household had a couple of spinning wheels and a hand-made loom. There was no chimney, the windows were tiny, and the single door opened into the stable. All the roofs were thatched. These people lived wretchedly, but they never complained, for they had been promised a place in heaven. The little money they earned, from their produce or livestock, went to the church or to the saloons. The five saloons in town did a thriving business.

When I was twelve years old I read Spinoza in my father's library and I lost my God. Spinoza did not deny the existence of God, but he destroyed my faith in a personal divinity. Whatever adversity befalls us is either the result of our own fault or that of others. In all the troubles I've had since my childhood I've always blamed myself for my misfortune, because I could not believe it was God's will.

It was a time when people were turning from ignorance and slavery to knowledge and freedom. A spirit of restlessness infected them. They became dissatisfied with the promise of a heaven to come and wanted to enjoy life on earth. Books and poems suddenly appeared, calling on youth to wake up and build a better world. Everywhere young people left the towns and villages of their birth and fled to the cities in search of something, they didn't know what.

My father's health declined, and his business became less and less profitable. No business could be conducted with the government honestly. Everyone demanded bribes. At the age of fourteen I left home and went to Kovno to earn my living as a clerk in a neighborhood store. My pay was fifteen rubles a year, with room and board. I felt very happy and considered myself lucky to live in the capital, where there were streetlights, sidewalks, paved streets, a nice park where the military band played every evening, and water drawn right from the faucet in the kitchen, at the back of the store, which served as my living quarters. I worked for Miss Amsterdam, a young unmarried lady—and when I say lady I really mean it, for she took an interest in me and treated me like her own child. She was well-educated, cultured, and lovable. In spite of being a rabbi's daughter she was not religious and had radical ideas. The few people she associated with were all radicals. Tolstoy was their God. Miss Amsterdam was not only my employer, but also my teacher. I remained with her for a number of years until she sold her business and moved to Saint Petersburg to live. In the meantime my father died, and I returned home at the request of my mother, who was ill and struggling to get along by renting out part of the house. Together with my younger brother we tended a vegetable garden and kept one cow and a few chickens.

To be poor in those days was more than an inconvenience, it was also a disgrace. I hated small-town life with all its discomforts, its public bath house open once a week for women, mud more than a foot deep in rainy weather, ignorance and superstition around you, everyone watching everything you did. I decided to go to America.

I scraped together the money needed for the voyage. My mother packed my trousseau, which she had been collecting since I was three, into two large wicker baskets with strong brass locks. My trousseau consisted of a feather bed and three large pillows, some seventy pounds of pure white down and goose feathers, with every quill removed by hand; dozens of hand-knit stockings of cotton or linen, which I could never wear in this country; all sorts of pure linen sheets, pillowcases, and towels; hundreds of useless objects; a few charms for good luck; and stacks of copper and silver household utensils passed down in the family for generations. My two baskets weighed close to three hundred pounds.

I left in August 1890, crossing the German border at night, since I had no passport, and boarded a train for Bremen. There I purchased my ticket for New York and stayed four days in a charity hotel called Emigranten Haus. On the fifth day we were put on a train bound for Antwerp, where we waited ten more days in the same sort of place. During this period agents approached us with offers of jobs. People with families were offered jobs in Fall River in the cotton mills. They were given tickets for the boat from New York to Fall River. Men from eastern Europe, mostly Slavs, were told of the prosperity awaiting them in the Pennsylvania coal mines. Those who took the jobs were advised to keep quiet about them on arrival, since a law had just been passed forbidding contract labor.

On the Red Star liner *Rhineland* we traveled steerage, four to a windowless cubicle deep in the hold. Our main meal consisted of potatoes boiled in their skins and herring served with bread and tea, but who cared about food on our way to the Golden Land? It was a rough trip, but I proved to be a good sailor and spent most of my time on deck, meeting all the passengers and listening to their plans. The men all planned to become successful merchants, worrying more about what they would do with their fortune than how they would earn it. They had almost nothing left after paying for their passage, but hope, courage, and ambition sustained them. Single girls counted on marrying rich men, of whom there were plenty in America. I listened to all, but my own heart was heavy.

At 9:30 A.M. on September 22, 1890, we passed the Statue of Liberty and docked at Castle Garden. It happened to be my twenty-fourth anniversary, but the day I landed in America was the day of my rebirth and my real birthday. I regret that twenty-four years—the best part of my life—were wasted.

With my two wicker baskets and my bundle I passed through the gates of Castle Garden and went out into the streets of New York in search of a new life.

I told my plight to a countryman of mine, himself a recent immigrant, who had come to meet his sister off the same boat. When she finally showed up, he volunteered to take me to a relative of his at 38 Chrystie Street on the Lower East Side, where I could spend the night. By the time we arrived, late in the afternoon, I was hot, tired, and hungry. We had to climb four flights to reach our haven, a two-room tenement at the rear, occupied by a family of five. In the long dark hall at each level were a sink and toilet, serving all four families on the floor. All the doors were open and all the neighbors were talking to one another, as they waited for their turn at the sink or to use the toilet. The lady of the house greeted me and made me feel at home. I stared out of the kitchen window at the opposite brick wall and studied the five-story-high lacework of clotheslines, which were drawn by pulleys—a real novelty to me. The display of faded bedding, infants' garments, and well-worn clothes made me think of flags of welcome. Since there was not room to spare, my wicker baskets and bundle were placed on the fire escape. Soon curious neighbors came in with all kinds of excuses to survey the new arrival. It was like a homecoming party. Everyone was helpful in those days.

About seven o'clock the man of the house arrived from work, accompanied by the family boarder. As soon as my presence was hastily explained, he was as friendly as could be and wished me luck in the land of opportunity. We all sat down, together with their two lovely children, who had been playing in the street, and shared dinner, which tasted delicious to me. From our conversation I could see that he was of the new generation that had sprung up in Russia, an intellectual. But here he had become a cap maker and worked in a sweatshop. The next morning, before I left for a room a couple of blocks away, I paid for my first meal in America—twelve cents. My new friend did not want to be paid, but I insisted, and she finally took the money. This was all her boarder paid her, and she certainly would not charge me more. I have never forgotten her.

I left to explore New York and to exchange my forty-four rubles – all my wealth—into American money. At Yarmulosky's Bank on Canal Street they gave me twenty-one dollars and some change for my good Russian rubles. I felt sad that my capital had shrunk so much and wondered how long I could live on what I had. The charge for my new room, with breakfast and dinner, was $3.50 a week – not much, but equivalent in Russian money to 7 rubles. One thing I could not understand was why so many little shops had wooden Indians standing in their doorways. Also I wondered how one man, named Ice Cream, could own so many stores. He must be very rich, I thought. When I had my first taste of ice cream a few days later, I was glad that I had not revealed my ignorance to anyone.

I did not know where to look for work. A girl I met promised to take me to the shop where she was working on men's shirts. The next morning she called for me at a quarter to seven. The shop was at 22 Bayard Street, in a tenement house, where the proprietors lived in the same room with their six or eight sewing machines. The operators were of both sexes, and the place smelled of cooking and perspiration, so mixed that I couldn't tell which was stronger. The noise was deafening, what with the clatter of the machines, the bawling of the children, and the loud singing of the operators. After looking me over, the boss said he was willing to hire me under the following terms: I would have to make a down payment of five dollars on my sewing machine, after which I would be charged three dollars a month for its use; the first three weeks I would work for nothing; then if I proved competent, I would be paid at the rate of three dollars for a whole week's work, amounting to seventy-two hours. I surveyed the room and its inhabitants and decided not to accept this wonderful opportunity. I did not like the people who worked there, the place itself, or the conditions of employment. So I left without the job.

On lower Broadway, at Howard Street, between Broadway and Center, I saw a sign: OPERATORS ON SHIRTWAISTS WANTED. I felt a little nervous as I climbed the stairs to the second floor. The foreman asked me whether I was an experienced operator, for they did not hire inexperienced help. I assured him I was, which was not the truth. At his instructions the forelady showed me to a machine and gave me some material to work on. In my broken English I told her that I was used to operating a Singer Sewing Machine, not a Wheeler and Wilson like the one in front of me. She agreed to show me how to thread it. I began sewing straight seams, but very slowly, of course, praying that the thread would not break, for I had no confidence I could fix it. Meanwhile the forelady, who had been watching me from a distance, reported to the foreman that I had lied about my experience. When I saw him approach, my heart began to beat faster. He told me I would have to leave, for they could not bother with beginners or run the risk of having their material spoiled. When I kept repeating that I could learn, he began to grow impatient with me. Nobody was a born operator, I said; they were all beginners once. If others had learned, so could I. As for his fears about my spoiling material, I was willing to pay for any damage I did. "Look!" I said. "Here is all the money I have. Take it as a guarantee." At this moment the manufacturer's wife came over from the cutting table to see what we were arguing about. When she heard my story, she took pity on me and handed back my money. Then she sat down beside me and gave me a few pointers about operating the machine. I worked very carefully and did not hurry, but tried to do the job well. In no time I picked up speed. My first week's pay, at piecework, was over nine dollars without overtime. Within four months I was promoted to working on samples and paid by the week – sixteen dollars, which was a small fortune. The firm's name was M.I. Nathan, The Magnet Waist Co. I stayed there until I left New York to be married in Worcester, Massachusetts.

Endnotes

PROLOGUE PAGE 7

1. Kunitz, 1985, p. 75.

2. Busa, 1982, p. 5.

3. Busa, in Ljungquist, p. 159.

CHAPTER ONE

THE LETTERS: TARRYTOWN, NEW YORK, 1945 PAGE 9

4. "Obituary for Stanley J. Kunitz, Poet, Teacher, and Former H.W. Wilson Editor." www.hwwilson.com.

YOU ASKED ME TO WRITE SOME OF MY MEMORIES, PAGE 9

5. Letter from Selective Service, January 14, 1941. Box 97, Folder 1, Stanley Kunitz Papers; Manuscripts Division, Department of Special Collections, Princeton University Library.

6. Pennsylvania, Veteran Compensation Application Files, World War II, 1950–1966; United States World War II Army Enlistment Records, 1938–1946. https://ancestry.com.

7. Letter from Stanley Kunitz to commanding officer, November 9, 1943. Kunitz was in an army hospital suffering from a chronic sinus infection, requesting reassignment. Box 97, Folder 1, Stanley Kunitz Papers; Manuscripts Division, Department of Special Collections, Princeton University Library.

8. Letter from Stanley Kunitz to Genevieve Taggard, March 19, 1944. Box 9, Folder 3. Genevieve Taggard papers, 1881–2001, Manuscripts and Archives Division, The New York Public Library.

IT KNOCKED ME OUT, PAGE 11

9. United States Federal Census 1900, 1910, 1920, 1930, 1940; Worcester

city housing directories 1902, 1903, 1904, 1924; Massachusetts Death Index, 1901–1980.

10. Letters from Stanley Kunitz to Genevieve Taggard, July 20, 1942; October 3, 1942; December 18, 1942; March 9, 1942. Box 9, Folder 3. Genevieve Taggard papers, 1881–2001, Manuscripts and Archives Division, The New York Public Library.

11. United States Federal Census 1930; San Francisco, California housing directories, 1934–37.

12. "Oral history interview with Joseph A. Danysh, 1964 December 3." Archives of American Art, Smithsonian Institution; Biography www.askart.com: Joseph A. Danysh (1906–1982).

13. Letter from Stanley Kunitz to Francis P. Murphy, January 14, 1946. Box 91, Folder 12, Stanley Kunitz Papers; Manuscripts Division, Department of Special Collections, Princeton University Library.

14. Telephone conversation with Gretchen Kunitz, M.D. , October 25, 2018. Correspondence from Ettore and Jessie Rella, and Mr. Rella's manuscripts span 1940's through 1989 Box 77, Folders 8, 9; Box 203, Folders 2, 3; Stanley Kunitz Papers; Manuscripts Division, Department of Special Collections, Princeton University Library. "Ettore Rella Dies: Wrote Dramas in Verse." *The New York Times.* October 21, 1988, p. B5.

15. Virginia, Marriage Records, 1936–2014, City of Richmond, November 21, 1939. Book 632, Page 8, Bucks County Recorder of Deeds, Doylestown, Pennsylvania. Ljungquist, Chronology, p. xxi.

16. Letter from Stanley Kunitz to Genevieve Taggard, January 19, 1943. Box 9, Folder 3. Genevieve Taggard papers, 1881–2001, Manuscripts and Archives Division, The New York Public Library.

17. Letter from Stanley Kunitz to Genevieve Taggard, January 5, 1943. Box 9, Folder 3. Genevieve Taggard papers, 1881–2001, Manuscripts and Archives Division, The New York Public Library.

18. Letter from Stanley Kunitz to Genevieve Taggard, March 19, 1944. Box 9, Folder 3. Genevieve Taggard papers, 1881–2001, Manuscripts and Archives Division, The New York Public Library.

19. "Liberty Ships and Victory Ships, America's Lifeline in War." National Park Service, U.S. Department of the Interior, www.nps.gov.

20. Letter from Karol Kramer, Interesting People Section editor, March 2, 1945. *The American Magazine: Collier's: Woman's Home Companion* answered Eleanor's request for prints, several of which were enclosed. Box 114, Folder 3, Stanley Kunitz Papers; Manuscripts Division, Department of Special Collections, Princeton University Library.

21. Percy Baker married Lily M. Goldberg in July 1943. New York, New York, Marriage License Indexes, 1907–2018; Telephone conversation with

Lucille Baker, wife of Stanton Baker, Percy and Sarah's son, October 30, 2018, verified they were "married during the war."

22. United States Select Military Registers, 1862–1985. https://ancestry.com. Mrs. Dine's youngest grandson, fifteen-year-old Conrad Isenberg, was too young to be drafted.

I'M TRYING MY BEST TO CALM DOWN, PAGE 20

23. A close look at Stanton Baker's arm patch, AA, signified that he was in an anti-aircraft battalion, a fact verified by his wife, Lucille. Telephone conversation, October 30, 2018.

24. Slater Isenberg "never received a single message or telephone call from Stanley or Eleanor." Email message, December 13, 2018.

25. Mrs. Dine's membership and donation receipts from Hadassah and the American Red Cross, which were sent to her Tarrytown address, spanned 1942–1950. Box 120, Folder 8, Stanley Kunitz Papers; Manuscripts Division, Department of Special Collections, Princeton University Library. An article on page D2 in *The Daily News*, Tarrytown, New York, Saturday, June 29, 1946, "To Conduct Polls for Zionist Vote," includes "Mrs. Yetta Dine" as a member of the committee working to elect women delegates to the 22nd World Zionist Congress. http://Fultonhistory.com.

CHAPTER TWO
LITHUANIA: A LIFE WITH NO FUTURE, 1866–1890 PAGE 25

WRITERS AT WORK, PAGE 25

26. "Constantine R. Jurgėla." *Contemporary Authors Online*, Gale, 1998. *Literature Resource Center.*

27. Greenbaum, 1991. Oral history interview.

28. Jurgėla, p. 528.

RESISTANCE, PAGE 27

29. Greenbaum, 1995, p. 181.

30. According to Jurgėla, p. 420, conscription began for 16 to 18-year-olds for a five-year period. Non-Russian soldiers, especially Jews, were "harshly punished for minor deviations from military discipline: late arrival after a leave of absence was treated as desertion, arguing with an immediate commander as disobedience, carelessness in handling armament as self-mutilation." Petrovsky-Shtern, Yohanan. "Military Service in Russia." YIVO Encyclopedia of Jews in Eastern Europe 2 September 2010.

31. Jurgėla, pp. 426–448.

32. ---, pp. 426–454; Greenbaum, 1995, pp. 180–181.

33. ---, pp. 469–480. In Jurgėla's Part II, The Period of Renaissance and Democratization (1863–1918), consequences of the 1863–1864 Insurrection are described.

THE SHROUD, PAGE 28

34. Jurgėla, p. 446.

35. ---, p. 473.

36. ---, p. 470. A knout is "a whip or scourge formerly used in Russia for the punishment of the worst criminals...its effect was so severe that few of those who were subjected to its full force survived the punishment." Whitney, The Century Dictionary: An Encyclopedia Lexicon of the English Language, Vol. III, 1891, p. 3307.

37. Jurgėla, pp. 421, 472, 475–76.

38. , p. 121.

INTERSECTIONS, PAGE 30

39. Greenbaum, 1995, p. 183.

40. ---, 1995, pp. 89–90.

41. ---, 1995, p. 74.

42. ---, 1995, p. 96.

43. ---, 1995, pp.104–110.

44. Pacernick, in Ljungquist, p. 185. Kunitz, 1985, p. 75.

JEWS IN LITHUANIA, PAGE 31

45. Stanley Kunitz's only child Gretchen's recent DNA results revealed her paternal genetic history as solely Ashkenazic, not Sephardic. Telephone conversation with Gretchen Kunitz, M.D., January 15, 2022.

46. Greenbaum, 1995, p. 2.

47. ---, 1995, p. 3.

48. ---, 1995, p. 160.

49. ---, 1995, p. 183.

FLICKERS OF AUTONOMY, PAGE 32

50. Greenbaum, 1995, p. 182.

51. ---, 1995, p. 90.

52. ---, 1995, p. 180.

53. ---, 1995, p. 183.

54. February 9, 1919; March 15; April 7, 1927. Kunitz's note on the set of letters reads: "September 28, 1982 'Letters to my mother-found among her papers.'" Box 27, Folder 8, Stanley Kunitz Papers; Manuscripts Division, Department of Special Collections, Princeton University Library.

THE FATE OF LITHUANIAN JEWS, PAGE 34

55. Greenbaum, 1995, pp. 188–193.

56. ---, 1995, pp. 338–339.

57. ---, 1995, p. 343.

THE MEMOIR BEGINS: YASHWEN, PROVINCE OF KOVNO, PAGE 36

58. In 1842, the territories of Lithuania were redrawn into three provinces of Kovno, Vilna and Grodno. Jurgėla, p. 421. Josvainiai, called Yosvain, Yasven in Yiddish, is located twenty-four miles north of Kovno or Kaunas. https://www.jewishgen.org/database/Lithuania/VitalRec.htm.

AN INCIDENT, PAGE 41

59. *Graf* is the German word for Count, a member of the nobility.

JEWISH LIFE IN YASHWEN, PAGE 42

60. Yetta Dine's view of village literacy conflicts with Jurgėla's. "Lithuanian book printing had continued to grow in quality and volume. The books in Lithuania gained an ever growing and expanding circulation among the petty gentry and peasants." Jurgėla, p. 424.

RECORD KEEPING, CONSCRIPTION AND BRIBES, PAGE 43

61. There is a conflict of information among the three authors regarding conscription: Greenbaum describes a sixteen-year duty (p. 180), while Jurgėla describes a five-year duty for sixteen to eighteen-year-old eligible men (p. 420). Requirements fluctuated according to the czar's needs during wartimes, a condition mentioned by Yetta Dine.

62. Lime is a staple in the production of plaster, mortar and cement.

63. Yetta Dine's sister Rive Mere (Rebecca Mary), who was nine years older, married Abel Mavsha Kesher. Children raised by Harry and Ida Jasspon were half-sister/cousin Sifre, Max, Rebecca, Yetta, Abe and Charlie.

Geneanet/Ancestry.com, LitvakSIG, Census and Family Lists from Various Districts, 1795-1900.

64. Shavel was the provincial capital of northern Lithuania. "... Šiauliai's Jewish population of about 8,000 was second only to that of Kaunas [Kovno]; its leather industry expanded and an important Bata shoe factory, owned by Jews, was located there, as well as linen, furniture, and chocolate factories. There were fifteen synagogues...including prayer houses of caters, merchants, tailors, shoemakers, butchers, and grave diggers, as well as of Hasidim; a yeshiva; and both traditionally and modern Jewish schools. Its Jewish residents were active in both internal and Jewish cultural life and civic affairs; indeed, a Jew served as vice-mayor." Michael Stanislawski, "Šiauliai."

65. "During World War I, Shavli was the site of a battlefield, and many Jews and other residents fled, never to return." Michael Stanislawski, "Šiauliai."

NAMING, PAGE 50

66. Kunitz's first line in "The Portrait," "My mother never forgave my father/," has a similar ring to Yetta Dine's "My children never forgave me for the names, especially the names I gave them and changed them later." Yetta Dine's use of plurals *children* and *them* deflects attention away from Stanley Jasspon, born Solomon S., who was her only child to actually change his name. Sarah Agnes and Sophia Alysson did not change their names, unless she was referring to their married names.

THE STORY OF GETCHEL, PAGE 52

67. Poet, satirist, journalist Chaim Harry Heine (1797–1856) converted from Judaism to the Lutheran religion and took the name Heinrich to find employment as a civil servant, which was forbidden to Jews. Clashes with the oppressive Prussian government forced him to move to Paris. Bruce Murphy, editor. Benet's Reader's Encyclopedia, 4th Edition. New York: HarperCollins, 1996, p. 54.

68. Of the three rabbis mentioned, Dr. Stephen Samuel Wise (1874–1949) is the most prominent. The Stephen S. Wise Collection (Number MS-49) at the American Jewish Archives in Cincinnati, Ohio, documents his life as a founding Zionist activist, social reformer, and civic leader. Coincidently, he is buried in Westchester Hills Cemetery, as is Yetta Dine.

DISSATISFACTION, PAGE 59

69. Abraham Issac Asher (1862–1942) ran A.I. Asher & Sons pants manufacturing business on Harding near Green and Water streets, where

Yetta Kunitz worked in a dry goods store prior to managing the Dine Manufacturing Company. He was one of the founders of Congregation Shaarai Thorah; "Mrs. Yetta H. Kunitz" is listed as shareholder, purchasing one bond for $5. Census reports and city directories show Asher's wife, Miriam, to be two to three years older than he; documents list the age difference between Asher and his oldest daughter, Rose, ranged between fourteen and seventeen years. In Norma Feingold's *Shaarai Torah: Life Cycle of a Synagogue*, he is pictured with a caption: "Abraham I. Asher, d. 1942, age 80." Asher's son Jacob became an attorney and Special Justice in the Central District Court in Worcester. Yetta Dine's reference to Abraham Asher's death added support for the year her memoir was written.

HOPE, COURAGE AND AMBITION, PAGE 62

70. "Overview departures from Antwerp" Immigrant Ships Transcribers Guild. http://www.redstarline.eu/. The *S.S. Rhynland* was built in 1879.

71. www.CastleGarden.org assessed the entry of "11 million immigrants from 1820 through 1892, the year Ellis Island opened."

A GOOD SAILOR, PAGE 62

72. The 1885 Contract Labor Law, known as the Foran Act, made it "unlawful for any person, company, partnership, or corporation ... to prepay the transportation, or in any way assist or encourage the importation or migration of any alien ... under contract or agreement ... to perform labor or service of any kind in the United States, its Territories, or the District of Columbia ... and pay for every such offense the sum of one thousand dollars ... the master of any vessel who shall knowingly bring within the United States ... any alien laborer ... who had entered into contract or agreement ... shall be deemed guilty of a misdemeanor, and ... punished by a fine of not more than five hundred dollars for each and every such alien laborer and may also be imprisoned for a term not exceeding six months." http://library.uwb.edu.

73. Red Star Line documents for the *S.S. Rhynland*'s 1890 September voyage from Antwerp to New York sets the arrival as September 17th. www.norwayheritage.com.

CHAPTER THREE

NEW YORK'S LOWER EAST SIDE, 1890–1893 PAGE 65

MY FIRST JOB IN AMERICA, PAGE 76

74. The *New Yorker Staats-Zeitung*, a German-language newspaper published in the United States since 1834, grew in circulation; by the late 1800s, it became one of New York City's major daily newspapers. *New Yorker Staats-Zeitung*. https://en.wikipedia.org/wiki/New_Yorker_Staats-Zeitung.

75. In this section of the memoir, Yetta Jasspon explicitly maintained that she never worked in a sweatshop, while her son wrote and repeated in interviews that her "only school was the sweatshops of New York, to which she had come alone as a young woman from Lithuania" (Kunitz, 1985, p. 74). This was the legend he constructed around his mother's life, as was his story about her writing her memoir at his suggestion because she was bored with her life in a rest home.

76. The aim of Harkavy's dictionaries, the first of which was published by Yiddish lexicographer Alexander Harkavy in 1891 as *The English-Yiddish Dictionary*, was to "acquaint English-speaking people with Yiddish and to instruct Yiddish-speaking people in English." Despite its being a valuable resource, it was riddled with difficulties for both English and Yiddish speakers attempting to learn the language. http://www.cs.uky.edu/~raphael/yiddish/harkavy/0003.png.

77. Welfare Island, now known as Roosevelt Island, was situated in the East River. "After New York City gained ownership in 1828 [from Robert Blackwell, who used it for farming], construction began on a series of public institutions, including a prison, an almshouse, and several hospitals... Eventually the thin strip of land became known as Welfare Island because the prison and the workhouse gained a reputation for overcrowding, violence, and drug trafficking." "Lunatics, Inmates, and Homeowners: The History of Roosevelt Island. https://blog.mcny.org.

THE DAY WAS NEVER LONG ENOUGH, PAGE 79

78. Yetta's mother Ida Jasspon died on July 23, 1891. https://ancestry.com/findagrave.com/memorial.

79. The *Morgen-Journal* was a German-language newspaper published in New York from 1890 until 1912. The Library of Congress, Chronicling America, Historic American Newspapers. http://chroniclingamerica.org. *The New York Journal*, founded in 1882, underwent name changes until 1902 when it became the *New York American*. https://onlinebooks.library.upenn.edu.

80. Born into a Jewish family, Samuel Gompers (b. London 1850, d. San Antonio, Texas 1924) followed his father's trade as a cigar maker at the age of ten. Soon after emigrating with his family to New York's Lower East Side in 1863, he joined Local 15 of the United Cigar Makers and became a union organizer. He devoted his life to labor-management relations through collective bargaining and worked to secure shorter working

hours and higher wages. Gompers was the first president of the American Federation of Labor (1886–1924). https://aflcio.org/about/history/labor-history-people/samuel-gompers; Van Doren, pp. 411–2.

81. Dedicated on November 8, 1891, The Educational Alliance at 197 East Broadway was first named The Hebrew Institute when The Young Men's Hebrew Association and The Hebrew Free School Association combined. "[T]he ultimate object of their work [was] the Americanizing, as far as possible, of the large mass of foreign-born Jews in this city, [which] will be attained all the more rapidly by this concentration of their energies." "For Work Among Hebrews. The Dedication of the New Building of the Institute." *The New York Times,* November 9, 1891.

Rabbi, writer and medical doctor Henry Pereira Mendes (b. 1852 Birmingham, England, d. 1937 New York City) helped to establish several organizations, including the Jewish Theological Seminary in 1886 and the Young Women's Hebrew Association of New York in 1902. Professor Felix Adler (b. Germany 1851, d. 1933 New York) was "a German-American professor of political and social ethics, rationalist, influential lecturer on euthanasia, religious leader and social reformer who founded the Ethical Culture Movement." https://en.wikipedia.org/wiki/Felix_Adler.

MARBLE HALLS AND FLOOR, PAGE 84

82. On March 31, 1905, *The New York Times* published "East Side Honors Poet of Its Masses" about Lithuanian-born Yiddish-language composer, poet and entertainer Eliakum Zunser (1840–1913), who came to New York City in 1889 and worked as a printer. In gratitude for his songs and in recognition of his penury, a pension fund was awarded to the sixty-five-year-old. He wrote only a few songs after his arrival in America, "The Golden Land" among them, p. 7.

83. Sholem Yankev Abramovitsh (1835–1917). In 1873, he published *Di klyatshe,* an allegorical novel comparing the plight of Jews in Russia to the fate of a broken-down nag who was unwilling to rebel against her tormentors (Jews not active in seeking reforms). The book was also an indictment of czarist policies which oppressed the Jewish minority. http://brittannica.com/art/Yiddish-literature/Modern-Yiddish-literature.

CHAPTER FOUR: A FEAST OF LOSSES, 1893–1950 PAGE 99

SOLOMON KUNITZ, 1893–1905, PAGE 100

84. Lyford, pp. 12–15.

85. July 30, 1893, Box 2, Folder 5. The George Maynard Diary Collection. Worcester Historical Museum.

86. Southwick, p. 38.

87. ---, p. 42.

88. Ceccacci, p. 2.

89. Yetta Dine's son-in-law, Alfred Isenberg co-founded the *Jewish Civic Leader* in 1926. He became a prominent member of the Jewish community and was interviewed for his 90th birthday. "Jewish Civic Leader's Founder at 90." *The Jewish Chronicle-Leader*. Vol. 47, No. 22, October. 8, 1981, p. 6. "Alfred Isenberg, 91; Jewish Civic Leader Founder, Publisher." *Worcester Telegram*. June 18, 1983. Clipping file, Biography, Isenberg, Alfred G., Worcester Public Library, 3 Salem Street.

90. Gold paint was a commodity used in decorative arts and printing. July 1, 1890, Primary Declaration of Intention, Massachusetts, State and Federal Naturalization Records, 1798–1950; December 31, 1892, Rhode Island, State and Federal Naturalization Records, 1802–1945; 1892 House Directory, Providence, Rhode Island City Directory, p. 176. https://ancestry.com.

91. A wrapper was "a loose garment meant to envelop the whole, or nearly the whole, person: applied to both indoor and outdoor garments, such as dressing gowns, overcoats, and shawls." *The Century Dictionary*, Vol. VI, p. 6986.

92. Copy of Record of Marriage, City of Worcester, Office of the City Clerk, #111965, Registered #565.

93. City and House Directories, 1896, p. 165; 1898, p. 370.

94. "Women's Wrappers." June 16, 1897. *The Fitchburg Sentinel* (Fitchburg, Massachusetts), https://newspapers.com.

95. "Independent Order of the Sons of Benjamin." http://www.phoenixmasonry.org/masonmuseum/fraternalism/jewish_orders.htm.

96. Massachusetts Birth Records, 1840–1915. Massachusetts Death Records, 1841–1915 https://ancestry.com/. Child mortality was high, by today's standards. Federal census statistics for 1890 and 1900 reports that children five and under accounted for approximately one in three deaths. The Hebrew word *shakul* means bereaved or robbed of one's offspring. biblehub.com/hebrew/7909.htm.

97. "BIG LOSS. Parisian Wrapper Company IS BADLY GUTTED." *The Worcester Spy*. Worcester, Massachusetts. Friday, January 20, 1899, pp. 1–2. Microfilm. Massachusetts, Death Records, 1841–1915, https://ancestry.com.

98. Massachusetts, Death Records, 1841–1915, https://ancestry.com.

99. Twelfth Census of the United States. Massachusetts, Marriage Records, 1840–1915. https://ancestry.com.

100. Twelfth Census of the United States; Massachusetts, Mason Membership Cards, 1733–1990. Provo, UT, USA https://ancestry.com.

101. 1902 Worcester House Directory, Real Estate Record, p. 762. 1903 Worcester Directory, p. 374.

102. 1904 Worcester City Directory, 58 Providence Street.

103. Death by drinking sweet-smelling, clear liquid carbolic acid results in an ending marked by severe burns in the mouth and esophagus and wrenching abdominal pain. "Death from accidental poisoning by carbolic acid." California State Journal of Medicine, Vol. XVII, No. 10, pp. 366–67. http://europepmc.org.

104. "Swallows Carbolic. Solomon Kunitz Ends His Life in Elm Park." *Worcester Daily Telegram*. Saturday, June 3, 1905, p. 14. "Solomon Kunitz Elm Park Suicide." *The Evening Post*. Second Edition. June 2, 1905, p. 1. Solomon's death certificate #1024 lists Yetta's brother Abe Jasspon as "INFORMANT." Microfilm.

105. Stitt, in Ljungquist, p. 125. The 1900 United States census report lists Dr. James Nightingale, physician, as a resident at a Front Street boarding house.

106. City of Worcester, Office of the City Clerk, #609011, Registered #1858. Record of Birth, Solomon S. Kunitz, July 29, 1905. Date of Record, January 1, 1906.

107. Rodman, p. 96.

108. Millier, p. 155. During 1952–54, Kunitz had an affair with poet Jean Garrigue. After nineteen years of marriage to Eleanor Evans, he divorced her in 1958 and married artist and poet Elise Asher.

MARK DINE, 1906–1925, PAGE 113

109. Kunitz, 1993, pp. 69–70.

110. Mark Dine: Declaration of Intention, Bureau of Immigration and Naturalization, No. 10784; June 5, 1914, Petition for Naturalization, U.S. Department of Labor, No. 12102. His son, Max, spelled his surname Dain. https://ancestry.com.

111. In letters written in 1977 to Kunitz from Carol Dine, granddaughter of Kunitz's stepbrother Herman, he learned that Mark Dine and Yetta Kunitz met through a relative. Dine emigrated to America with three sons, Herman, Max and Mitchell, while daughters Sonia and Clara stayed in Lithuania and became dentists. Box 27, Folders 5–7, Stanley Kunitz Papers; Manuscripts Division, Department of Special Collections, Princeton University Library. Marriages Registered in the City of Boston for the Year 1910, #6339: Mark Dine, 53, Yetta Jasspon Kunitz, 43, p. 276. Massachusetts Archives, 220 Morrissey Blvd., Boston, MA.

112. By 1912, Mrs. Dine was working at a 79 Green Street dry goods store and still owned one Ellsworth street property. By 1914, she had no real estate listed in the directories. The Dine Manufacturing Company made children's dresses.

113. Ferrara, 2012, pp. 150–53. The 1900 census lists Annie Johnson as "servant" in the Kunitz household; the 1910 census names Mary Cashis, a servant who may have been the inspiration for Frieda in "The Magic Curtain."

114. Feingold, 1991, p. 26.

115. Nancy Greenberg, Cultural Arts/Senior Adult Director, Worcester Jewish Community Center. Ms. Greenberg talked with her retired men's group about their memories of the small "Deutche" shul. Email, October 7, 2015.

116. Pacernick, in Ljungquist, p. 182, 185.

117. January 3, 1979, *Boston Globe* obituary for Herman Dine (b.1894) described his coming from Lithuania to Boston at 13 years of age, graduating from Harvard in 1916. An expert in municipal finances, he became Director of Accounts in the Massachusetts Department of Corporations and Taxes. A May 29, 1961 letter from Mitchell's wife Jennie Dine to Kunitz described their living together and "being in business with your mother and Mr. Dine," adding "you were such a cute little boy and I would help you take a bath, brush your hair and even dress you." Box 27, Folder 4, Stanley Kunitz Papers; Manuscripts Division, Department of Special Collections, Princeton University Library.

118. City Document, No. 67. Address of Hon. George M. Wright, Mayor of the City of Worcester, 1913 with the Annual Reports of the Several Departments for the Financial Year Ending November 30, 1912, p. 687. Collection of The Worcester Historical Museum.

119. A written communication from The Worcester Department of Code Inspections shows that the 1919 Building Permit Book, page 297, was issued by the Bureau of Building on March 22nd; city water service was installed May 20th. Mortgage: Worcester District Registry of Deeds, Book 2364, Page 367.

120. Telephone conversation with Carol Stockmal, January 10, 2019. Details of original interior were discovered as she and her husband restored the house. The memory of stained-glass windows was supplied by Stanley Kunitz during one of his post-1985 visits. In letters to the Stockmals, he created a word to show shared possession of 4 Woodford Street as "y/our house." The Stanley Kunitz-Stockmal Collection, Archives and Special Collections, Clark University.

121. Kunitz, 2004. Kunitz discussed his living in "the last house in town" and his isolation "far from his schoolmates." SK/S, 1-2, Folder 59, pp. 12–13,

2004. The Stanley Kunitz-Stockmal Collection, Archives and Special Collections, Clark University.

122. *The Wild Braid: A Poet Reflects on a Century in the Garden. Working Materials. 9.26.04.* SK/S 1-2, Folder 59, p. 19. The Stanley Kunitz-Stockmal Collection, Archives and Special Collections, Clark University, Worcester, Massachusetts.

123. Max Dain, who spelled his surname differently from the rest of the family, is listed in the 1920 United States Census at 943 Massachusetts Avenue in Cambridge.

124. "A Youth Looks at His World 1922–28." Box 136, Folder 32, Stanley Kunitz Papers; Manuscripts Division, Department of Special Collections, Princeton University Library, pp. 6–7.

125. Kunitz, 2004. SK/S 1-2, Folder 59, The Stanley Kunitz-Stockmal Collection, Archives and Special Collections, Clark University, Kunitz, 2004, p. 21. Mark Dine's City of Worcester death certificate 613748, #7 specifies his cause of death on January 1, 1920, as "arteriosclerosis, angina pectoris."

126. Letter from Kunitz to Carol Dine, 1977. Box 27, Folder 5, Stanley Kunitz Papers; Manuscripts Division, Department of Special Collections, Princeton University Library.

127. *Boston Daily Globe*, 1920. Historical Newspapers, Birth, Marriage, & Death Announcements, 1851–2003. 1920 United States Census. Somerville, Massachusetts, City Directory: 1925, p. 184. Massachusetts, Birth Index, 1860–1970, Births 1921–25. https://ancestry.com.

128. Worcester House Directory, 1924, p. 366. The Isenbergs lived at 967 Pleasant Street.

129. *The Aftermath of the Class of Nineteen Twenty-two of Worcester Classical High School*, 1922, p. 32, 127. Collection of Worcester Historical Museum.

130. Parker and Siegel, in Ljungquist, p. 172.

131. Kostelanetz, in Ljungquist, p. 33.

132. Worcester County Registry of Deeds, Book 2365, pp. 24–25.

SOPHIA ISENBERG, 1926–1933, PAGE 124

133. Telephone conversations with Slater Isenberg, October 8, 2018, October 12, 2019, November 3, 2019.

134. 1927 Somerville Directory. 1927 Yetta H. Dine Passport. Box 182, Folder 10, Stanley Kunitz Papers; Manuscripts Division, Department of Special Collections, Princeton University Library.

135. December 23,1929. Box 28, Folder 3, Stanley Kunitz Papers; Manuscripts Division, Department of Special Collections, Princeton University Library.

136. Bube (pronounced buh-bee) is Yiddish for grandmother.

137. Given her limited resources, the financial support for Mrs. Dine's trip to Palestine remains a mystery. A search of *The Somerville Journal, The Boston Jewish Advocate* and Worcester papers yielded no articles that shed light on organizational sponsorship, such as Somerville's Hadassah chapter.

138. Kunitz's note on the set of letters reads: "September 28, 1982, Letters to my mother-found among her papers," February 9, 19; March 15; April 7, 1927. Box 27, Folder 8, Stanley Kunitz Papers; Manuscripts Division, Department of Special Collections, Princeton University Library.

139. Busa, 1982, p. 23.

140. "Who should go to college?" *Liberty: A Weekly for the Whole Family.* Vol. 3, No. 14, August 7, 1926, pp. 4–5. Box 133, Folder 1, Stanley Kunitz Papers; Manuscripts Division, Department of Special Collections, Princeton University Library

141. Kunitz, 1985, p. 101.

142. *Sunday Telegram,* July 11, 1926. Box 125, Folder 2, Stanley Kunitz Papers; Manuscript Division, Department of Special Collections, Princeton University Library. In 2001, Kunitz's literary agent forwarded a request to him from Book of the Month Club to republish 1931's *Living Authors,* which Kunitz edited under the nom de plume "Dilly Tante." Kunitz declined, writing "I chose to adopt a pseudonym as a joke, but mostly because I had just published my first book of poems, *Intellectual Things,* and wanted to avoid any confusion of identity." January 26, 2001. Box 153, Folder 3, Stanley Kunitz Papers; Manuscripts Division, Department of Special Collections, Princeton University Library.

143. "Alfred Isenberg at 90 looks back." *The Jewish Chronicle-Leader.* Vol. 47, No. 22, October 8, 1981, p. 8. Isenberg, Alfred G., Biography, Clipping File, Worcester Public Library. Print.

144. "Mrs. A.G. Isenberg Dies at Princeton." *Worcester Daily Telegram.* August 24, 1932. Microfilm.

145. The back cover of February 1929 issue of *The Dial* lists the biography and publishing credits submitted by Kunitz to editor Marianne Moore.

146. June 13, 1929. Box 27, Folder 8, Stanley Kunitz Papers; Manuscripts Division, Department of Special Collections, Princeton University Library.

147. Kunitz, 1993, p. 22. Helen Pearce Downer was three years Kunitz's senior and mother of a six-year-old daughter. The 1925 New York State Census shows three-year-old Lee Downer living with her father Donald G. Downer's parents, physician Mortimer and Lillian, on their farm in

Woodstock, New York. Dr. Mortimer likely died, because the 1930 census reported that his son, Dr. Mortimer, Jr. was head of the household, and niece Lee lived with them.

148. Kunitz's novel *Hartrex* is unpublished. His title was a created compound word: hart, an adult male deer, and trek, a long, difficult journey on foot. Box 12, Folders 1–8; Box 13, Folders 1,2. Stanley Kunitz Papers; Manuscripts Division, Department of Special Collections, Princeton University Library.

149. December 23, 1929; January 23, 1930. Box 28, Folder 3, Stanley Kunitz Papers; Manuscripts Division, Department of Special Collections, Princeton University Library.

150. The series of letters Kunitz sent to his mother were marked with a notation: "Stanley Kunitz, September 28, 1982 Letters to my mother—found among her papers." Quotations in this section span the 1929-30 period when he and Helen Pearce Downer were traveling in France and Italy: June 13, 21, July 9, September 4 and 11, October 19, December 8, 1929 and March 13, 1930. Box 27, Folder 8, Stanley Kunitz Papers; Manuscripts Division, Department of Special Collections, Princeton University Library. Kunitz and Pearce-Downer returned to New York on the S.S. Berlin, April 21, 1930 (New York Passenger Lists, 1820–1957).

151. *The Nation*, June 18,1930. *The Worcester Daily Telegram*, May 18, 1930. Kunitz scrupulously collected reviews of his books; as his career matured, he hired a literary clipping service in Walton, New York. Box 128, Folder 1, Stanley Kunitz Papers; Manuscripts Division, Department of Special Collections, Princeton University Library.

152. Kunitz, 1930.

153. July 7, 1931. Box 27, Folder 8, Stanley Kunitz Papers; Manuscripts Division, Department of Special Collections, Princeton University Library.

154. July 16,1931. Box 27, Folder 8, Stanley Kunitz Papers; Manuscripts Division, Department of Special Collections, Princeton University Library.

155. Undated [July 20,1931]. Box 27, Folder 8, Stanley Kunitz Papers; Manuscripts Division, Department of Special Collections, Princeton University Library.

156. Mansfield, Connecticut Registry of Deeds, Vol 48, page 209; Volume 55, p. 394.

157. Letter from Helen Pearce to Genevieve Taggard, August 5, 1931, Genevieve Taggard papers, *1881–2001*, Series 1, Box 9, Folder 3. Manuscripts and Archives Division, The New York Public Library.

158. Kunitz, 1993, p. 16. As much as he wanted to break free from the confines of his editing job, Kunitz eventually produced 7 reference books for H.W. Wilson between 1931 and 1975. Box 172, Folder 8, Stanley

Kunitz Papers; Manuscripts Division, Department of Special Collections, Princeton University Library.

159. Undated. Box 27, Folder 8. Stanley Kunitz Papers; Manuscripts Division, Department of Special Collections, Princeton University Library.

160. August 29, 1932. Box 1A, Folder 3, Stanley Kunitz Papers; Manuscripts Division, Department of Special Collections, Princeton University Library.

161. Telephone conversation with Slater Isenberg, October 8, 2018.

162. "Mrs. A.G. Isenberg Dies at Princeton." *Worcester Daily Telegram*, August 24, 1932. Conversation with Dr. Luigi Ceccacci, February 2013. City of Worcester, Record of Death, Number 1914.

163. 1932 August. Box 1A, Folder 3, Stanley Kunitz Papers; Manuscripts Division, Department of Special Collections, Princeton University Library.

164. Telephone conversation with Slater Isenberg, October 8, 2018.

165. Massachusetts, Marriage Index, 1901–1955, https://ancestry.com.

SARAH BAKER, 1933–1944, PAGE 134

166. Box 116, Folder 8, Stanley Kunitz Papers; Manuscripts Division, Department of Special Collections, Princeton University Library. Sixteenth Census of the United States-1940.

167. Letter from Stanley Kunitz to Genevieve Taggard, June 14, 1935. Box 9, Folder 3. Genevieve Taggard papers, 1881–2001, Manuscripts and Archives Division, The New York Public Library.

168. Volume 57, Page 468, Town of Mansfield, County of Tolland, State of Connecticut, Town Hall, Storrs, Connecticut. Book 633, p. 8, Bucks County Office of Recorder of Deeds, Doylestown, Pennsylvania.

169. December 3, 1936, Vulcania Passenger List for Helen Kunitz, born in Fort Washington, New York, March 17, 1902, Lurgan Green, New Hope, Pennsylvania. New York, Passenger Lists, 1920–1957 for Helen Kunitz. https://ancestry.com.

170. Matousek, p. 297. The 1940 census lists Helen Pearce, divorced, with no occupation living at 47 E. 9th St., New York with eighteen-year-old Lee, an unemployed waitress. Kunitz and Eleanor lived at 126 E. 24th Street.

171. Chronology, in Ljungquist, p. xxi.

172. Sixteenth Census of the United States.

173. Number 18258, Certificate of Death for Sarah Baker, Bureau of Records, Department of Health, Borough of Manhattan. Telephone conversation with Dr. Stuart Baker and his mother, Lucille, October 30, 2018.

174. Letter from Yetta Dine to Stanley Kunitz, February 14, 1944.

Miscellaneous Documents, "Yetta Helen Jasspon Kunitz Dine, 1866–1952 Transcription & Photocopies of Her Memoir and Supporting Documents, Volume Two of Two," Gretchen Kunitz Collection. Since 1935, the Social Security Act has provided federal assistance for the elderly. Coincidentally, it was drafted by President Franklin D. Roosevelt's Secretary of Labor, Frances Perkins, who spent her childhood in Worcester, Massachusetts.

175. New York, New York, Marriage License Indexes, 1907–2018. Telephone conversation with Stanton's wife, Lucille Baker, and her son Dr. Stuart Baker. She verified they were "married during the war." October 30, 2018.

176. 1976. Box 8, Folder 44, Stanley Kunitz Papers; Manuscripts Division, Department of Special Collections, Princeton University Library.

ROSILYN LEVITAN, 1944–1951, PAGE 139

177. Box 120, Folder 9, Stanley Kunitz Papers; Manuscripts Division, Department of Special Collections, Princeton University Library.

178. Slater Isenberg, 2019, MRI Sales Consultants, Morris County, NJ/ LinkedIn.

179. Dine, Y.H. Correspondence. Box 120, Folder 7, Stanley Kunitz Papers; Manuscripts Division, Department of Special Collections, Princeton University Library.

180. April 1945, Box 133, Folder 1; January 14, 1946. Box 91, Folder 2, Stanley Kunitz Papers; Manuscripts Division, Department of Special Collections, Princeton University Library.

181. New Hope property Book 775, Page 91. Bucks County Office of Recorder of Deeds, Bucks County Courthouse, 55 East Court St., Doylestown, PA.

182. Ljungquist, p. xxi; Kunitz, 1993, p. 23.

183. Dine, Mrs. Y.H.: Correspondence. Box 120, Folder 7, Stanley Kunitz Papers; Manuscripts Division, Department of Special Collections, Princeton University Library.

184. Parker and Siegel, in Ljungquist, p. 173.

185. July 29,1950; October 5,1950; December 7, 1950; February 16, 1951; April 17, 1951; June 11, 1951. Box 84, Folder 6, Stanley Kunitz Papers; Manuscripts Division, Department of Special Collections, Princeton University Library.

186. June 24, 1950. Box 27, Folder 8, Stanley Kunitz Papers; Manuscripts Division, Department of Special Collections, Princeton University Library.

CHAPTER FIVE: MOUNT VERNON, NEW YORK, 1951 PAGE 143

JOURNEY'S END, PAGE 143

187. January 16,1951. Box 120, Folder 7, Stanley Kunitz Papers; Manuscripts Division, Department of Special Collections, Princeton University Library.

188. Jacqueline's sister was opera singer Mimi Benzell, February 6, 1951. Miscellaneous Documents, "Yetta Helen Jasspon Kunitz Dine, 1866–1952 Transcription & Photocopies of Her Memoir and Supporting Documents, Volume Two of Two." Collection of Gretchen Kunitz, M.D.

189. Telephone conversation with Dr. Stuart Baker and his mother, Lucille Baker, October 30, 2018.

190. July 9, 1951. Box 120, Folder 8, Stanley Kunitz Papers; Manuscripts Division, Department of Special Collections, Princeton University Library.

THE DIARY, PAGE 147

191. Great-grandson Stuart (Stanton and Lucille Baker's son) was almost two years old when Mrs. Dine was in the Mt. Vernon rest home. Stuart Baker, M.D., email communication, February 13, 2021.

192. Undated; undated. Box 120, Folder 7, Stanley Kunitz Papers; Manuscripts Division, Department of Special Collections, Princeton University Library.

193. Two consecutive entries are dated "Saturday, April 28th."

194. Lawrence and Jacqueline Baker became the parents of twins, Donna and Karen. Telephone conversation with Dr. Stuart Baker and his mother Lucille, October 30, 2018.

195. Yetta Dine seemed to echo Nietzsche's statement in *The Twilight of the Idols*, "Skirmishes in a War with Age":"The sick man is a parasite of society. In certain cases, it is indecent to go on living. To continue to negotiate in a state of cowardly dependence upon doctors and special treatments, once the meaning of life, the right to life, has been lost, ought to be regarded with the greatest contempt by society," quoted in Bartlett, p. 728.

196. June 2, 1951; May 12, 1951; June 3, 1951; May 12, 1951. Box 120, Folder 7, Stanley Kunitz Papers; Manuscripts Division, Department of Special Collections, Princeton University Library.

197. October 12, 1951. Box 84, Folder 6, Stanley Kunitz Papers; Manuscripts Division, Department of Special Collections, Princeton University Library.

198. The Kunitzes may have rented the six-acre Fleecydale Road property in Lumberville, Pennsylvania prior to purchasing it on November 23, 1951. It was ten miles from their former 14-acre property on Lurgan Road, which they had sold in 1946 [Book 1016, Page 100]. Following Kunitz's 1958 divorce from Eleanor and marriage to Elise Asher, he sold Fleecydale Road in 1959, and they shifted their summer home to Provincetown, Massachusetts. Book 1492, Page 1. Bucks County Office of Recorder

of Deeds, Bucks County Courthouse, 55 East Court St., Doylestown, Pennsylvania.

199. Spinoza stated in *Ethics,* Definition XIII that "Fear cannot be without hope nor hope without fear," quoted in Bartlett, p. 282.

200. June 21, 1951. Box 120, Folder 7, Stanley Kunitz Papers; Manuscripts Division, Department of Special Collections, Princeton University Library.

201. February 6, 1951. Miscellaneous Documents, "Yetta Helen Jasspon Kunitz Dine, 1866–1952 Transcription & Photocopies of Her Memoir and Supporting Documents, Volume Two of Two." Collection of Gretchen Kunitz, M.D.

202. In 1951, Shavuot was celebrated one week earlier, on June 10th and 11th. It is a commemoration of the Israelites receiving the Torah from God on Mount Sinai. www.hebcal.com/holidays/shavuot.

203. Undated. Box 120, Folder 7, Stanley Kunitz Papers; Manuscripts Division, Department of Special Collections, Princeton University Library.

204. July 24, 1951. Box 120, Folder 7, Stanley Kunitz Papers; Manuscripts Division, Department of Special Collections, Princeton University Library.

205. August 4,1951. Box 27, Folder 8, Stanley Kunitz Papers; Manuscripts Division, Department of Special Collections, Princeton University Library.

206. August 22, 1951. Box 27, Folder 8, Stanley Kunitz Papers; Manuscripts Division, Department of Special Collections, Princeton University Library.

207. September 29, 1951. Box 120, Folder 7, Stanley Kunitz Papers; Manuscripts Division, Department of Special Collections, Princeton University Library.

208. Charles Jasspon died on December 29, 1951. https://www.findagrave. com/memorial. Undated, "Statement for Services to Dine Yetta Helen." Miscellaneous Documents, "Yetta Helen Jasspon Kunitz Dine, 1866–1952 Transcription & Photocopies of Her Memoir and Supporting Documents, Volume Two of Two." Collection of Gretchen Kunitz, M.D.

CHAPTER SIX: FAMILY TIES PAGE 169

I HAD NO FAMILY, PAGE 169

209. Rodman, p. 97. Kunitz misstated the year as 1963.

210. Anderson, Karl Oscar Emanuel. Presentation of Stanley J. Kunitz. 1961. History of University, Box R 2-4. Clark University Archive. Worcester, Massachusetts.

211. February 1961. Box 42, Folder 5, Stanley Kunitz Papers; Manuscripts Division, Department of Special Collections, Princeton University Library.

212. May 29, 1961. Box 27, Folder 4, Stanley Kunitz Papers; Manuscripts

Division, Department of Special Collections, Princeton University Library.

213. Cocola, pp. 134–153. Through analysis of poems and interviews, Cocola traced Kunitz's relationship with his Jewish identity.

214. Isenberg, Alfred. Box 57, Folder 13, Stanley Kunitz Papers; Manuscripts Division, Department of Special Collections, Princeton University Library. Eleven letters and memos between Isenberg and Kunitz chronicle the mending of their relationship.

215. Telephone conversation with Slater Isenberg, November 3, 2019.

216. Busa, in Ljungquist, p. 160.

217. *The Aftermath of the Class of Nineteen Twenty-Two of Worcester Classical High School*, p. 32. Worcester Historical Museum.

218. Ferrara, 2012, p. 149.

219. "Local Store Owner Is Cousin of Pulitzer Prize Poet." *The Berkshire Evening Eagle,* May 8,1959, https://newspapers.com.

220. Gottesman, October 31, 1985, pp. 2, 7. October 16, 1985, p. 3.

221. August 27, 1986, SK/S 1-1, 1986, Folder 9, The Stanley Kunitz-Stockmal Collection. Clark University Archive. Clark University. Worcester, Massachusetts.

222. Wunderlich, 1997, in Ljungquist, pp. 189–90.

223. Paniker, in Ljungquist, p. 112.

224. Beckman, in Ljungquist, p. 116.

225. Kelen, in Ljungquist, p. 149. Kunitz co-founded the Fine Arts Work Center in Provincetown and Poets House in New York City.

MOTHER AND SON, PAGE 176

226. Busa,1992, in Ljungquist, p. 161.

227. Wednesday, March 9. Notebook D. Box 2, Folder 3, Stanley Kunitz Papers; Manuscripts Division, Department of Special Collections, Princeton University Library. His companion "J" is Jean Garrigue. Given the subjects covered and people named, entries are likely to have been written in the mid-1950s.

228. Toufexis, Anastasia. "Behavior: The Most Powerful Bond of All: A mother-son relationship can sometimes exact a heavy price." *Time,* October 1, 1984, p. 86. Toufexis referenced psychologist and sociologist Carole Klein. Box 18, Folder 7, Stanley Kunitz Papers; Manuscripts Division, Department of Special Collections, Princeton University Library.

RECONCILIATION, PAGE 178

229. Kelen, in Ljungquist, p. 151.

SYMPATHETIC VIBRATIONS, PAGE 180

230. Russell, in Ljungquist, p. 20.

231. Zuckerman, Amy. "The Day Kunitz Came Home." May 25, 1980, *Sunday Telegram*, p. 11. SK/S 1-1, 1980, The Stanley Kunitz-Stockmal Collection. Clark University Archive. Clark University. Worcester, Massachusetts.

232. Prose, p. 23.

THE POEMS, PAGE 181

233. "The Summing-Up - 1952–53 New Poems." Box 9, Folder 17, Stanley Kunitz Papers; Manuscripts Division, Department of Special Collections, Princeton University Library. Published in the "The Coat Without a Seam" section of *Stanley Kunitz: Selected Poems 1928–1958*, (Little, Brown and Company, 1958), *The Poems of Stanley Kunitz 1928–1978*, (Little, Brown and Company, 1978), and *The Collected Poems/Stanley Kunitz*, (W.W. Norton and Company, 2000).

234. October 1969 draft of "The Portrait." Box 9, Folder 3, Stanley Kunitz Papers; Manuscripts Division, Department of Special Collections, Princeton University Library.

235. The undated copy of Solomon Kunitz's death certificate that Kunitz purchased is found in Box 182, Folder 3, Stanley Kunitz Papers; Manuscripts Division, Department of Special Collections, Princeton University Library. Pinpointing the date of purchase was more challenging, but it was after Mrs. Dine's 1952 death. The certificate is signed by City Clerk Robert J. O'Keefe, who served from 1953–1998 (Nick Kotsopoulos. "Longest-tenured City Clerk O'Keefe dies at 88" *Telegram & Gazette*, November 22, 2012). Documented visits to Worcester were few after he left in 1927: Kunitz returned in August 1932 for his sister Sophia's funeral and in 1961 to receive an honorary degree from Clark University. A decade later, when the Worcester County Poetry Association was launched, he was invited to read at the Worcester Public Library with Robert Bly and Denise Levertov. From that time on, Kunitz read in Worcester on several occasions, when he could have obtained his father's death certificate ("True to give poetry reading tonight in Worcester." October 4, 2011. www.telegram.com.

236. Busa, 1982, p. 3.

237. Moyers, p. 247.

238. Two articles appeared in the local newspapers: "SOLOMON KUNITZ ELM PARK SUICIDE" *The Evening Post* (June 2, 1905) and "SWALLOWS CARBOLIC ACID. Solomon Kunitz Ends His Life in Elm Park." *Worcester Daily Telegram* (Saturday, June 3, 1905, p. 14).

Worcester Public Library. Microfilm.

239. Worcester City Hall birth certificate 1858#: Solomon S. Kunitz, date of birth July 29, 1905; date of record January 1, 1906.

240. Busa, 1982, pp. 3–4.

241. In *Stanley Kunitz: An Introduction to the Poetry*, Gregory Orr discusses Stanley Kunitz's use of the dramatic lyric form in which a single character, addressing a silent auditor at a critical moment, reveals himself or herself and the dramatic situation. When discussing his poem, "Father and Son," Kunitz described the dramatic lyric as being akin to "the dramatic monologue" where the stanzas should be regarded as "narrative blocks or paragraphs" (Kunitz, 1975, p. 126).

AFTERWORD: WORCESTER, MASSACHUSETTS, 2016 PAGE 185

SEARCH AND RESCUE, PAGE 185

242. Worcester City and Housing Directories: 1904–1920. Green Street was in a bustling district of mixed-use buildings with businesses and offices on the lower floors and apartments on the third floor.

243. "The Day Kunitz Came Home." *Worcester Sunday Telegram*, May 25, 1980. SK/S 1-1, 1980, Folder 1. The Stanley Kunitz-Stockmal Collection. Clark University Archive. Clark University, Worcester, Massachusetts.

244. SK/S 1-1, 1985, Folder 7, The Stanley Kunitz-Stockmal Collection. Clark University Archive. Clark University, Worcester, Massachusetts.

245. Johnson, "A Glimpse of Stanley Kunitz's Childhood Home, Worcester, Massachusetts." *The Worcester Review*. Vol. XXVI, No. 1&2, p. 25.

246. SK/S 1-1, 1989, Folders 15, 16, The Stanley Kunitz-Stockmal Collection. Clark University Archive. Clark University, Worcester, Massachusetts.

247. 1989; Box 8, Folder 43, Stanley Kunitz Papers; Manuscripts Division, Department of Special Collections, Princeton University Library.

248. "Stanley Kunitz letters are donated to Clark." *Telegram & Gazette*. October 23, 2009, p. B9.

249. "Boyhood home of Stanley Kunitz in Worcester, Mass. named a Literary Landmark." *The Voice for American Libraries*. ISSN 1084-4694 Vol. II, Issue 5, September 2010.

250. "Awards laud recognition of city's architectural gems." *Telegram & Gazette*. January 17, 2019, p. 1, A5.

251. 2014. Box 209, Folder 5, Stanley Kunitz Papers; Manuscripts Division, Department of Special Collections, Princeton University Library.

252. Moyers, p. 243.

253. Busa, in Ljungquist, pp. 155–56.

254. Moyers, p. 244.

255. Undated. Box 147, Folder 11, Stanley Kunitz Papers; Manuscripts Division, Department of Special Collections, Princeton University Library.

MOVING CLOSER, PAGE 191

256. Email correspondence with Gretchen Kunitz, M.D., October 1, 2016.

CHALLENGES, PAGE 192

257. Kunitz, 1985, p. 75.

258. 1951; 1940–1950. Box 27, Folder 8; Box 120, Folder 7, Stanley Kunitz Papers; Manuscripts Division, Department of Special Collections, Princeton University Library.

259. 1924–26. Box 28, Folder 4, Stanley Kunitz Papers; Manuscripts Division, Department of Special Collections, Princeton University Library.

260. "Community Briefs." *The Daily News, Tarrytown*, New York. May 21, 1937; New York State Census, 1925.

261. 1910; 1920; 1930 United States Federal Census. "Louis Levitan, Merchant and Community Booster, Dies Suddenly." *The Daily News, Tarrytown*, New York, February 22, 1940.

262. January 5, 1943. Box 27, Folder 8, Stanley Kunitz Papers; Manuscripts Division, Department of Special Collections, Princeton University Library.

263. Massachusetts, Death Index, 1901–1980, Vol. 99, p. 461.

264. Undated. Box 97, Folder 2; Box 115, Folders 14, 15, Stanley Kunitz Papers; Manuscripts Division, Department of Special Collections, Princeton University Library.

ABOUT YETTA DINE'S WRITING, PAGE 197

265. An Internet search showed various styles of cursive handwriting. The one that most closely resembles Mrs. Dine's is 19th-century Russian, which supports the description in chapter 2 of her education in Lithuania, following its Russian occupation.

266. Kunitz, 1985, p. 75.

HIS MOTHER'S STORY, PAGE 199

267. 1983. Box 91, Folder 11, Stanley Kunitz Papers; Manuscripts Division, Department of Special Collections, Princeton University Library.

268. Undated. Box 115, Folder 15, Stanley Kunitz Papers; Manuscripts Division, Department of Special Collections, Princeton University Library. Yetta Dine's image may have been cropped from a photograph of her and grandsons, Slater (1925–2020) and Conrad Isenberg (b. 1929), c. 1930s.

269. Email communication from Jennifer Freed, September 24, 2019, Ferrara, 2019, p. 76.

Acknowledgments

MY DEEPEST THANKS to Gretchen Kunitz, M.D., without whose cooperation the preservation and transcription of her grandmother's memoir would not have been possible and without whose encouragement this book would not have been written.

There would have been no intense study of Stanley Kunitz's life and poetry without Carol Stockmal and her late husband Greg, who provided the initial impetus and inspiration for the research reflected in this book.

Correspondence and discussions with Mrs. Dine's family members brought her and her writing to life. Slater Isenberg, who died in October 2020, shared memories of his grandmother during our telephone conversations and emails. Mr. Isenberg remembered her as "an intriguing woman, resilient, creative and surprisingly lucid. I always admired her." My gratitude also goes to Ruth and Seth Isenberg, Stuart Baker, M.D. and his mother Lucille Baker who died in March 2021. She said, "Make sure you tell how loving she was."

I am indebted to Babette Gehnrich, Paper Conservator, American Antiquarian Society, Worcester, Massachusetts, who gave me advice on preserving primary documents in the Collection of Gretchen Kunitz, M.D.

One of the distinct pleasures of doing research is meeting archivists and librarians, who are a group of gifted and dedicated professionals: Rodney Gormé Obien and Renée Fox; Gabriel Swift, Brianna Cregle, AnnaLee Pauls and the staff at Princeton

University's Department of Special Collections; Patrick Raftery, Librarian, Westchester County Historical Society; the staffs of the New York Public Library's Berg Collection and the Brooke Russell Astor Reading Room for Rare Books and Manuscripts; Joy Hennig and Jennifer Marien, Worcester Public Library staff; Fordyce Williams and the staff of the Archives and Special Collections at the Robert H. Goddard Library, Clark University in Worcester, Massachusetts; Corinne Gabriele of the College of the Holy Cross, Archives and Special Collections; Michael Basinksi, Curator of The Poetry Collection at the University of Buffalo; Curators Vital Zajka and Gunnar Berg, YIVO Institute for Jewish Research, New York; Wendy Essery, Library and Archive Manager and William D. Wallace, Executive Director, Worcester Historical Museum; Beverly Gill, Research Services, Boston Public Library.

Visits to town halls in pursuit of records were successful because of the cooperation and assistance shown by Stephanie Huber and Sara-Ann Chaine of the office of the Town Clerk, Mansfield, Connecticut; Nancy Takach, Recorder of Deeds, Bucks County Courthouse, Doylestown, Pennsylvania.

My appreciation to Brett C. Millier, Reginald L. Cook Professor of American Literature, Middlebury College; documentarian Tobe Carey; Edward R. Cronin; Nancy Greenberg, Cultural Arts/Senior Adult Director, Worcester Jewish Community Center; Charles Skillings, Holden Historical Society; the late Michael True, professor emeritus, Assumption University.

Many thanks to Francine D'Alessandro for her research in support of the Stanley Kunitz Boyhood Home docent program and Linda Robinson, who located archival newspaper material. I am grateful to Linda Chadwick, whose editing and genealogical talents are reflected throughout this book.

Writers appreciate having friends and family who listen and understand a project as it grows in its own unpredictable manner: my husband, John Gaumond, the late J. Philip O'Hara, Patricia H. O'Hara, Susan McDaniel Ceccacci and Luigi Ceccacci, M.D., Julie

Pantano, Phyllis Edinberg, bg Thurston and Tim Millunzi, Susan Roney O'Brien, Dee O'Connor and Curt Curtin, Esther Martin, Robert Gill, Pete Gaumond, James Schifferle, Susan Elizabeth Sweeney and Michael Chapman, Lucille Cormier, James Dempsey, Nan Hass Feldman and Alan Feldman, Norm and Linda Schifferle, the late Jennie and late David Benigas.

Special thanks to the 2016 and 2017 participants in two courses of study, "Stanley Kunitz and Worcester: 'Make room for the roots!'" and "'My name is Solomon Levi'": Family and Place in the Poems of Stanley Kunitz," Worcester Initiative for Senior Education (W.I.S.E.), hosted by Assumption University. Our discussions prompted my initial search for Mrs. Dine's memoir.

Finally and without hyperbole, this publication would not have become a reality were it not for my editors at TidePool Press, Jock and Frank Herron and Ingrid Mach, whose talents and vision transform manuscripts into books.

Works Cited

Abramovitsh, Sholem Yankev. http://brittannica.com/art/Yiddish-literature/Modern-Yiddish-literature.

Adler, Felix. https://en.wikipedia.org/wiki/Felix_Adler_(professor).

"Alfred Isenberg, 91; Jewish Civic Leader Founder, Publisher." *Worcester Telegram*. June 18, 1983. Clipping file, Biography, Isenberg, Alfred G. Worcester Public Library, 3 Salem St. Print.

Anderson, Karl Oscar Emanuel. Presentation of Stanley J. Kunitz. 1961. History of University, Box R 2-4. Clark University Archive. Worcester, Massachusetts. Print.

"Awards laud recognition of city's architectural gems." *Telegram & Gazette*. January 17, 2019, p. 1, A5. Print.

Bartlett, John. *Familiar Quotations by John Bartlett: A Collection of Passages and Proverbs Traced to Their Sources in Ancient and Modern Literature*. Boston: Little, Brown and Company, 1955. Centennial Edition. Print.

"BIG LOSS. Parisian Wrapper Company IS BADLY GUTTED." *The Worcester Spy*. Worcester, Massachusetts. January 20, 1899, pp. 1–2. Microfilm.

Boyer, Paul S., ed., *The Oxford Companion to United States History*. New York: Oxford University Press, Inc., 2001. Print.

"Boyhood home of Stanley Kunitz in Worcester, Mass. named a Literary Landmark." *The Voice for American Libraries*. ISSN 1084-4694 Vol. II, Issue 5, September 2010. Print.

Busa, Chris. "The Art of Poetry #29: Stanley Kunitz." *The Paris Review*. 1982, pp. 2–45. Print.

Cahan, Abraham. *Yekl: A Tale of the New York Ghetto*. New York: D. Appleton. Internet Archive CNsrif_ucla:LAGE_681645.1896.

Ceccacci, Susan McDaniel. "Jewish Background." *Worcester Ethnic Groups*. Unpublished manuscript. Worcester Heritage Preservation Society [Preservation Worcester], 1983. Print.

Census Reports, Volume IV, Twelfth Census of the United States, Taken in the Year 1900. Vital Statistics, Part II: Statistics of Deaths. https://ancestry.com.

City Document, No. 67. Address of Hon. George M. Wright, Mayor of the City of Worcester, 1913 with the Annual Reports of the Several Departments for the Financial Year Ending November 30, 1912, p. 687. Collection of The Worcester Historical Museum. Print.

Classical High School Yearbook Collection. Worcester Historical Museum. Worcester, Massachusetts. Print.

Cocola, Jim. "Stanley Kunitz's Cracked Vocation." *Studies in American Jewish Literature*, Vol. 34, No. 1, 2015. pp. 134–153. Print.

"Community Briefs." *The Daily News, Tarrytown, New York.* May 21, 1937. https://newspapers.com.

"Constantine R. Jurgėla." *Contemporary Authors Online*, Gale. 1998. *Literature Resource Center* http://lionk.galegroup.com.

Danysh, Joseph A. "Oral history interview with Joseph A. Danysh, 1964 December 3." Archives of American Art, Smithsonian Institution; Biography, Joseph A. Danysh(1906–1982). www.askart.com.

"Death from accidental poisoning by carbolic acid." California State Journal of Medicine, Vol. XVII, No. 10, pp. 366–67. http://europepmc.org.

Department of the Interior, Census Office Report on Vital and Social Statistics in the United States at the Eleventh Census: 1890, Part III: Statistics of Deaths. https://ancestry.com.

Dine, Yetta. *Yetta Helen Kunitz Dine: 1866–1952, Transcription & Photocopies of Her Memoir and Supporting Documents, Volumes One and Two.* Judith Ferrara, transcriber. 2017. Collection of Gretchen Kunitz, M.D. Print.

"1885 Contract Labor Law." Session II, Chapter 164; 23 Stat. 332. 48th Congress; February 26, 1885. U.S. Immigration legislation online. http://library.uwb.edu.

"East Side Honors Poet of Its Masses." *The New York Times.* March 31, 1905, p. 7. http://nytimes.com.

East Side Stories: A Film by Tobe Carey. Willow Mixed Media, 2008. Film.

"Ettore Rella Dies: Wrote Dramas in Verse." *The New York Times.* October 21, 1988, p. B5. http://nytimes.com.

Feingold, Norma. *Water Street: World Within a World.* Worcester Historical Museum, 1983–4. Print.

---. *Shaarai Torah: Life Cycle of a Synagogue.* Worcester Historical Museum, 1991. Print.

Ferrara, Judith. "The House on Woodford Street: Memory and Imagination in the Poems of Stanley Kunitz." *The Worcester Review*, Vol. XXXIII, Nos. 1 & 2, 2012, pp. 144–157. Print.

---. Reference Guide for the Stanley Kunitz Boyhood Home Docent Program. Revised edition, 2019. Unpublished manuscript. Print.

"For Work Among Hebrews. The Dedication of the New Building of the Institute." *The New York Times,* November 9, 1891. http://nytimes.com.

Gompers, Samuel. https://aflcio.org/about/history/labor-history-people/samuel-gompers.

Gottesman, Jan. October 31, 1985. "World Renowned Poet Kunitz Comes Home." *The Jewish Chronicle-Leader.* Vol. 59/No. 21, pp. 2, 7. https://chroniclingamerica.loc.gov.

---. "Stanley Kunitz on the Occasion of a 5-Day Celebration of His 80th Birthday." October 16, 1985. Cassette tape. Judith Ferrara, transcriber. September 4, 2009, Worcester Historical Museum, Worcester, Massachusetts. Print.

Greenbaum, Masha. *The Jews of Lithuania: A History of a Remarkable Community – 1316–1945.* Lynbrook, NY: Gefen Books, 1995. Print.

---. "Oral history interview with Masha Greenbaum." Sandra Bradley, interviewer. 1991 October 08. The Jeff and Toby Herr Oral History Archive, United States Holocaust Memorial Museum Collection. http://ushmm.org/search/catalog/irn513295.

Harkavy, Alexander. *The English-Yiddish Dictionary.* New York: Hebrew Publishing Company, 1891. http://www.cs.uky.edu/~raphael/yiddish/harkavy/0003.png.

Hénault, Marie. *Stanley Kunitz.* Boston: Twayne Publishers, 1980. Print.

"Independent Order of the Sons of Benjamin." http://www.phoenixmasonry.org/masonmuseum/fraternalism/jewish_orders.htm.

Isenberg, Alfred G., Biography, Clipping File, Worcester Public Library, 3 Salem Street, Worcester, Massachusetts. Print.

Jewish Genealogy Data Bases. https://www.jewishgen.org/database/Lithuania/VitalRec.htm.

Johnson, Carle. "A Glimpse of Stanley Kunitz's Childhood Home, Worcester, Massachusetts." *The Worcester Review,* XXVI, 1&2, 2001. Print.

Jurgéla, Constantine. *History of the Lithuanian Nation.* New York: Lithuanian Cultural Institute, 1947. Print.

Kotsopoulos, Nick. "Longest-tenured City Clerk O'Keefe dies at 88." *Telegram & Gazette,* November 22, 2012. http://telegram.com.

Kunitz, Stanley. *Intellectual Things.* New York: Doubleday, Doran and Company, 1930. Worcester Author Collection, Worcester Public Library. Print.

---. *Passport to the War.* New York: Henry Holt & Company, 1944. College of the Holy Cross Archives and Special Collections. Print.

---. *Stanley Kunitz: Selected Poems 1928–1958.* Boston: Little, Brown and Company, 1958. Print.

---. *A kind of order, a kind of folly: Essays and Conversations by Stanley Kunitz.* Boston: Little, Brown and Company, 1975. Print.

---. *The Poems of Stanley Kunitz: 1928–1978.* Boston, Little, Brown and Company. 1979. Print.

---. *Next-to-Last Things: New Poems and Essays.* Boston: The Atlantic Monthly Press, 1985. Print.

---. *Interviews and Encounters with Stanley Kunitz.* Stanley Moss, ed., Riverdale-on-Hudson, New York: The Sheep Meadow Press, 1993. Print.

---. *The Collected Poems: Stanley Kunitz.* New York: W.W. Norton & Company, 2000. Print.

---. "Stanley Kunitz on Paul Celan and the Poetry of the Holocaust," *Crossroads #58*, Fall 2003. https://poetrysociety.org.

Stanley Kunitz Papers; Manuscripts Division, Department of Special Collections, Princeton University Library.

The Stanley Kunitz-Stockmal Collection. Archives and Special Collections, Robert H. Goddard Library, Clark University. Worcester, Massachusetts.

"Liberty Ships and Victory Ships, America's Lifeline in War." National Park Service, U.S. Department of the Interior, www.nps.gov.

The Library of Congress, Chronicling America, Historic American Newspapers. www.loc.gov/collections/chronicling-america.

Ljungquist, Kent P., editor. *Conversations with Stanley Kunitz.* Jackson: University Press of Mississippi, 2013. Print.

"Local Store Owner Is Cousin of Pulitzer Prize Poet." *The Berkshire Evening Eagle.* May 8,1959. https://newspapers.com.

"Louis Levitan, Merchant and Community Booster, Dies Suddenly." *The Daily News, Tarrytown, New York*, February 22, 1940. http://Fultonhistory.com.

"Lunatics, Inmates, and Homeowners: The History of Roosevelt Island." https://blog.mcny.org.

Lyford, Joshua. "Diary of Worcester: One Man's Account of Worcester, 1862–1909." *Worcester Magazine*, May 18–24, 2017. pp. 12–15. Print.

Massachusetts Birth Records, 1840–1915. https://ancestry.com.

Massachusetts Death Index 1840–1915; 1901–1980. https://ancestry.com.

Massachusetts, Marriage Records, 1840–1915. https://ancestry.com.

Massachusetts, Mason Membership Cards, 1733–1990. Provo, UT, USA. https://ancestry.com.

Massachusetts, State and Federal Naturalization Records, 1798–1950. https://ancestry.com.

Matousek, Mark. *When You're Falling, Dive: Lessons in the Art of Living.* New York: Bloomsbury USA, 2008. Print.

The George Maynard Diary Collection. Worcester Historical Museum. Worcester, Massachusetts. Print.

Millier, Brett C. *Flawed Light: American Women Poets and Alcohol.* Urbana and Chicago: University of Illinois, 2009. Print.

Moore, Marianne, ed. *The Dial.* Volume LXXXVI, February 1929. The Poetry Collection of the University Libraries, University at Buffalo. Print.

Moyers, Bill D. *The Language of Life: A Festival of Poets.* James Haba and David Grubin, Editors. New York: Doubleday. 1995. Print.

"Mrs. A.G. Isenberg Dies at Princeton." *Worcester Daily Telegram.* August 24, 1932. Worcester Public Library. Microfilm.

"Mrs. Yetta Dine, Former Resident." *Tarrytown Daily News, 4-1-1952*, p. 2. http://Fultonhistory.com.

Murphy, Bruce, editor. *Benet's Reader's Encyclopedia, 4th Edition.* New York: HarperCollins, 1996. Print.

Museum of the City of New York. https://blog.mcny.org.

The New York Journal. https://onlinebooks.library.upenn.edu.

New York, New York, Marriage License Indexes, 1907–2018. https://ancestry.com.

New York Passenger Lists, 1820–1957. https://ancestry.com.

New York State Census, Tarrytown, 1915, 1925. https://ancestry.com.

New Yorker Staats-Zeitung. https://en.wikipedia.org/wiki New_Yorker_Staats-Zeitung.

"Obituary for Stanley J. Kunitz, Poet, Teacher, and Former H.W. Wilson Editor." www.hwwilson.com.

Orr, Gregory. *Stanley Kunitz: An Introduction to the Poetry.* New York: Columbia University Press, 1985. Print.

"Overview departures from Antwerp." Immigrant Ships Transcribers Guild. http://www.redstarline.eu.

Pennsylvania Veteran Compensation Files, WWII, 1950–1966. https://ancestry.com.

Petrovsky-Shtern, Yohanan. "Military Service in Russia." YIVO Encyclopedia of Jews in Eastern Europe 2 September 2010. 21 November 2018.

http://www.yivencyclopedia.org/article.aspx/Military_Service_in_Russia.

Prose, Francine. *The Lives of the Muses: Nine Women and the Artists They Inspired*. New York: Harper-Collins, 2002. Print.

Red Star Line. www.norwayheritage.com.

Rodman, Seldon. *Tongues of Fallen Angels*. New York: New Directions Book, 1974. Print.

Skillion, Anne, editor. *The New York Public Library Literature Companion*. New York: The Free Press. 2001. Print.

"Solomon Kunitz Elm Park Suicide." *The Evening Post*. Second Edition. June 2, 1905, p. 1. Microfilm.

Southwick, Albert B. *150 Years of Worcester: 1848–1998*. Worcester, Massachusetts: Chandler House Press. 1998. Print.

Stanislawski, Michael. "Šiauliai." YIVO Encyclopedia of Jews in Eastern Europe, 18 October 2010. 22 November 2018. http://www.yivoencyclopedia.org/article.aspx/Siauliai.

"Stanley Kunitz letters are donated to Clark." *Telogram &Gazette*. October 23, 2009, p. B9. Print.

Stanley's House: A Film by Tobe Carey. Willow Mixed Media, 2007. Film.

"Swallows Carbolic. Solomon Kunitz Ends His Life in Elm Park." *Worcester Daily Telegram*. Saturday, June 3, 1905, p. 14. Microfilm.

Genevieve Taggard papers, 1881–2001. Manuscripts and Archives Division, The New York Public Library. Print.

Taylor, W.E. "Death from accidental poisoning by carbolic acid." California State Journal of Medicine, Vol. XVII, No. 10, 1919. pp. 366–67. https://core.ac.uk.

"To Conduct Polls For Zionist Vote." *The Daily News. Tarrytown, N.Y.* June 29, 1946. http://Fultonhistory.com.

United States Federal Census Reports: 1900, 1910, 1920, 1930, 1940, 1950. https://ancestry.com.

United States Select Military Registers – 1862–1985. https://ancestry.com.

United States World War II Army Enlistment Records, 1938–1946. https://ancestry.com.

Van Doren, Charles and Robert McHenry, editors. *Webster's American Biographies*. Springfield, Massachusetts: G. & C. Merriam Company, 1975. Print.

Waller, Jason. "Benedict de Spinoza: Metaphysics." Internet Encyclopedia of Philosophy. https://www.iep.edu/spinoz-m.

Williams, John Taylor. *The Shores of Bohemia: A Cape Cod Story*

– *1910–1950.* New York: Farrar, Straus and Giroux, 2022. Print.

Whitney, William Dwight. *The Century Dictionary: An Encyclopedic Lexicon of the English Language.* Volume III. New York: The Century Company, 1891. Print.

Wilkerson, Dale. "Fredrich Nietzsche (1844–1900)." Internet Encyclopedia of Philosophy. https://www.iep.edu/nietzsche.

"Women's Wrappers." June 16, 1897. *The Fitchburg Sentinel.* https://newspapers.com.

Zuckerman, Amy. "The Day Kunitz Came Home." *Sunday Telegram,* May 25, 1980. SK/S 1-1, 1980, The Stanley Kunitz-Stockmal Collection. Clark University Archive. Clark University. Worcester, Massachusetts. Print.

City and House Directories:

- Michigan City, Indiana, 1945. https://ancestry.com.

- Providence, Rhode Island, 1892. https://ancestry.com.

- San Francisco, California, 1934–1937. https://ancestry.com.

- Somerville, Massachusetts Directory 1927. Print.

- Worcester, Massachusetts, 1896–1982. Print.

Municipal Offices:

- Bucks County Office of Recorder of Deeds, Bucks County Courthouse, 55 East Court St., Doylestown, Pennsylvania.

- Town of Mansfield, County of Tolland, State of Connecticut, Town Hall, Storrs, Connecticut.

- Worcester County Registry of Deeds, 110 Front St., Worcester, Massachusetts.

- City of Worcester, Office of the City Clerk, 455 Main St., Room 206, Worcester, Massachusetts.

- Office of Vital Records, Bureau of Vital Statistics, New York City Department of Health and Mental Hygiene, 125 Worth St., Room 125, New York, New York.

Permissions

Permissions granted from the following:

- The Literary Estate of Stanley J. Kunitz, Gretchen Kunitz, M.D. and Chuck Verrill, Darhansoff and Verrill Literary Agency, Coexecutors.
- Stanley Kunitz Papers. Manuscripts Division, Department of Special Collections, Princeton University Library. Princeton, New Jersey.
- W. W. Norton & Company, New York for reprint of selected poems and excerpts from *The Collected Poems: Stanley Kunitz* (2000) and *Passing Through: The Later Poems, New and Selected: Stanley Kunitz* (1995).
- The Archives at YIVO Institute for Jewish Research, 15 West 16th Street, New York, NY 10011-6031.
- The Museum of the City of New York, 1220 Fifth Avenue, New York, NY 10029.
- The Worcester Historical Museum, 30 Elm Street, Worcester, Massachusetts 01609.
- Aubyn Freed
- John Gaumond
- Slater Isenberg
- Carol Stockmal
- Bérge Ara Zobian

Index

NOTE: Unless otherwise indicated, family designations shown in parentheses (), such as (son) or (sister) refer to the subject's relationship to Yetta Jasspon Kunitz Dine (YJ). References to Stanley Kunitz, poet: (SK). Page numbers in italics refer to illustrations.

About the Author

Judith Ferrara, Ph.D. holds degrees from the University of New Hampshire, Fitchburg State University and the State University College at Buffalo. Her publications in the field of education include *Peer Mediation: Finding a Way to Care* (Stenhouse Publishers). Her poems, essays and artwork have appeared in three collections and in journals. She received a Worcester Cultural Commission/ Massachusetts Cultural Council Creative Arts Fellowship in 2003. In 2018, she received the Stanley Kunitz Medal from the Worcester County Poetry Association. Ferrara lives in Worcester, Massachusetts, with her husband John Gaumond.